M000295040

# TOURS OF DUTY

# TOURS OF DUTY

## The Best Vietnam War Stories
## from the Men Who Served

### Edited by Michael Lee Lanning

STACKPOLE
BOOKS

*Guilford, Connecticut*

Front cover photo: U.S. Army Bell UH-1D helicopters airlift members of the 2nd Battalion, 14th Infantry Regiment from the Filhol Rubber Plantation area to a new staging area, during Operation "Wahiawa," a search and destroy mission conducted by the 25th Infantry Division, northeast of Cu Chi, South Vietnam, 1966. Photo courtesy of James K. F. Dung, SFC, photographer. Available in the holdings of the National Archives and Records Administration, cataloged under the National Archives Identifier (NAID) 530610.

Published by Stackpole Books
An imprint of The Rowman & Littlefield Publishing Group, Inc.
4501 Forbes Blvd., Ste. 200
Lanham, MD 20706
www.rowman.com

Distributed by NATIONAL BOOK NETWORK
800-462-6420

Copyright © 2014 and 2019 by Michael Lee Lanning

*All rights reserved.* No part of this book may be reproduced in any form or by any electronic or mechanical means, including information storage and retrieval systems, without written permission from the publisher, except by a reviewer who may quote passages in a review.

British Library Cataloguing in Publication Information available

**Library of Congress Cataloging-in-Publication Data available**

ISBN 978-0-8117-3848-4 (paperback)
ISBN 978-0-8117-6879-5 (e-book)

♾™ The paper used in this publication meets the minimum requirements of American National Standard for Information Sciences—Permanence of Paper for Printed Library Materials, ANSI/NISO Z39.48-1992.

**DEDICATED TO**

1LT William F. (Bill) Little     KIA November 11, 1969
CPL Delma L. Reed     KIA July 2, 1967
SP4 Stanley D. Ross     KIA October 20, 1969
1LT Andrew D. (Dave) Smith     KIA May 28, 1970
CPL William O. (Bill) Vaughn     KIA December 30, 1969

. . . and the other 58,204

# Contents

# Introduction

Half a dozen fellow veterans sat with me around our usual chipped laminate corner table in the worn neighborhood café drinking coffee and waiting for the morning to pass. In the afternoon we would drift to our individual televisions to watch ESPN, Turner Classic Movies, or the History Channel. If the weather was just right, one or two might venture out to the golf links and another couple to a local fishing hole. All of us were well over sixty years of age; veterans of the more recent wars in the Middle East were still in uniform or out trying to make a living.

As happened nearly every morning, conversation drifted from politics to sports and then local gossip. Occasionally, one of the guys would bring up sex, but its mention was usually more nostalgic than salacious. And inevitably, someone would bring up Vietnam, which then sparked a series of war stories that had often been told and retold. I pretty much kept quiet, as I was new to the group and not much on talking freely to people I did not know well.

A fellow joined us one morning for the first time; I don't remember if he was the guest of one of the regulars or just passing through. After a few often-repeated war stories, the new guy joined in. He told us about being the only survivor of his platoon after a VC ambush and then how he escaped and evaded enemy patrols for more than a month before making his way to friendly lines. He concluded that none of this was in his records because it was all classified "Top Secret."

Eyes rolled around the table but everyone remained silent. Finally, I could stand it no longer and started to stand to tell this "veteran" that truth must be a stranger to him or perhaps something a bit more profane. Just as I began to rise, an older vet—whom I believed to have been a private in Korea and a senior sergeant in Vietnam, though I don't know for certain because we never discussed rank—grasped my arm and held me in my seat.

He said to me, but loud enough for everyone to hear, "Never question the virtue of a man's wife or the veracity of his war stories."

The war stories, at least for that morning, ended, and the stranger quickly made his way to the door. At first, I resented the old sarge's remark, but then realized that it really did not make much difference. Real veterans recognize made-up war stories within seconds of their being told. While some of us might embellish, slightly or extremely, our war stories, truth prevails among those who were really there. It must also be understood that two soldiers in the same fight, separated by only a few feet, often see thing entirely differently. Every soldier's war is limited to a space measured in mere meters. For the overall picture, we can only listen to or read the stories of others.

It is most often the war stories themselves that tell the tales of combat—not the teller or the war itself. While serving in the Florida Phase of the U.S. Army's Ranger School in 1970, I and my fellow instructors used war stories as examples of the teaching points to help inform our students, many soon to be in Vietnam themselves, and to bring our points to life. When a fellow instructor ended his Ranger tour, often returning to Vietnam, we threw going-away parties centered around liquid refreshment and more war stories. By the end of the night's festivities, we instructors, always looking for teaching material, began to divide the departing soldier's war stories. One would say, "I'll take his ambush tale," while another claimed "the hot LZ story." As the years passed it often became difficult to determine just what had happened to whom. It made no difference. The stories were true, or mostly so, and that is one of the offspring of battle. War stories are as much as part of a man's service as is that old green duffle bag, a few rows of colorful ribbons, and a pride that does not diminish.

What follows are war stories of Vietnam. I can personally testify to the veracity of some because "I was there." Others were related to me over the years by soldiers whom I hold in high regard. Names have been left out to protect both the guilty and the innocent. Regardless of who originated each of the following stories, all are presented in the first-person for ease of reading and continuity. Each story is identified by its teller's unit, Corps area, and year in country. (Corps Tactical Zones [CTZ] were designated Military Regions [MR] on July 1, 1970. For this book, Corps areas are given for location regardless of the time frame.)

Any time Vietnam veterans get together—whether two or twenty—war stories follow. The tales they relate about the paddies, the jungles, the highlands, the waterways, and the airways provide the vets themselves with an even greater understanding of the war they survived and allow the nonparticipants glimpses into the frequent dangers of intense firefights, often hilarious responses to inexplicable situations, and strong bonds that only they can share. All too often, these individual stories from soldiers, airmen, marines, and sailors remain only oral, are never captured or compiled in any meaningful way that would more fully complete the whole of the Vietnam War. This is but a small effort to record some of our stories.

Michael Lee Lanning
Bolivar Peninsula, Texas
March 2014

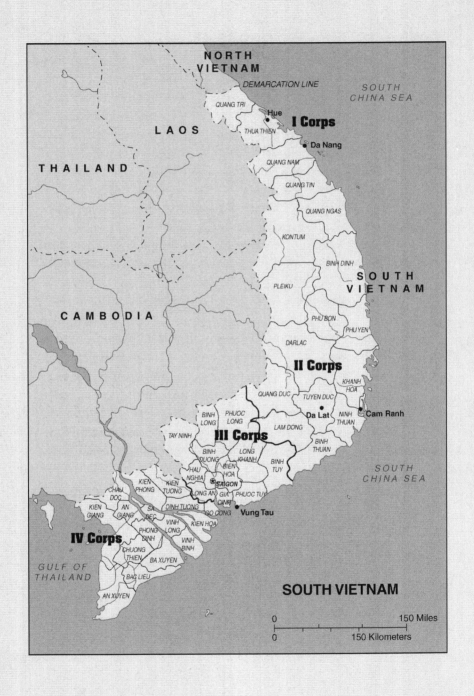

SOUTH VIETNAM

# Vietnam War Stories

War stories are usually brief and often interrupted by groans from someone who has a similar tale to tell or by laughter from those who have "really been there" and understand the true humor of an event. This book begins with a lengthy story that deserves to be told in its entirety—if nothing else, out of respect for the dead and wounded.

I was raised in the home of a career air force noncommissioned officer. In 1965 I received a commission in the infantry from the ROTC program at Texas A&M University. I attended the infantry officers basic course and then airborne and ranger schools before volunteering for Vietnam. After a brief tour at Fort Polk, Louisiana, I reported to Vietnam, where I served as a platoon leader in the First Cavalry Division. When I arrived in 1966, the First Cav had captains with eight to ten years of service and NCOs with ten to twenty years in uniform—many of whom were veterans of Korea and even a few of World War II. With that amount of experience around, it was a good place to be a green second lieutenant.

By the time I returned to the States in 1967, I had decided that I would make a career of the U.S. Army. My first tour and its aftermath enlightened me, however, on what it meant to be a professional soldier and a combat veteran. I had become hard in my mind and in my soul. That hardness was not all that pleasant because, although you become aloof from physical and mental pain and suffering, you also separate yourself from love and joy. Your soul does not die, but it does become hardened. Family and friends lose some of their closeness, and the only place you feel comfortable is with other combat veterans. The upside is that it makes you a very dangerous adversary.

I was fortunate during the dark days after my first tour that I was assigned to the Florida Camp of the U.S. Army Infantry School's Ranger Department. As an instructor I was surrounded by officers and NCOs just back from Vietnam. Not only did I learn from them, but also they helped shed light on darkness. More important, during this time I married an ex-nun who delivered me from my former depths.

In late 1968 I bid the Ranger Camp, my wife, and newly born son farewell to return to Vietnam for my second tour. I was extremely happy to be assigned to 3rd Brigade of the 101st Airborne Division and then further assigned to the 3rd Battalion, 187th Infantry (Airmobile), known as the Rakkasans, at Camp Evans, northeast of Hue. For about a month, I was in charge of Echo Company, which contained the battalion's recon platoon, 4.2-inch mortars, and other support units, mostly remaining in a rear firebase.

In January 1969 I assumed command of Delta Company and returned to the field. By now the senior captains had been promoted to field grade and the old NCOs had received direct commissions, had retired, or were dead. Most of the NCOs were now products of the Noncommissioned Officers Course at Fort Benning. These "shake and bakes," as they were known because of their near instant rank, acted as platoon sergeants and often as platoon leaders as we were nearly always short at least one lieutenant. Many of the squad leaders were SP4s. Fortunately, my first sergeant was a professional NCO whom I had met as a fellow instructor at the Florida Ranger Camp. It was a unit of young men leading young men. It worked because our functions were limited to combat—tactics, maneuver, and supply. The company could have never passed a muster in a peacetime setting, but in the jungle we were a formidable force.

For the next several months, we operated in the interior of I Corps. Lots of airmobile insertions and long search-and-destroy missions in the mountains and jungles. There was ample combat, but I doubt if this period differed much from the experiences of other infantry companies in Vietnam at the time.

On May 9, 1969, my battalion air-assaulted from Camp Evans into a river valley near the A Shau Valley. The lush valley, about one kilometer wide, was covered with low elephant grass and had a fair size stream in its middle. We immediately set up a perimeter and dug fighting holes.

We had already been given our missions for the next day. My company, Delta, would lead the air assault to the base of Dong Ap Bia (Hill 937) and then move east upon the arrival of the next company. According to G-2 (Intelligence), there was a large NVA supply center on and around the mountain. I was sure we had drawn this mission because we had been successful in finding enemy supply dumps on the other side of the valley the previous week.

The battalion commander and his command group were to follow my company up the hill while Alpha Company moved to the northwest and Charlie Company to the south. Bravo Company would remain in reserve. We knew there was going to be some heavy fighting, but not more so than many other fights in which we had been engaged.

After an uneventful night, May 10 dawned clear, beautiful, and relatively cool. We ate a C-ration breakfast and waded the stream to the pickup zone (PZ) on the other side. There were supposed to be division pathfinders to guide the helicopters into our exact pickup spots, and the battalion commander was raging mad when they did not show up. We popped smoke and managed to bring in the choppers with no problems. This was the first and only time while I was with Delta that the entire company was airlifted all at one time. Usually, we had four helicopters to shuttle us into an LZ over an hour or so.

The NVA had antiaircraft guns in the A Shau, so our helicopters flew no more than twenty feet above the treetops. Terrain, or nap-of-the-earth, flying is very exciting because you can look down only a few feet into the trees. When the helicopter nears a mountain, the pilot pulls up at the last second, tops the peak, and dives down the other side. It is better than a roller coaster, but perhaps not as safe.

During the flight I saw a large deer with a huge set of antlers standing in a jungle clearing. He just stood there watching us fly over. He was majestic.

We could see friendly artillery rounds exploding on the LZ just as our flight was on final. The fires lifted as we neared and four helicopter gunships swept in prepping the sides of the LZ. Our helicopters hovered six feet above the ground with their skids touching the top of the elephant grass. We had to jump to the ground with our eighty-pound rucksacks. No one was hurt by the drop, but it pissed off a lot of guys that the choppers had not set us on the ground. Several of my soldiers shot the departing birds the finger and shouted obscenities at them.

My platoons immediately deployed to secure the LZ for the arrival of the remainder of the battalion. I dispatched a reinforced squad to the west toward a wood line that dominated the LZ. Within an hour Alpha and Charlie Companies were on the ground, as was the battalion CP. About 11:00 a.m., my recon squad received two sniper rounds from somewhere on Hill 937. The rifle fire did no damage, but those were the opening rounds of the long fight that followed. I later came to the conclusion that these sniper rounds were an announcement to all of us that the NVA occupied the hill and that we were welcome to try to take it. They had well-constructed defensive positions, complete with bunkers and connecting trenches that were less than two kilometers from the safe haven of the Cambodian border to which they could either escape or from which they could receive reinforcements and supplies. They knew we would pursue the snipers and they were correct.

The ridgeline we followed was virgin jungle with visibility limited to only ten or twenty meters. After we moved about 1,500 meters, my point reported spotting several NVA running up the ridgeline. We continued to pursue, but a few minutes later, the battalion commander called me on the radio to tell me to find a place for his command post. I found a relatively flat piece of ground and met with the battalion operations officer (S-3), who approved the location. My platoons established a perimeter and began to put out observations posts.

A forward air observer and the division's air reconnaissance had spotted a number of NVA in our area, and the battalion commander had already requested that Bravo Company come forward from its reserve position. Bravo soon arrived and passed through our perimeter and continued up the ridge. Half an hour later, they were in a heavy firefight, with enemy rounds passing over and through Bravo into our positions. I alerted a platoon to be prepared to reinforce Bravo, but other than keeping my head down, there was nothing else I could do.

The firefight continued until airstrikes finally sent the enemy back up the hill. Wounded began coming down the ridge, and my first sergeant coordinated their evacuation. A black sergeant made his own way on a badly wounded leg. He was angry and cussing. I went up to him and said, "Hey, you're out of here. Brighten up!"

He smiled and said, "Ain't no big thing, sir. Those mother-fuckers." We both laughed, and he limped off to the LZ.

As darkness fell, I sent squad ambushes both up and down the ridge. The flanks were both so steep that we could merely roll hand grenades down on any approaching enemy. The night passed quietly.

At dawn of May 11, I pulled the ambushes back into the perimeter. Bravo soon got into another fierce firefight, and again we took charge in evacuating their wounded. Alpha Company also made contact down the valley to our west. I was put out that Bravo had taken over our mission and left us guarding the battalion command post. I knew, however, that our time would soon come.

Things stayed fairly quiet until about 1600 hours. A couple of Cobra gunships rolled in, mistakenly taking us for the NVA. Their 2.75-inch rockets began to explode in the treetops start-ing on the southwestern part of the perimeter, then over the top of the battalion CP, and then into the northeastern side. I was caught in the open and decided there was no time to run to a foxhole. Instead, I hit the ground and tried to make my body as small as possible. About ten rockets exploded in our perimeter before the gunships turned away.

The battalion CP suffered one killed and twelve wounded. Among the wounded were the S-3 air operations officer and the battalion sergeant major. The battalion commander was bleeding from a back wound and had numbness in his legs but elected to stay on the ground rather than be evacuated.

My company had one dead and twenty-five wounded—30 percent of Delta's entire manpower. One of the wounded was a radio telephone operator, and another was the leader of the 1st Platoon. I saw the platoon leader limping toward the land-ing zone. He waved at me, and I waved back. I never saw him again. I was just too busy reorganizing the company to have the time to say a more formal good-bye.

The medics worked on the more seriously wounded. I saw my company head medic working on a Japanese-American kid who had a pin-size hole in his chest. There was only a single drop of blood on the outside, but he was bleeding to death internally. The medic frantically beat him on the chest and administered CPR. He finally saw that it was doing no good and sat back on his haunches and cried. Another soldier put his arm around the medic's shoulder and said, "Doc, you did all you could do."

Talking more to himself than those around him, the medic, "He died on me. The son of a bitch died on me." Then he got up and began working on other wounded.

While all this was going on, the NVA were shooting artillery in our direction from Laos. Fortunately, the rounds landed about 600 meters short of our perimeter. As I walked around our positions, I was amazed, as always, by the resiliency of American soldiers. Among the men there was a sense of outrage about being shot up by our own gunships, but generally, they quickly returned to business as usual. They ate their canned rations and prepared for night ambushes. The disaster had not affected our combat effectiveness—except by reducing our numbers by twenty-six men.

Bravo continued to hold in place and direct air strikes on upper regions of the hill. Alpha Company was ordered to join us around the CP, so I knew we would soon be going up the hill. Charlie Company was also ordered to close on the base of the hill. Elements of the 1st Battalion, 506th Airborne Infantry Regiment were on the way to help, but they were stopped by enemy contact in the valley below. The night passed with no further action.

During the day of May 12, we moved to positions to begin a general assault up the hill. Bravo would continue going up the ridge we currently shared. Charlie was to start up a ridge to the right flank and Delta on the left.

To get to our assigned ridgeline, we had to go down a 100-meter decline with almost vertical sides and then back up the other side to get to the hill's left flank. The sides of the gulch were so steep that it required ropes on both the descent and ascent. It was slow, grueling work. By late afternoon it was apparent that neither we nor Charlie Company would be in position to launch an attack before dark. The battalion commander ordered us to stop and establish defensive perimeters.

I thought that we had gotten out of the battalion CP perimeter undetected because we had stayed in deep foliage and had come across no new or old trails. I decided to take a chance and not have the company dig in because I did not want to make noise and be located by the NVA. This was risky, given the large number of enemy around us. We enforced strict noise discipline and did not allow poncho hooches for fear of light reflection. Actually, our position was very defendable. The only decent approaches were down or up the narrow ridgeline and I posted two machine guns on each. The night passed uneventfully.

Just after sunrise on May 13, the air force resumed their bombing of the ridgeline in front of Bravo Company. By this time we knew there were a large number of NVA on the hill in front of Bravo, but I don't think anyone fully realized the number of enemy soldiers and extensive fortifications we were up against.

About 1030 hours we, along with Bravo and Charlie Companies, continued our assault up the hill. Our route was not bad for about 600 meters. I hoped that we could reach the top undetected—sneak in the back door while Bravo and Charlie kept the NVA busy on our flanks. However, the ridgeline abruptly ended with an almost vertical drop into a streambed and with only a cliff on the other side. We would be exposed for more than 200 meters, but if we were going to cover Bravo Company's flank, we had to take the chance. I let battalion know what we were facing only to be told they wanted us on the top of the hill as soon as possible.

My 1st Platoon, previously on point, now took up an overlook position on the near side of the ravine to cover the rest of the company's crossing. The 2nd Platoon then started down the side of the near cliff, using ropes and holding on to vines and bushes to make their way to the streambed. I followed them with my headquarters group, and the 3rd Platoon came after us. The platoons put out flank security in the streambed following our company SOP.

The 2nd Platoon began climbing up the far side. I followed behind their first squad. My first sergeant remained in the streambed to help coordinate the crossing. The rest of the 2nd Platoon and then the 3rd Platoon came up the cliff behind me. My lead elements at the top of the cliff reported that no enemy were in sight.

During the crossing we could hear Bravo Company in a fierce firefight. I was still climbing when I heard a huge explosion followed by the fire between Bravo and the NVA dissipating. An air force bomb had fallen short and killed or wounded several of the Bravo soldiers, forcing them to break contact and withdraw down their ridge.

I was less than halfway up the cliff when the NVA opened up with rocket-propelled grenades (RPGs), machine guns, and small arms. The enemy fire came from up the ridge and struck troops on both sides of the ravine. Those of us still in the streambed or climbing the cliff were covered from the fire.

The initial RPG rounds wounded eight or nine soldiers, including the 1st Platoon leader, who was hit in his back on the near side and blown down into the streambed. His back was broken. A PFC had a sucking chest wound that required quick evacuation or he would die. Still another man was blinded.

The 1st Platoon sergeant, now the platoon leader, took charge of his survivors and began placing withering fire on the NVA. The men on the far side and those in the streambed who had a field of fire did likewise. All of this was automatic. I did not have to order them to return fire. It must have been effective because the NVA fire slackened.

My medics wanted to bring in a Dustoff immediately, but I wouldn't call for the medevac until we had secured the high ground on the other side of the stream. I continued to climb and to encourage the rest of the 2nd Platoon to reach the top as soon as possible—this, of course, is a relative term when climbing a cliff. Nonetheless, in half an hour, my RTOs, the 2nd Platoon, and I were on the high side of the streambed on a narrow ridge. We now controlled the high ground, or thought we did, and we had the 3rd Platoon in the streambed and 1st Platoon still on the downhill side.

Just as the last of the 2nd Platoon reached the top of the cliff, two events began to unfold. First, I could hear an approaching medevac in the air, and second, on the ground I could hear NVA crashing through the jungle down the ridge. They made no attempt to mask the sound of their movement. Just as they got about fifty meters from us, they stopped. Their company commander must have ordered them to block the ridgeline rather than attack. While they had stopped their advance, they did continue to lob RPG rounds into the company. This added to the tension but produced no more casualties—at least until the helicopter hovered above the streambed in an attempt to use a jungle penetrator cable and basket to evacuate the wounded.

About this time I heard an RPG fired from our right front, followed by an explosion behind and below me. I turned around, knowing beforehand that the helicopter had been shot down.

My confirmation of the crash came from one of the platoon sergeants who got on the company radio net in a panic, screaming, "The helicopter has been shot down! You've got to get us out of here! We'll all be killed."

Afraid that his panic would infect the entire company, I pressed the send button on my radio so no one else could hear or transmit. I then had my other RTO change the frequency on his battalion command net to the administrative net that was monitored by my first sergeant. I told him to take the radio away from the panicky NCO and to deck him if he had to. The first sergeant said he would take care of it. He also told me that three of our wounded had been killed in the chopper crash and that they were now working to get the crew out of the downed bird.

As I made my way back down into the riverbed, many things were going on at the crash site. A small fire had begun and everyone knew that the helicopter might explode within minutes, if not seconds. The urgency to get the five flight crewmen out of the wreck was immense.

The helicopter lay on its left side. One of my NCOs climbed up to where the pilot lay with a leg crushed and jammed into the rudder pedals, preventing his extraction. Fire began to lick its way up the side of the chopper. The sergeant took out his knife and cut away muscle and tendons until he freed the pilot's leg and pulled him out just as the entire helicopter burst into flame. Four Delta troopers were severely burned trying to rescue the remaining crewmen. All efforts were useless. We could only look on helplessly as the crewmen burned alive. Mercifully, all of the helicopter crew were unconscious from the crash and did not have to experience the hell of burning to death. By the time the fire was finally out, the aviators were reduced to half their normal size.

I now had one platoon on the uphill side of the ridge, one in the streambed with the crashed chopper, and one still on the downhill side. We had thirteen wounded, five of whom would have to be carried to the LZ at the base of the hill for extraction. In addition to the dead aviators, three Delta soldiers had been killed by the crashing helicopter. One was the soldier with the sucking chest wound who was in the chopper's extraction basket when it crashed on him. Two more soldiers were killed by the thrashing rotor blades. My first sergeant told me that one of the men was cut in two by the rotor blade. He said that the soldier remained conscious and looked down at the gaping wound. He added that the soldier's expression was one of horror and a realization that he was dead.

I could tell that the soldier's death and my first sergeant's own brush with mortality had deeply affected him. I had no idea of what to say to my subordinate and friend, so I did what soldiers do in these situations. I talked about something else. I think I asked him if all our weapons had been accounted for or something like that. We never discussed it again.

I called the battalion commander on the radio and gave
him a situation report on the helicopter crash and our number
of dead and wounded. I asked him if he wanted us to continue
up the hill or to bring the wounded down for evacuation. He
asked me what I thought. I told him that I didn't think we
could continue the attack and evacuate the wounded at the
same time. Each of the five litters would require four men to
carry it in the steep terrain. With the loss of the previously
wounded from the aerial rockets, the wounded and dead from
the current firefight and chopper crash, and twenty litter bearers, I was left with only forty-two effective fighting men. Twenty
of my soldiers on the uphill side of the ravine were all that
stood between us and the NVA. I recommended that he dis-
patch a platoon of Alpha Company from his perimeter to assist
our withdrawal to his position, and he concurred.

We began moving everyone back up the cliff to the downhill part of the ridgeline. I made the decision to leave the dead
behind. This is the kind of decision that is not covered in training and that no commander ever wants to make. *Never leave a
fallen comrade behind* is the unspoken code of infantrymen.
Most would willingly die in an attempt to recover their dead
fellow soldiers. My choice, however, came down to a simple
math problem. I did not have enough soldiers to retrieve the
dead in the ravine while also taking care of the wounded and
attempting to establish a 360-degree defensive perimeter—all
of this with the NVA only fifty meters or so up the high side of
the ridge. We would have to return after evacuating our
wounded to recover our dead.

The heat was oppressive, and the cliff remained almost vertical. We began about 1600 hours getting the wounded up the
embankment inch by inch with ropes, poncho litters, and
sheer muscle power. During this time the platoon from Alpha
Company joined us and took up security positions. We finally
got everyone out of the streambed and back on the lower level
of the ridge. The 2nd Platoon was still on the other side of the
streambed covering our withdrawal. They received sporadic
small-arms fire and an occasional RPG that did no harm. Once

we were all out of the ravine, I radioed the 2nd Platoon to join us. It was a great sense of relief when the 2nd Platoon sergeant, a brave, talented, experienced NCO, came into our perimeter and reported that all his men were safely back with us. He then dropped exhausted to the ground.

All the while, the men not carrying wounded had been digging in and establishing observation posts. No orders were needed. These were good infantrymen who knew their trade. After I checked the perimeter, I asked the head medic if any of the wounded were in danger of dying anytime soon. If they were, I knew we would have to hump them down the ridge in the now gathering darkness. Doc said he was worried about the helicopter pilot but thought he and the others would make the night. All of the wounded must have been in great pain despite the morphine Doc administered, but I did not hear a moan or whimper from any of them.

Three of the wounded men stood out. The first was the pilot, whose boot-encased foot stuck out at a strange angle despite the field splint on his leg. The second was the 1st Platoon leader, whose back had been broken in the initial fight and who had been again struck by pieces of the medevac's rotor blades. Finally, there was a small Puerto Rican who was always trying to be sent home on the claim he was the sole provider for his mother. He now leaned against a tree with bandages over his entire face to cover an eye wound. When I asked him how he was doing, he simply said, "Fine, sir."

The company, as well as myself, was exhausted. Fortunately, the NVA did not attack. I suppose they felt they were at the advantage in the defense and were waiting for us to resume our push up the hill. We could hear RPGs and mortars being fired into Bravo Company's perimeter to our flank, but the rest of the night passed without incident for us. I felt fairly at ease. But danger is a relative thing. When one goes from extreme danger to lesser degrees of danger, the lesser danger becomes very tolerable.

We began moving our wounded down the hill to the battalion CP and LZ on the morning of May 14. It took four hours for my 2nd Platoon and the attached platoon from Alpha Company to move the wounded the 600 meters. During that morning I had numerous conversations with the battalion commander. The first involved the platoon sergeant who had panicked down in the streambed. Even though he had only minor burns from the helicopter fire, I sent him to the rear— I wanted him gone forever.

The battalion commander questioned why I had sent back someone who could, and probably should, still be humping a rucksack. I told him that the sergeant had panicked, and his fear had nearly spread through the company. I warned that if he came back to the company, I would put him on point until he was shot, and if that did not work, I would shoot him myself. I was aware that this was an irrational response, but I was so angry that I meant what I said. I had become as radical as the circumstances that surrounded me, and I was operating with a different logic from that before the fight.

To the battalion commander's credit, he responded, "I understand. Is there anything else I can do for you?"

The second conversation focused on my request to go back up the hill to retrieve our dead. On the secure radio scrambler, I explained to the battalion commander that I thought we could recover the bodies without taking additional heavy casualties. I also emphasized the importance of the recovery to the company's sense of duty of not leaving anyone behind and that I felt it was important to their morale.

The three Delta soldiers we had left on the ridge, along with the helicopter crewmen who had come to our aid, were a part of our collective responsibility. No one in his right mind would risk lives for something as nebulous as morale, but this mission was different and had its own situational logic. We debated neither the fear nor the logic. The responsibility was simply embedded in our souls.

Beyond the responsibility as company commander, I had personal experiences to motivate me. A relative of my wife had been missing in action in one of the war's earlier battles. Even though his remains had been recovered five days later, I saw firsthand how the lack of knowledge and doubts had devastated the family. I knew that the mothers of my three men, and those of the aviators, had either received or were about to receive notice that their sons were missing. We had a responsibility to those dead men and their families.

During the planning process another problem arose. The 2nd Platoon had brought back four replacements from the LZ after they extracted the wounded. One of the replacements, who did not share our sense of obligation to our dead comrades, told his squad leader that he would not go. The staff sergeant with one punch knocked out the reluctant soldier—jungle justice with no investigation or court-martial. Once the medics brought the replacement back to consciousness, he picked up his rifle and joined his fellow soldiers. I don't know if he ever understood why he was asked to risk his life to recover men who were already dead. Regardless, he did his duty—and was wounded later in the day. I never saw him again.

The recovery plan was fair simple. One platoon would advance up a ridge parallel to our original route and provide overwatching fires for the recovery element. Another platoon would do likewise from the top to the ravine where our dead lay. A third platoon would go down the cliff and bring the bodies up and out. I would set up my CP behind the platoon overlooking the ravine.

The recovery teams were just beginning to lift and pull the bodies out of the ravine when the NVA opened up with small arms and RPGs. My two security platoons immediately returned fire with M16s, machine guns, grenade launchers, and even a 90 recoilless rifle we had drug from the LZ. The fire momentarily silenced the NVA weapons. When they renewed their fire, it lacked its original intensity.

My position was fairly well masked by the ridgeline, but one RPG gunner began to concentrate on the area of my CP. We were just below a bit of high ground, so the RPG rounds were falling a bit short. However, each explosion spattered us with sticks, rocks, and spent shrapnel. Several pieces of the still-hot shrapnel went down my collar of my shirt, burning my back. With each round I got madder and madder. Finally, despite the efforts of my RTO to stop me, I stood, charged to the top of the high ground yelling and cursing, and emptied a magazine on full automatic at my unseen enemy.

I then scurried back to my protected position and resumed being a company commander rather than just a shooter. It was a stupid thing to do, but firing those rounds relieved some of my stress and anger.

I don't think my shooting had much to do with it, but the NVA fire let up some, and we began to extract our dead. I was taken aback when I saw the first helicopter crewman as he was carried by me. His remains must not have weighed fifty pounds, blackened skin all over. His hands, feet, and face were burnt off, as was the flesh over his ribs, exposing the bones. All sense of a human being was lost.

The four men carrying the soldier who had been cut in two by the helicopter rotor blade were having a difficult time with the 200-pound body. At a steep portion of the ridgeline, they dropped him, and the body broke into two pieces. The four litter bearers jumped back in horror. One looked at me and implored, "Sir! He just broke in half!" The soldier was looking at something that was just unreal to him. It was beyond anything he could possibly conceive, and he wanted his company commander to fix it—or at least have it make a little sense.

Just then another RPG struck nearby, blowing several sticks into my face. I became angry at the enemy, angry at the soldier for getting cut in two, angry at the litter bearers who dropped him, and angry at the delay in getting my company out of the danger area. I ran up to those poor guys, grabbed the dead soldier's legs, threw them on the litter, and yelled at the men to pick up the rest of the body and quickly get their asses down the ridge.

While we were retrieving our dead, Charlie Company was getting chewed up 500 meters to our west. Parts of Bravo were dispatched to reinforce Charlie. Although I knew Charlie's fight was only half a kilometer away, it seemed like it was miles in the distance and not related to us. I did plot the best route on my map to go to the aid if called upon. Air strikes and artillery continued against the mountain for most of the day.

At the battalion CP, I saw that the battalion commander was making all decisions, large and small. The battalion S-3 had pretty much been frozen out of the decision-making process. One of the battalion commander's many prejudices was a hatred for West Point graduates, one of whom our S-3 happened to be.

Back at my company, I was standing and talking with my RTO and my artillery forward observer and his RTO when an RPG round suddenly exploded in a tree ten feet behind us, tearing off the top of my helmet and splattering my back with shrapnel. My FO was flung backward, and his RTO crumpled to the ground with chest wounds.

My back was burning from the pieces of the RPG, but I could tell the wounds were not significant. I ran to my FO, who was gasping for air. I ripped his shirt open to find tell-tale bubbles of a sucking chest wound coming from three one-inch holes in his left chest. I covered the wounds with my hands to keep air from escaping from his lungs and prevent them from collapsing as I yelled for a medic.

The artillery RTO had a six-inch hole in his chest. He stared straight into the sky, blinked a few times, and died. His blue unseeing eyes still looked alive, filled with incredible anger, I started a profane rant. My RTO said, "Sir, let's get out of here. This isn't safe."

I could tell that he was concerned because I was still cursing. He then said, "You should see your helmet. It's shot to hell."

His concern calmed me. I took off my helmet and found that four inches of the steel top were missing and a large section of the plastic liner was gone as well. There were sharp shards of metal around the edge of the hole like it had blown outward from the inside. I realized that I had escaped death or a severe brain injury by less than an inch. I went from feeling a powerful rage to being filled with an overwhelming joy at just being alive. Most people go through their entire lives and never experience these extreme emotions. I told my RTO that we had lived a lot of life in a very short period of time.

As we walked into the Delta perimeter, one of my soldiers saw my helmet and shouted, "Who do you think you are, sir, Captain Combat?" We shared a laugh. I was happy again.

While a medic picked tiny bits of shrapnel from my and my RTO's backs, I remembered that I was named for a great uncle who returned from World War I with a bullet hole in his helmet. My father was so impressed with the artifact hat he always said he would name his first son after the old veteran. I said a little prayer to my great uncle and told him that we might be taking this "hole in the helmet tradition" a bit far. The old man's spirit and I shared a laugh.

We maintained 50 percent alert that night, and I frequently checked the perimeter to be sure half of the men were awake. About midnight I looked up the hill to see more than fifty small fires twinkling in the night. At first I thought they were from our artillery and air strikes, but then noticed that the fires ran in three rough yet distinct bands across the front of the hill. I realized that they were cooking fires. Never before had I seen the NVA so blatantly advertise their positions. It was as if they were saying to us, "We're up here—come kick us off if you can."

The rest of the night passed uneventfully. Early the next morning, Alpha and Bravo Companies once again attacked up the hill. They made little progress before the Bravo Company commander was severely wounded by our own helicopter gunships. That pretty much stalled the attack, and by afternoon the two companies had returned to the battalion perimeter. A new captain took over Bravo Company. I began to wonder if we would run out of captains before we got to the top of the hill.

There was intelligence that the NVA would attack our perimeter that night so we remained on 100 percent alert. Our area remained quiet, but Charlie Company was hit by satchel charges. They countered with hand grenades, some of which we collected from our men and sent over to Charlie.

By the morning of May 16, I was beginning to feel intensely tired. Less than four hours of sleep in the last two days, combined with the pressures of combat, had taken its toll. I decided that I had to work in some catnaps during the day. Our artillery and air strikes continued to rock the hill.

The assistant division commander, a brigadier general, flew in about midday with some staff officers and reporters. When I saw the *Time* magazine reporter and his photographer, it confirmed that a major battle was shaping up. It was entertaining to watch the clean, spit-shined division staff officers and the reporters do double takes when they saw my damaged helmet. It was one of those moments in time where I took great pride in being a combat infantryman—everyone else is just *less than.*

A lieutenant colonel from division asked me some questions about the operation. I was careful not to criticize the battalion commander in any way. I really did not care for the man at all, but he was my commander and therefore deserved my loyalty.

Our battalion remained in the perimeter while the 1st Battalion, 506th Airborne Infantry, moved to the other side of the hill. The plan was for a two-battalion attack on May 18. I did get in a few catnaps, alternated with watching air strikes on the hill. The night passed without incident.

We spent May 17 watching air strikes on the hill. The 1/506 continued to move into position so we could have a coordinated attack. The battalion commander told us that Alpha Company would assault up the ridgeline on the same path as the day before. Delta would attack up the ridgeline on which Bravo had been fighting. He also told us that flak jackets would be issued as would gas masks because the plan called for CS (tear gas) to precede our attack.

As I walked back the company, I knew that Delta's turn had come up again and that we were going to take terrible casualties. We were going to attack over bare ground into dug-in machine-gun bunkers and spider holes. Both my heart and mind knew that half of us were going to be dead or wounded within the next twenty-four hours. An almost overwhelming sadness filled me, mixed with fear and excitement. The knowledge that my leadership and intelligence were going to be tested like never before was humbling. It was apparent to me that the next day would be the most important of our lives.

I called together my platoon leaders and first sergeant to give them my warning order. I didn't pull any punches and told them that we were going to suffer a lot of casualties the next day and to prepare themselves and their men to accept that fact. The wounded who could walk would be expected to make their own way down the hill. We would do our best to get the others out. The first sergeant and platoon sergeants then began to issue the gas masks and flak jackets along with extra ammo to the troops.

I took a platoon and began to recon our next day's route up the hill. Because of the narrowness of the ridge and steepness of its sides, there was really no way up the hill except the same route Bravo had attempted earlier. It was eerie walking up the ground where Bravo had fought for the past six days. There was battlefield debris everywhere. Bloody bandages, spent rifle and machine-gun cartridges, shredded rucksacks, uniforms, and other flotsam from the fights lay among trees shattered by artillery fire and air strikes. I counted seven dead enemy soldiers. Decomposing bodies lose their facial features after a very short time and look less human the longer they are left to rot. Although I respected the dead soldiers as fellow warriors, their death and condition had no effect on me. They were simply a natural part of what had become my life. I did feel a profound respect for the infantrymen of Bravo Company.

Where our trail intersected a horizontal one, there were two fully loaded U.S. rucksacks leaned up against a tree. One of my soldiers, fearful of booby traps, looked at me and said, "I'm not touching those rucks, sir."

I replied, "Good idea because I'm not touching them either." We smiled at each other and continued up the ridge. We stopped when we could just make out the top of the hill through the vegetation. I then took a fire team of four soldiers,

and we leap-frogged from one tree to the next for another
thirty meters. We were very careful to stay behind cover as we
had no desire to get in a firefight at that moment. From there
I was greeted with the worst possible ground on which to conduct an assault that anyone could imagine. The entire mountain, from about twenty meters to my front, was completely
denuded except for a large tangle of trees near the top—
which was an obstacle in its own right. The ridgeline narrowed
at the tree line from forty to ten meters across with steep
sides and continued that way for at least a hundred meters up
the hill.

I recognized that it would be a gauntlet we would have to
negotiate the next day. If we made it through the narrow gap,
we would then face a steep uphill climb of at least forty-five
degrees for at least 400 meters. It got even steeper near the
summit. There was no concealment that would block the
vision of the NVA gunners anywhere along the nearly quarter
mile. I did spot a shallow depression near the top that might
offer a little cover.

Making the situation even more untenable was that the
vegetation-covered ridgeline on our right flank, which was to
be Alpha Company's line of advance, was only seventy meters
from ours. If Alpha slowed from pushing the NVA up the hill,
it meant we would begin receiving flanking fire. Also there was
a tree line on the ridge to our left about 300 meters away
where the Medevac had been shot down. It would provide the
NVA an additional opportunity to fire on our flank.

I could not see the dug-in, reinforced NVA with trenches,
tunnels, and machine-gun bunkers that waited for our attack
to the top, but I knew they were there. I knew we were going to
be in trouble. There was no "schoolbook–Fort Benning solution" for the situation we faced, but I had to come up with a
plan that gave us the best chance of success or at least survival.
I honestly did not know if such a plan existed. I kept thinking,
"I wish the NVA would just withdraw tonight."

When we returned to the battalion perimeter, I went to the
Alpha Company sector and talked to their commander. I told

him what I had seen on the hill and asked if he had any solutions. He looked down and said, "No, I don't. It's going to be a tough nut to crack. I think we are going to be involved in a blood bath tomorrow."

I trusted the Alpha Company commander's integrity and his skills as a soldier, so I asked, "What do you think would happen if we refused to go up the hill again or if we told the battalion commander that we had serious doubts about our chances of success?"

He responded with the wisdom that I expected, saying, "It would not make one damn bit of difference. Everybody from the division commander down is involved in this. The 1/506th is attacking the other side. It's too late to stop. If we said no, they would fire us, and one of our lieutenants would take our companies up the hill tomorrow."

I had never questioned an order, even a foolish one, in my entire career. I was in unmapped territory. I had no training to help me through this dilemma. It was a situation that really was not discussed at any level. This was the United States Army, and we always carried out our orders no matter how difficult.

I acknowledged the Alpha Company commander's logic and said, "You are right. The troops have a better chance with us in command than with any of our platoon leaders." I concluded, "When we start up that hill, I need you to cover my right flank or we're dead."

He looked me in the eye and said, "You can count on it."

I then went and reported what I had seen on my recon to the battalion commander. My only attempt to get him to change the orders for the following day was to say, "Sir, the flanking fire and no concealment means that Delta Company is going to suffer a lot of casualties."

He looked at me, put his hand on my shoulder, and said, "You'll do fine tomorrow."

That was it. Our future was set. I went back to my CP and began to plan. As I saw it, we had two courses of action. We could attack with one platoon to keep pressure on our line of advance and wait until Alpha Company moved far enough up the hill to protect most of our right flank. This would mean that most of my lead platoon would be sacrificed and few would survive. My gut told me that this was a losing tactic because I would be committing my force piecemeal.

I decided that we would attack up the narrow, seventy-meter gauntlet ridge with the platoons in column. Upon completion of navigating through the gauntlet, the lead platoon would go to the right and the following platoon to the left. The trail platoon would stay in the tree line to provide fire support and to serve as a reserve. I would commit them in response to how the situation developed.

I was well aware that we had to keep moving forward until we overran the enemy positions and occupied the top of the hill. If we stopped in front of their positions on that denuded mountain, we would receive fire from three sides—and die.

After I was satisfied with my plan, I briefed my first sergeant to see if he had any ideas for alternatives. We had shared many a patrol in the Florida Ranger Camp and trusted him completely. He said he could not see any other rational approach. Along with being my first sergeant, he was also my friend. In Florida I had met his wife and children. We both realized that there was nothing further we could do—we were professional soldiers caught up in our roles.

I assembled the platoon leaders and issued my orders. The 3rd Platoon would lead, followed by the 2nd, and then the 1st. Management of the wounded was one of my top priorities—we could not let our wounded slow or stop our attack.

As I was walking around the perimeter inspecting the preparations, a PFC asked me, "Do you know what they are calling this place, sir?"

When I replied no, he said, "Hamburger Hill."

This was the first time I had heard the term, so I asked why.

He smiled and said, "We go up—hamburger comes down." He paused, raised his fist, smiled again, and said, "It ain't no big thing, sir."

When I returned to the company CP, there were six replacements waiting. The first sergeant had already assigned them to their platoons, and they were waiting for my welcome and briefing. I told them that we were going to make a tough attack the next day and that all they had to do was follow their fire team and squad leaders and they would be fine. I had nothing else to offer. I wondered how many would be standing at the end of the next day.

A PFC came to the CP asking to speak to the first sergeant. After he did so, the first sergeant said that the man was scheduled for point the next day for the lead platoon—in other words he would be the point man for the entire company. The man was distraught and said he was sure that he would be killed. The first sergeant sent him back to talk to his platoon sergeant. Fifteen minutes later, the PFC returned and told me with a proud smile that he was the point for tomorrow. I wished him luck. That was the last time I saw him alive.

I was pumped with adrenaline. I spent the rest of the day trying to anticipate all the things that could go wrong the next day, but I could think of nothing that made me adjust my plan. That night the NVA artillery once more fired from Laos at us, but the rounds again fell short. I slept well.

Early the morning of May 18, we began our move from the battalion perimeter to our line of departure—about 1,000 meters. Our approach to the LD was along a relatively flat ridgeline that varied in width from fifty meters to as narrow as twenty meters and was covered with virgin jungle growth. There were several well-worn trails from Bravo's assaults up the hill. Nothing had changed from my recon the day before.

Our own artillery, high explosives mixed with CS rounds, prepped our axis of advance. We had on our gas masks, and I could see artillery rounds landing in the trees fifty meters to our front. A large piece of artillery shrapnel hit my helmet, nearly knocking me down. It felt like someone had hit me on the top of my helmet with a two-by-four. I kept moving, with only a brief moment to think that my helmets had certainly taken a beating over the past days. I also wondered if this was a foreshadowing of what was to happen.

The line of departure was the tree line where the jungle ended and the denuded ridgeline began its ascent to the top of Hamburger Hill. By the time we reached the tree line, we were already receiving intense small-arms fire. Fifty meters past the tree line was the narrow ridgeline only ten meters wide, with steep drop-offs on each side.

My RTOs and I followed the lead platoon. As we stepped out of the jungle into the gauntlet, we were greeted by thousands of bullets breaking the sound barrier around us, the audio equivalent of a thousand bullwhips cracking about a foot from our heads. Bullets were whacking the ground all around us, kicking up dirt and debris. Grenades were crumping, and I could see their light gray smoke puffs only ten or fifteen meters away.

In this totally alien environment were also the sights of the dead and wounded. The point man who had come to the first sergeant with concerns about his death was correct in his prediction. He had made it only ten meters into the open area. He now stood dead, his body impaled on a tangle of branches, arms stretched out as if he had been crucified. His bloody face hung back with pink buck teeth exposed. He had been shot in the heart and lungs, and blood still dripped from his mouth.

Wounded soldiers followed my orders to evacuate themselves if possible. A man with a shoulder wound was followed by a soldier with his nose shot off. Despite the bullets flying and the general turmoil, a man without a nose leaves a lasting impression. It is an ugly, disfiguring wound.

In those first few minutes, I had much more to do than look around and dodge bullets. I had to evaluate the situation to see if we needed to make adjustments to our plan of attack. It quickly became obvious that there was no cover or any way up the ridge other than straight forward. We had to push on into the NVA defenses and kill them. If we stalled, we would die.

The situation quickly became worse. I came upon a machine gunner firing into the tree-covered ridgeline to our right where Alpha Company was attacking. I shouted for him to stop because Alpha was on the other ridgeline, and he hollered back that we were receiving fire from that flank. I looked down and saw bullets striking the ground and kicking dirt to my right, which meant he was correct. I told him to resume firing. I radioed battalion and asked for them to have Alpha's lead platoon pop smoke. To my horror I saw that the smoke marked their progress only ten meters beyond the tree line—a hundred meters to our rear. Alpha was in their own bad fight, and that left our right flank exposed.

About this time an enemy soldier sprang from his defensive position twenty meters to my front and began running up the hill. I shot him. To this day I hate to admit it, but that kill was a great stress reliever. It gave me a small sense of payback.

The lead platoon leader informed me that he could go no farther because of enemy fire and because he could see huge Claymore mines to his front. I ordered him to keep moving and suggested that he shoot the Claymores with his M79 grenade launchers to cause predetonation. He acknowledged just before I saw him blown six feet into the air by a hand grenade, flailing like a rag doll as he fell. The last thing he heard in his life was me yelling at him to keep moving.

Our attack was stalling, so I ordered the reserve platoon forward along the right side away from the claymores. It was the last order I gave as company commander. I was on one knee; bullets were hitting all around me. I ignored them because they were not hitting me or anyone else. It was not really bravery. The simple fact was that bullets were striking everywhere and one place was as safe as the next.

I was reaching back to grab a radio handset from an RTO when a machine-gun bullet hit me in the right arm, six inches below the shoulder on the triceps side and exiting out the front in my arm pit. Being hit sounded like a wooden bat hitting a baseball. I was spun around to my left and pitched forward on my left side. Arterial blood spewed from the wound. I knew instantly that I had been badly hit because I felt the same body sensation that I had when being badly tagged in a fistfight. There was no initial pain—just a sensation of being seriously damaged.

I pushed my thumb into the bullet hole as far as it would go. The spurting blood stopped, and I regained color vision. I happily noted that my arm was still somewhat connected to my body. At the same time I realized that I was facing death. I did so with no fear or joy, just a calm sense of resignation and acceptance. But with the combination of shock and my thumb, a quarter-inch blood clot had formed, thus saving my life. I had no idea at the time that my thumb might stop the arterial bleeding. I was acting strictly out of reflex. Whatever, I was just thankful that it worked.

Taking a handset from one of the RTOs, I informed the battalion commander that I had a chunk of my arm missing and that I was turning over command of the company to the lone surviving platoon leader. Both RTOs pulled me into a bomb crater twenty meters down the ridge and then departed immediately to look for their new company commander— brave men. They left behind a damaged radio that would receive but would no longer transmit.

The pain began to come in waves—I mean serious pain, the kind that makes one groan and wither. A medic jumped into my hole, put a battle dressing on the wound, and wrapped a large bandage around my arm and body, using my body as a splint. The wound was too far up the arm to use a traditional tourniquet.

The body splint and morphine helped dull the pain a bit. Over the next hours, I had periodic fantasies that I could get out of the crater and again lead the company, but each time I moved, I was rewarded with disabling pain. The pain likely saved my life. If I had done much movement, the clot would have broken loose and I would have bled to death. I had to accept the fact that the battle was over for me.

I was alone in the crater, but I did have the damaged radio, so I heard the battle progress. I felt pride when I heard the surviving lieutenant whom I had placed in my command tell the battalion commander that he would stay on the hill as long as he lived, but that if he did not get some more ammunition soon, there was no chance of making it to the top. That was my company—and they were not backing up.

A short time later, a soldier ran down the hill and jumped into my crater. I recognized him as the company screw-up who always dodged his duties. He smiled at me and said he was going after ammo. I figured he was going down the hill with no intentions of returning, but he proved me wrong when he returned carrying a heavy load of ammo. He made this run two more times.

An artillery sergeant joined me in the crater as he called in artillery on our left flank. Delta was now receiving fire from the front as well as both flanks.

I have no idea how long I stayed in the bomb crater—an hour, or two, or maybe three—I just don't know. I think I was conscious most of the time. At some point I heard the lieutenant acting as company commander on the radio pleading for more ammunition. I tried to get the radio to transmit to tell battalion to either get ammo to Delta or pull them back but the radio transmitter remained inoperable.

Finally, a soldier from Charlie Company jumped into the crater, receiving a bullet wound in his leg on his way. Apparently, Charlie was now attempting to come up the ridge in support of Delta. In my mind I said, "To hell with it," and I crawled out of the crater and made my way down the denuded ridge. NVA bullets whacked the ground all around me from the flanks, but I no longer really cared. I actually felt invincible, likely a result of shock and loss of blood.

As I neared the tree line, the Charlie Company commander yelled at me to get down before I got shot. I kept walking, pausing only long enough to shout back, "Fuck you." I have no idea where that response came from, but it was as good as any. I walked about fifty meters beyond Charlie's line and collapsed on the trail. Soon other wounded joined me. We were mostly covered from enemy fire, but I realized that all the enemy would have to do is come in from the unprotected flanks and finish us off. I attempted to get a defense organized, but I had absolutely no strength remaining. I lay back down and waited for what came next. Pain again radiated from my shoulder throughout my body.

I have no idea how long I remained on the trail—I was fighting pain so severe that time no longer existed. It started to rain heavily, and I began to shiver from the cold as well as from the loss of blood. I tried to stop the shivering because it made me feel like I was out of control and I did not want others to think I was weak. At some time I began to negotiate with God, promising he could have my arm if he just let me live.

More wounded joined us. A medic gave me some additional morphine, but it did little to diminish the pain. A small helicopter began picking up the wounded and shuttling them 400 meters down the hill to the battalion CP. I believe I was in the second group but am unsure about that and about just how I got on the helicopter.

At the battalion CP, I was placed on a regular stretcher under some trees. I was still shivering uncontrollably. Sitting next to me was one of my RTOs who had been shot in the elbow; he was in tremendous pain. There were four or five news photographers snapping pictures of the wounded. The RTO and his pain ended up published in *Time*. I turned away. I did not want them to take a picture of me shivering.

More Delta troops were coming off the hill. My first sergeant, with a leg wound, limped by and said, "Thank God you're alive. I thought you were dead." The battalion commander came by and said the same thing.

The battalion doctor finally made his way to my litter, felt my pulse, and said, "I want him out of here right away." He had found no pulse in my wounded arm and said that I would finish bleeding to death if the clot did not hold. He wrote something on a tag he tied to my boot. As I waited for the medevac, a sergeant from Bravo Company gave me a cup of warm C-ration coffee. He tenderly raised my head so I could swallow. What a kindness—and I don't even remember his name.

I was carried to a Dustoff helicopter and strapped onto the second tier of stretchers. Most of my company were dead or wounded. I grieved for them as I still do today. Yet as the helicopter rose off the ground, turned, and dropped off the hill to

gain climbing air speed, I experienced one of the greatest feelings of my life. A great darkness was lifted from my soul to be
replaced by a simple, consuming joy. I knew that I would live—
that I had survived Hamburger Hill. There are no words to
describe the freedom I felt. I have never before or since experienced such a moment of pure exhilaration.

Life is sweet. Although I faced eighteen months of severe
pain, healing, and recovery, I always came back then, as I do
now, to that purest fleeting minute of hope.

(Two days later, May 20, at about 1700 hours, elements of
the 3/187 topped Hamburger Hill and eliminated the last of
its defenders. More than 670 NVA were killed by verified body
count, and three were taken prisoner. Hundreds, if not thousands, more NVA died from artillery and airstrikes along their
withdrawal route. American losses were 72 killed and 372
wounded. Two weeks later, on June 5, the 101st Airborne Division abandoned Hamburger Hill, giving it back to the jungle.)

**—101st Airborne Division, I Corps, 1969**

It was nearly dark when my squad set up a linear ambush
along the abandoned railroad track that paralleled Highway
1 between Long Binh and Xuan Loc. The old rail right-of-way
offered an easier path into the villages than the thick jungle
that surrounded it.

A little after midnight, I saw movement in my night-vision
scope and alerted the squad leader to warn the rest of the
men. The gook kept coming, his rifle slung over his back. We
let him get close, hoping there were more behind him but
soon decided he was alone. When he reached the edge of our
kill zone, he spotted one of our Claymore mines. I thought he
would run, but apparently, he had never seen one of the U.S.
explosive devices. He picked it up to inspect it just as my squad
leader clicked the igniter.

In the light of the explosion, I saw the top half of the gook literally disappeared in a pink cloud. Oddly, his legs and lower torso remained standing for a few seconds. I swear they even took a couple of steps before they fell over.

**—199th Light Infantry Brigade, III Corps, 1969**

★ ★ ★

My LRRP team went in with the helicopters that were extracting an infantry company. We were to stay behind to see what the enemy would do once they thought the Americans had departed the area. As the choppers with their infantry cargo lifted off the pickup zone, the six of us eased into the edge of the tree line and placed Claymore mines on the most likely approach. Less than an hour later, we heard movement in the jungle. The noise rapidly increased as the VC neared our position. As we had hoped, they thought everyone had left on the choppers. They were soon to learn just how wrong was this assumption.

The enemy point man was only a few feet from one our Claymores when our team leader blew the mine and initiated the ambush. We filled the kill zone and its screaming mass of men with M16 fire and hand grenades. In seconds, twelve VC lay dead. They had not returned a single shot. We gathered their weapons, equipment, and documents, and less than ten minutes after the first shot, we were on our bird back to base camp.

It had been a perfect ambush, a perfect mission. I would have remembered it regardless, but it remains a bit more vivid in my mind because it was my first patrol.

**—9th Infantry Division, IV Corps, 1968**

We had been on company operations in the jungles and mountains of the Central Highlands for more than two weeks. Other than a couple of light contacts, everything had been pretty quiet. That changed about midday. Our lead elements stumbled upon a dug-in NVA unit. We maneuvered to put as much firepower on them as possible. Unfortunately, the thick monsoon clouds hovered near the ground, preventing our use of air power. We were also at the max artillery range, and their fire was mostly ineffective.

The firefight settled into a sustained battle, with neither side gaining an advantage. After more than an hour of fighting, we had sustained several killed and even more wounded. I don't know how the enemy was faring, but they were likely also hurting.

During a lull in the battle, a GI yelled out, "Hey Charlie, you quit fucking with us and we will quit fucking with you." Someone on the other side must have understood English. The sporadic gun fire from both sides ceased. Everything became quiet again. After a few minutes all we could hear was the clanking of equipment as the enemy slipped away into the jungle. We stayed in place for a while and then began withdrawing to the nearest clearing to evacuate our dead and wounded. None of our officers ever mentioned what had brought an end to the battle.

**—25th Infantry Division, II Corps, 1966**

The enemy ambush caught our lead platoon by surprise. Rifle and machine-gun fire sent GIs diving for cover and returning fire. Typical of many fights, this one did not last long. Several of our guys were wounded; two lay dead. One had been shot several times in the chest and had died almost immediately. The second body did not have a visible mark. A couple of the guys noted that the dead soldier was a new guy and wondered if he had died of a heart attack or maybe simply fright.

A few days later, we got a report from the mortuary that a single AK round had entered the soldier's anus and punctured most of his internal organs before lodging in the base of his throat. Either he had turned to find cover or reached behind for more ammo during the fight. Bullets have no respect for rank or anatomy.

**—173rd Airborne Brigade, III Corps, 1967**

We were in the edge of a rubber plantation east of Bear Cat when the third man in our column hit a booby-trapped grenade. Fragments ripped through his neck sending a geyser of blood from his jugular into the air. A buddy tried to stop the flow with his hands, but the arc of blood continued to flow. The blood stopped only when the wounded soldier's still-beating heart emptied his body. Soon that organ stopped, leaving a stream of blood that ran for more than six feet along the plantation floor.

Another GI had been hit with multiple frag wounds in both legs. Both extremities were punctured by hundreds of bits of metal ranging from pinpoint pricks to gashes several inches in length. Most of the damage appeared to be on the left side. As we cut off his fatigue trousers, the soldier managed between groans and suppressed screams to calmly ask if he still had his balls. An affirmative answer seemed to comfort him more than the bandages we were applying.

The initial leg tourniquet failed to stem the blood flow. It began to look as if he would bleed out like his fellow soldier now lying dead a few feet away. The company commander, who had been standing aside to allow the medics to work, stepped forward. He took the web belt out of the cut-off trousers and made it into an additional tourniquet. When the blood still flowed, he placed his boot on the wounded soldier's upper thigh for leverage and began pulling the belt tighter.

This brought new screams from the wounded man, but he quieted when the blood flow finally stopped. He was silent while the medic reached in his bag for morphine with built-in needle and found a small area void of shrapnel punctures on the less injured leg. The medic pushed the needle into the soldier's thigh. I'll be damned if he didn't yell. Hundreds of holes in his legs, and he reacted to a thin needle. Maybe he had something about medical shots.

In a misting rain we put the dead and wounded on the same Dustoff. I heard later that the man with the leg wound survived. I hope so.

—**199th Light Infantry Brigade, III Corps, 1969**

The UH-1 helicopter had gone down as a result of ground fire just across the border in Laos after inserting a recon team along the Ho Chi Minh Trail. Another chopper landed and quickly evacuated the injured door gunners and deceased copilot. The dead pilot, however, was tightly wedged in his seat by the instrumental panel and the aircraft's nose being forced backward during the crash landing, and they could not free him.

Someone up the chain of command ordered my Special Forces Studies and Observation (SOG) Team to recover the body. We carried in several iron crowbars and metal saws, but we were barely on the ground before we began receiving fire from all directions. Our support gunships kept the enemy off of us for a while, but it soon became apparent that we could not free the pilot's body and that the NVA were preparing to overrun our position.

Our team leader called in additional fire support as well as our extraction bird. With no comment, he took his machete and cut off the pilot's head and placed it in a parachute bag with the tools. Minutes later, we were safely in the air on the way back to our South Vietnam base. We had failed in recovering the entire body, but the head would be sufficient for identification. There would be no addition to the roll of missing in action. I have no idea what they told the family, but I suspect they recommended that they not open the casket.

**—5th Special Forces Group, I Corps/Laos, 1968**

Upon arrival at the 315th Tactical Air Wing in Phan Rang in 1970, I was assigned the primary duty of navigator on a C-123. My secondary job, or additional duty, was to act as the wing's Civic Action coordinator. This meant I was to work with the locals to win their hearts and minds. I saw it just as a way to help some poor folks.

A few weeks after my arrival, I attended a meeting of the Ninh Thuan Civic Action Council. There were many projects ongoing, and all appeared to be well coordinated between the Americans and Vietnamese. A representative of the Luong Giang hamlet asked the council for "electricity." I initially thought he meant an electrical system with lines to every house in his village. Not so. He explained that all he was asking for was a small gasoline-powered generator and enough wire to have a single light in their hamlet office/school and one more light on the village perimeter so artillery spotters would know where they were and not fire on them. I took care of it. It was a simple request, and we had lots of generators and wire.

A month later, I escorted seven Vietnamese Boy Scout leaders to Da Nang for a conference. It was mostly a way to get out of our base for a while, but it was interesting to see that such a normal activity as the Boy Scouts could exist in the war zone.

About this time, I started going out in the C-123 parking area late at night, after the maintenance men had finished

their work. I usually found a group of men in one of the revet-
ments shooting dice. The first time I did this, I could see they
were worried that I was going to reprimand them, so I said,
"Peace. I'm not after your buns. I have a proposition for you to
consider." I told them about Dollars for Scholars and showed
them a picture of one of the Vietnamese students with his
name, grades, and special need situation on the back. Then I
said, "This is my proposition: if you all agree, I'll put the picture in the pot. Whoever wins the pot gets the picture. I get
the pot and the winner's name, unit, and phone number.
Then, when I go downtown to deliver the scholarship, I take
the winner with me. He can present the scholarship personally
or just be there." They never turned down my proposition. I
didn't do this very often, and I never played for more than one
scholar per night, but I got several scholarships this way.

On one of my Civic Action missions, I stopped by province
headquarters to see what happened to two VC who recently
surrendered. One was now a farmer. They had given him a job
carrying rice sacks to tide him over and two hectares of irri-
gated land. He had planted onions. The other was a wood-
worker. They had given him a foot-operated lathe, and he
made rungs for ladders and railings.

By the beginning of June, word was getting around that
Civic Action had a friend in airlift, so I started getting phone
calls asking for help. One was from an Army Civil Affairs lieu-
tenant near Cheo Reo. There had been a flood in that area.
They had plenty of help from Buddhist Boy Scouts, Catholic
Boy Scouts, CORDS, etc., but the flood had filled the under-
ground bins where people stored rice and spoiled the grain.
He asked, "Can I get them some rice?"

I said, "I'll see if I can." The next morning, I went to the
early briefing and looked at the flight schedule. Four crews
were going into Djamap near the Cambodian border. I asked
one of the pilots if he was coming out of there empty, and he
replied in the affirmative. I said, "Why don't you ask the troops
at Djamap to load six pallets of the captured NVA rice that is
just sitting there, then shoot a practice assault landing at Cheo

Reo on the way back, and give the rice to the Army Civil Affairs lieutenant."

He asked, "Civic Action?" and I said, "Yes, Civic Action." I talked with the other three pilots, and the result was that they moved twenty-four tons of rice in less than twenty-four hours based on the army lieutenant's telephone call, all with no paperwork. He telephoned again that night to thank me, saying it was enough rice to last until the next scheduled truck convoy arrived.

There was other work to be done. At the end of June, I went to an Air Force Red Horse construction squadron and talked with their chief master sergeant about the poor condition of the 600 meters of access road to Luong Tri hamlet. The chief said he had some new troops who needed practice operating the road grader. When I added that the hamlet also needed a culvert, he said, "No problem."

All he needed from me was a note stating that this was a Civic Action project so they could get off the base. A few days later, he sent the road grader along with a backhoe to install the culvert.

Hoai Trung was a Montagnard hamlet in a more remote part of the province. We took agriculture tools (hoes, shovels, rakes), salvaged parachute shroud line (which they really liked and used for everything from sewing thread to tying their houses together), and packages from people in the States. One package had a doll that opened and closed its eyes and said, "Mama," when someone sat it up or laid it down. Several of the old Montagnard men sat around and played with it, saying, "Heh, heh"—which is their way of laughing uproariously. After dark, a team from CORDS showed a movie of the moon landing a year earlier. The Montagnards weren't impressed— they only knew that the moon got high enough to clear the trees and that was enough information for them. They did, however, like the Donald Duck cartoons. They called the Disney character "Mister very angry duck!"

In early August I got a call from the air freight terminal saying they had a large pallet for me. When I arrived, I found about a half a ton of small strawberry plants from the U.S. Department of Agriculture, all nicely packed in little boxes with cardboard dividers, wooden floors, and risers for the layers. The pallet was addressed to me as the Civic Action officer, Phan Rang, Vietnam. I had not ordered it and didn't know it was coming, so it must have been arranged by the university professor to whom one of the lieutenants had sent soil, water samples, and climate data several months earlier.

I assembled about twenty volunteers to start delivering the strawberry plants and went with the first delivery to Luong Tri. The volunteers put the plants in holes cut in the sides of fifty-gallon barrels filled with dirt, and they also planted some along the banks of irrigation ditches. I went back to my office, and they took the rest of the strawberry plants to the Rural Development Cadre for distribution around the province. I don't know if the strawberries survived in Ninh Thuan Province, but they were spreading rapidly along the banks of irrigation ditches when I left. I recently read that Dalat is famous for strawberries, but not ours—theirs were brought there by the French in the 1930s.

In September, the 7th Air Force basically killed the Civic Action Program by replacing it with the Community Relations program. Under the new 7th Air Force directive, all donations, either by an organization or an individual, had to be made to the fund and not directly distributed to the Vietnamese recipients. This included both money and material goods. The fund would receive, store, and distribute all donations based on the needs of the community. This was not a popular decision.

I followed the new regulations the best I could. One exception was when I received in the mail two gallons of slate paint I had requested from my mom. She bought them at a local hardware store in Arkansas and had to get the covers brazed shut before the post office would take them. In early November, a lieutenant and I used the paint to refurbish blackboards at An Phuoc High School.

Shortly before I finished my tour, a local official invited me to his home in Phan Rang City for the evening to thank me for my work in Civic Action. At supper with his family, they gave me a plate of chicken heads. I said I knew this was an honor, but the honor should go to the oldest man present. After a few seconds, I could no longer stand my hypocrisy and said, "And besides, I don't like to eat chicken heads."

There was a long silence. Then the aged Vietnamese head of household leaned over and whispered something to my host. He translated: "My father says he thinks you are the only honest American ever to eat here."

I said, "Thank you." Everyone smiled, the chicken heads were transferred to my host's father, and we continued with the meal.

**—315th Tactical Airlift Wing, II Corps, 1970**

Our battalion recon platoon had a unique method of keeping up with its kills. The platoon RTO carried a skull on a short stick tied to his radio carrier. I am not sure where the skull had come from; some of the guys who had been around a while said it was from a graveyard in the Delta.

The platoon tradition was that each successful contact was recorded by taking an eighteen-inch length of inch-wide ribbon and writing the date and number of kills on this "streamer." By the time I joined the platoon, there were dozens of streamers attached to the bleached skull. This was good for platoon morale, but our lieutenant and platoon sergeant knew that everyone might not be in total agreement about the skull's redeeming values. So whenever we were going to the rear or even to a major firebase, the ribbon-covered skull went into someone's rucksack. Everything worked well until one day we hurried out the jungle hoping to get a hot meal at an isolated artillery firebase.

What awaited us was not only the chow but also a *Stars and Stripes* photographer. Of course he snapped a picture of our

RTO, skull and all, as we passed through the wire. It did not make the front page, but it got enough attention so that we were told to get rid of the skull—and to do so immediately. Several of the old-timers took charge of burying the relic—and maybe they did. However, I heard later that one them boxed it up and mailed it home. I kind of hope that is the correct story; it would be satisfying to think the skull with its records of our kills sits today in someone's basement or storage closet somewhere in the U.S.

**—199th Light Infantry Brigade, III Corps, 1969**

Our helicopter gunship fire team was scrambled for "troops in contact" early in the afternoon of February 19, 1968. We were sent to Thu Duc, where a company of the 1st Battalion, 28th Infantry, 1st Infantry Division, was heavily engaged, having sustained several serious wounded soldiers. Ground communications, which told us what direction the enemy fire was coming from, reported that a Dustoff was en route. We coordinated the evacuation with the Dustoff on the radio, but as soon as the chopper flew in low level, he began receiving fire.

I was flying trail. Our lead ship went in on his gun run alongside the Dustoff and also took fire. The Dustoff ignored the incoming and landed to load the wounded. I rolled in and knew the exact target I was shooting at—I could see enemy fire coming out of a hooch in the nearby jungle. We received fire during the entire gun run but kept going in hopes of taking some of the pressure off the defenseless Dustoff. I shot a rocket and then another that almost hit the target. I shot one more rocket, and it hit head center, blowing up the hooch.

About this same time our helicopter cabin turned into chaos. Other enemy fire sent bullets into our helicopter that made loud noises. Plexiglas powder exploded through the cockpit from a large hole in the windshield in front of the copilot. The left door gunner yelled, "I'm shot, I'm shot. Get me to a hospital!" I looked back in the crew area and saw blood spurting from a wound in his thigh with protruding meat and splintered bone. The copilot's face was oozing blood from the bits of Plexiglas that had been in the windshield just seconds before. I pulled up and radioed lead, "We've got a crewmen hit. I'm headed to the hospital."

I suddenly realized that even though I knew the general direction to the aid center, I didn't have any idea as to its exact heading. The Dustoff pilot, who had just lifted off the LZ with the wounded, must have been monitoring our radio frequency. He called and asked, "Do you know how to get to the hospital?" He did not wait for an answer, saying, "Just follow me, that's where I'm headed."

Our aircraft had taken many hits, and some of the instruments weren't working, but the helicopter kept flying. The crew chief slowed the gunner's bleeding. We had him to the hospital in fifteen minutes. He was also shot in the hand, but his leg wound was the most serious. The copilot's wounds were superficial.

For years I wondered what became of these guys. Thirty-four years later, I was reunited with the door gunner. His leg was saved, though it is now a few inches shorter than the other. A couple years later, we were reunited with the other pilot. We have never been able to locate the crew chief who saved the gunner's life.

**—1st Infantry Division, III Corps, 1968**

It is not often that we encountered the enemy out in the open with their having little chance of escape. This time, however, we were on a company-size sweep when we caught about thirty NVA in relatively clear territory. A blistering firefight erupted. The company commander put in artillery to block the enemies' escape and then rolled in a pair of F-4s carrying bombs and napalm.

The bombs mostly ended any resistance, killing or wounding the majority of the dinks. When the napalm hit, we were close enough to feel the air sucked into the inferno. Seconds after the napalm strike, a single gook began to fire at us. Suddenly he appeared out of the smoke with his uniform and even his pith helmet, which he had somehow managed to keep on his head, ablaze. Despite being on fire, he continued to work the bolt action on his SKS rifle. I don't know if he was simply showing his bravery or hoping we would shoot and put him out of his misery. Either way, he was successful.

**—4th Infantry Division, II Corps, 1967**

Irecall sipping a Ba Muoi Ba in Simone's one night on Tran Hung Dao when someone remarked to an old master sergeant that the bar girl he was hanging out with had screwed just about everyone in Saigon. The master sergeant replied, "Well, hell, Saigon ain't *that* big of a town!"

**—MACV, III Corps, 1965**

You do a tour in the infantry in Vietnam and you were sure to see some unusual wounds on your fellow soldiers—and perhaps yourself. Once, in I Corps, our patrol discovered a high-speed trail that showed lots of recent activity. A fire team paralleled the trail for a ways looking for a good ambush spot for the rest of us.

A burst of fire, outgoing and incoming, suddenly roared from the area of the fire team. We immediately rushed to their support. In the minute it took for us to reach the team, the fight ended. On the ground lay three dead NVA. One member of the fire team was propped up against a tree with his entire jaw shot away and hanging from his face by only a few pieces of muscle and flesh on his right side. The platoon and company medics went to work on him, placing his jaw about in its original position and then wrapping his entire head in first aid bandages. A Dustoff soon had him on the way to the hospital. I heard that he survived, but I have no idea in what condition.

**—101st Airborne Division, I Corps, 1969**

Soldiers in Vietnam received their mail addressed to their unit via an APO (Army Post Office). Each address was APO San Francisco, followed by five numbers designating the unit—similar to zip codes back home. One of the guys in my company was always asking for info on San Francisco from anyone from there or who might have visited the city.

We finally made him reveal that he did not want his parents back in Tennessee to worry about him so he had told them he was a cook at the Presidio in San Francisco rather than a grunt in the Vietnam jungle. Since each of his letters had the return address of APO San Francisco, his story held up.

**—25th Infantry Division, II Corps, 1966**

As the deputy advisor to the 5th Battalion of the Republic of Vietnam (ARVN) Airborne Division, I participated in Operation Lam Son 719—the South Vietnamese Army's incursion into Laos. The 5th Battalion, famous for its airborne assault into Dien Bien Phu in 1953 in an unsuccessful effort to

defend the French base, was one of the elite ARVN units. We
had just spent an easy month as the "Palace Guard" securing
the residence of the president of South Vietnam. On February
3, 1971, we were ordered to pack and assemble our gear for
deployment. Since the Airborne Division worked hot areas all
over South Vietnam, we had no idea where we were going.

At Tan Son Nhut Air Base, we boarded C-123 airplanes
and flew north. It had been hot and balmy in Saigon, but it
was cold and rainy when we landed in Dong Ha. There we set
up camp for the night and learned we were joining the huge
invasion of Laos to finally cut the Ho Chi Minh Trail and to
neutralize the North Vietnamese resupply depots and rest stations there.

The next morning, we marched to Khe Sanh, where the
Tactical Operations Centers (TOCs) for the ARVN Airborne,
Ranger, and 1st Infantry Divisions were located. My battalion
then assembled between Khe Sanh and the old Lang Vei Special Forces Camp, which had been overrun back in 1968 by a
NVA infantry and tank attack. On February 8, we joined the
other units moving west. We advisors had already been
informed that we were not to accompany our ARVN units
across the border. It was a difficult order to follow, as I was
close to my ARVN counterpart and had spent time in his
home dining and celebrating the Tet holiday only a week earlier. We found out just how serious the order was when we
reached border checkpoints manned by U.S. Military Policemen enforcing the order posted on large signs "No U.S. Personnel Allowed Beyond This Sign."

On the way back to our base camp, where we would monitor the operation by radio and prepare resupply missions, I
stopped at Lang Vei and walked the grounds. The concrete
bunkers were still there, as was the NVA tank that made the
final assault up to the command bunker—the first use of Russ-
ian-provided armor in the war. It was a very eerie site.

Back at the assembly area, I worked on marshaling and rig-
ging loads of thousands of rounds of small-arms ammunition
and artillery shells as well as tons of food and water. These

were to be delivered by American helicopters that, unlike we ground forces, were allowed to cross the border.

My secondary job was to serve a shift as a watch officer and monitor the radios. The first couple of days the operation seemed to be going okay. Soon, however, the radio traffic indicated the fighting had intensified and some of our units were not doing well. The Rangers inserted north of the Airborne took the brunt of the initial NVA assaults, and we began to hear the death throes of their firebases as they were overrun.

Soon the Airborne units were in the same condition. Within a couple of days, we lost a brigade headquarters, an entire artillery battalion, and an infantry battalion. The pleas for help coming across the radio were disheartening beyond anything I have ever experienced, but we were helpless to do anything other than listen to our Vietnamese comrades fight and die. We also monitored the U.S. helicopter communications nets and frequently listened to the cries and screams of American U.S. pilots and air crews as they crashed to the ground.

The ARVN Airborne lost more than 450 killed, 2,000 wounded, and hundreds missing. The U.S. lost more than 100 aircraft in the operation. When the survivors of the 5th Battalion were finally extracted, we immediately got them onto aircraft out of Khe Sanh and back to Tan Son Nhut. They had been badly mauled; the entire operation lasted only about five weeks, but the toll was terrible. The war had escalated to a degree that I did not think possible.

**—MACV, I Corps, 1971**

Vietnam sucked. If you weren't sweating your ass off, it was raining so hard nothing stayed dry. And then you got shot, or shot at, lost a buddy, had diarrhea, or couldn't shake the boil on your shoulder where the strap of your hundred-pound rucksack rubbed. A shithole had more going for it than the Nam.

But then one day my platoon set up our night defensive position along a quiet stream flowing with fresh clean water set in a location so picturesque only a classic landscape artist could paint it with any accuracy. The air was cool; it hadn't rained for days. For a moment you could close your eyes and actually think you were home—or at least somewhere outside the war zone.

We had had a major firefight two days before where we kicked butt with three NVA killed and only one minor wound on our side. We knew the dinks had di-di-mau'd (departed) from the area, so everyone took in the quiet calm engulfed in his own thoughts.

It was the platoon medic who broke the mood with an announcement, "Hey LT, there's two fucking bodies partially buried facedown over by 1st Squad."

"Okay, let's take a look," I said. Sure enough, the two bodies were half exposed and their bloated bodies made them look like inflated, albeit smelly, dolls ready to float off into the sky. I said to my RTO, "Call it in and let higher know they can add two more enemy KIA to our last firefight." It was only a short while before we got instructions to dig the bodies up to see if there were any weapons or identifications. When Doc heard this he said, "That's fucked. Those bodies have been stewing for days and the only thing under them are worms and maggots."

Nevertheless, 1st Squad got the honors of digging them up. They dug around the first body and then with their entrenching tools attempted to roll the body over. Or that was the plan—they quickly learned that rotting flesh really doesn't roll. Eventually, half of the body was face up. The escaping gases and stench added just the right ambience. We all took a look—there really was nothing else to do during an afternoon in the jungle. No one said anything until the RTO summed up what many of us were thinking, "Shit, that looks just like Vietnam."

**—4th Infantry Division, II Corps, 1970**

One interesting assignment enjoyed by all the pilots in my unit was chasing tigers away from local villages—accomplished by low-level flight in our OH-58 scout aircraft. When a village reported a marauding tiger, we took to the air to look for the rogue feline to drive it back into the jungle. More often than not, we did not find a tiger, but we had fun and left a good feeling with the reporting village that we had tried to help.

One hot day I walked into operations and was told that I had a phone call from Saigon. I answered and was surprised to hear the voice of my college freshman roommate. I'd thought he was in Germany. He explained that he had been reassigned as an ARVN advisor and that he had been in the Delta for about six months. He had been wounded by shrapnel and been in a medical facility in Saigon for three weeks. He wanted to know if I could drive up to Saigon (about an hour's drive on Highway 1 from LZ Plantation, Bien Hoa) and pick him up because his doctors said he could enjoy the Saigon area for a couple of days before going back to his unit. He told me he would like to see a friendly face from back home.

I told him I would fly to Tan Son Nhut (Hotel 7 LZ) and pick him up and then we could spend the night at the Plantation before I flew him back to Saigon the next day. He reluctantly agreed, not telling me until we were airborne that he was not really comfortable in helicopters. Having flown only in Hueys before, he was dismayed when I showed up single pilot in an OH-58 with no doors. He sat in the copilot's seat, a place in the front of the 58 that does feel like you are sitting on the edge of nothing because the doors are open on both sides and there is only a thin bubble beneath your feet.

We departed Tan Son Nhut with flight instructions to remain at low level until we passed though the key hole of the Saigon River—a spot that served as a landmark for many helicopter pilots approaching and departing Tan Son Nhut. I was clearing the vegetation on the riverbanks by at least ten feet (demonstrating scout flying techniques), and my friend was drawing up his feet like we were going to hit every tree. I was

enjoying getting even with him for all of the shit he had pulled
on me during our freshman year.

I cleared the key hole, climbed to 1,000 feet, and headed
for the island on the Nha Be River outside of Long Binh and
Bien Hoa. Just as I was clearing the checkpoint, I got a radio
call from flight ops asking, "Blackjack 910, how long would it
take you to reach Trang Bom?"

"About twelve minutes if I step on it," I replied.

"The village has sighted a tiger on the edge of the jungle.
Can you chase it away?" flight ops asked.

I replied affirmatively and headed east on Highway 1 past
LZ Plantation and descended to treetop level as I approached
the village. I doubted that we would see a tiger, but I would put
on a show for the village and my friend. I started a serpentine
flight pattern near the edge of the village and slowly worked it
out toward the jungle. My friend was looking down into the
elephant grass and scrub palm to help me out. Suddenly, he
yelled, "There he is! We flew right over him."

I did a fast pedal turn and found the tiger crouching and
looking up at us. The chase was on. I dropped the collective,
pushed the cyclic forward, and sped toward the tiger at grass-top
level. The tiger started running, spinning, and backtracking.
The trick was to stay with the big cat and push it into the jungle and away from the village—just like working cattle with a
horse back in Texas. After a few minutes, the tiger was in the
triple-canopy jungle and we could no longer see him.

After we landed at LZ Plantation, my friend and I had dinner then and hit every club in the II Field Force and USARV
complexes. Having spent his entire tour in the field, he
thought he had died of his wounds and gone to heaven. He
slept late the next day, and I woke him about noon to see if he
was ready to have lunch and fly back to Saigon. He was ready
for lunch, but what he really wanted to know was if we could
chase another tiger on the return flight.

**—1st Aviation Brigade, III Corps, 1970**

During Operation Paul Revere in far western II Corps, my platoon dug in along a ridgeline. Suddenly, large NVA units charged through the jungle and were in the midst of our positions. Just as we had killed most of them and sent the survivors into retreat, one of them toppled into my foxhole. I tried to strangle him, but he was too strong. I shouted for one of my nearby buddies to shoot him, and I could feel the blast of his rifle when he did so. Despite being strangled and shot, the NVA still did not give up. Another GI came over and started punching him with his fist with little results.

Finally, I remembered a machete I had on my rucksack for cutting through the thick jungle. I grabbed it and began hacking at the enemy soldier. He screamed but continued to fight. My final blow cut his arm off and broke the machete blade. First time I ever saw one break. They were well-made tools.

**—25th Infantry Division, II Corps, 1966**

There are few comforts for the infantry soldier in the field. At times a pair of dry socks seems heaven-sent, and a favorite C-ration tastes like fine cuisine. But the one thing that makes a soldier feel really good, raises his morale, and strengthens his resolve to survive is mail. In the spring of 1970, even that was taken away from us.

For those of us in Vietnam, there were a few connections via ham radio operators that could arrange for a telephone call back home—albeit you had to be in the rear and learn to say "over" each time you were ready for the other person to talk. This developed into some amusing, "I love you, over," and "I love you, too, over" exchanges. Otherwise we had to rely on the U.S. mail to communicate with loved ones. In those days before e-mail and the Internet, we accepted the average of five or more days for a letter to make it home and for another week to receive a response. One of our few combat zone benefits was that we could write "free" in the upper right corner of outgoing envelopes instead of affixing a stamp.

Mail call was held daily in rear areas, but we in the field had to wait for resupply helicopters that arrived every three days or so. Usually, the company commander's RTOs broke down the mail for each of the platoons. Knowing that we might receive several letters from the same person at one time, many of our correspondents numbered each letter on the back of its envelope.

On March 18, 1970, more than 210,000 U.S. Postal Service employees walked off the job in protest of receiving a mere 4 percent pay raise and being denied collective bargaining. Apparently, our fellow uniform-wearing government workers had forgotten their creed of getting the mail delivered in spite of "snow nor rain nor heat, nor gloom of night." The postal workers, like many others in the United States at the time, simply ignored those of us who were fighting our nation's war, however unpopular.

Mail already in the military postal system continued for a few more days and then trickled to nothing. Our final link with "the world" and everything precious was cut off. I had less than a month remaining in-country and already had my orders for my next assignment. Word was out that everyone was getting a few days dropped from their 365-day tour. The rumor was that they had to fill the return airplane seats now vacated by the dead.

President Nixon negotiated a settlement with the postal workers, and in a couple of weeks they were back on the job. It took a while to get the mail on the way to Vietnam again; I never received any more mail while in country.

In one of my last letters to my wife, I had given her an estimated date of my arrival at Travis Air Force Base, California, where she planned to meet me. With no mail to tell her of my exact arrival, I had no idea if she would be there. Finally, I used a method that predated mail service. I sent a courier. A friend was manifested on a freedom bird about six hours before mine. He promised to call my wife when he landed to let her know I was supposed to be on the next plane and to tell her the arrival time.

My flight stopped in Anchorage, Alaska, to refuel, and I was able to telephone my wife to be sure she had received the message. It was a wonderful homecoming, but some forty years later, I've yet to really regain any good feelings about the U.S. Postal Service.

**—199th Light Infantry Brigade, III Corps, 1970**

My company commander hailed from Georgia. I was the only southerner among his lieutenants. During field operations, the CO would often give orders such as, "I need someone to mosey over yonder and check out that tree line." My fellow lieutenants responded with puzzled or blank stares.

The CO would get frustrated and then turn to me asking if I knew what he was talking about. When I assured him I did, he would assign the mission to my platoon. My ability to understand him resulted in extra duty for my platoon—but I sure got along well with my company commander.

**—101st Airborne Division, I Corps, 1969**

In April 1971 I was an advisor to the ARVN 5th Airborne Battalion. After flying from our base at Saigon to the Dak To airfield, we marched west for about thirty-five miles before we were picked up by helicopters for an air assault onto a low ridgeline several miles from Firebase 6. This artillery and infantry defensive perimeter, as well as nearby Firebase 5, were under attack by NVA units that had poured across the Laotian border following Lam Son 719. We were told that without our help both bases might soon be overrun.

Several low hills masked our insertion from NVA observers, but we were still a two-day march from the firebase. After an exhausting march across difficult terrain, we arrived at our attack position for a night assault through the NVA to link up with the firebase defenders.

We waited uneasily until darkness enveloped; however, we still had nearly a full moon with a light cloud cover—so we could see fairly well. I was in my normal position alongside the C Company commander, prepared to provide assistance with air, helicopters, and artillery support. The attack kicked off at approximately 9:00 p.m., with Charlie Company in the lead. This was the first time I had participated in a night attack, and I quickly learned that it is very difficult to control an assault in the dark.

Despite the fact that we had thoroughly prepped the area with artillery and air-delivered bombs and napalm, the NVA met our advance with intense small arms, rocket-propelled grenades, and machine-gun fire. Confusion and chaos reigned from the noise of firing by both sides, and the crossing of red and green tracers, the dust of the battle, and the screaming of the wounded.

I lost track of my Vietnamese counterpart and then got separated from my radio operator. I simply crawled forward from stump to fallen log to any low spot I could find. Soon I could see the objective . . . about 1000 meters away. I kept crawling and moving in that direction. The area had been hit with napalm earlier in the day, leaving the ground burnt and smelling of the jellied gas fumes. I thought I was going to be sick if I couldn't stick my head up to grab a deep breath of fresh air. I kept crawling and making short rushes toward the objective, which was now about 500 meters up the hill.

Green NVA tracers were coming from that direction, and I kept having thoughts one of them might have my name on it—in big letters. After another 250 meters, an illumination flare went off overhead, and I spied several ARVN paratroops from C Company about twenty-five meters away. We waved at each other and continued up the hill. The attack now had lasted about five hours, and I was beyond exhaustion.

The ARVN soldiers moved slowly toward me as I threw a hand grenade in a NVA position directly to my front. In the light of more illumination rounds, I saw a couple more fortified foxholes directly up the hill. The ARVNs moved to flank the nearest bunker while I moved straight up the hill. When I came to the lip of the fortification, it was all quiet and I determined that it must be empty. I slipped over the side only to discover I was very wrong. Two very surprised NVA soldiers reached for their rifles. My .45-caliber pistol was in my hand, cocked and loaded. I shot several rounds as quickly as I could . . . I have no memory of the sound.

My ARVN comrades joined me and helped remove the bodies of the two NVA soldiers. We took ownership of the hole and hunkered down to wait for the arrival of the rest of the company. Within fifteen minutes the ARVN Charlie Company commander arrived and made our little hole his command post (CP). The firing died down, and I pulled out my poncho, covered up, and immediately fell asleep. I awoke a couple of hours later at first light and looked around in awe. Five meters from where I was sleeping were the remains of an NVA soldier who had been hit directly with napalm. His charred body was sitting up and melted to the machine gun he was still holding in a firing position. Next to the hole were the two dead NVA soldiers we had thrown out a few hours earlier. A few feet down the hill were nearly two dozen dead bodies . . . mostly ARVN.

As we began to move up the hill to actually enter the firebase, we found more piles of dead soldiers, mostly NVA. Many of the corpses had been decaying in the hot sun for a couple of days. The stench of death was penetrating and everywhere. Nearly six hundred men—NVA, ARVN, and American advisors died on those hilltops only about one kilometer apart.

For the rest of the day, we watched the U.S. Air Force deliver Arc Light (B-52) missions several miles down the hill directly on the border with Laos and Cambodia. It was a terri-fying sight; how anybody could survive was beyond me. On our last night on the hilltop, we observed a convoy of NVA trucks with lights on moving down the Ho Chi Min Trail.

The next morning, as we moved off the hill, I came upon an ARVN helmet. I thought I would give it to one of my ARVN counterparts. As I picked it up, I noticed it was full of hair and brains. I quickly dropped it. I was happy to leave it and the stench, death, and grime of Firebase 6 behind.

My horror, however, wasn't over. As we walked down a steep ridgeline with thick bamboo thickets, we came under mortar attack. My senior advisor was walking with the battalion CP, approximately two hundred yards behind my company. A mortar round struck the captain, killing him instantly. He was not only my boss, but also a good friend.

Two days later, we were back in Saigon. It was the largest and bloodiest battle that I had seen in my tour—and it was my last. In a few days I was on a "freedom bird" on the way back home. My year in Vietnam was finally over.

**—MACV, I Corps, 1971**

When one of our five-ton trucks was destroyed by a road mine outside of Phan Thiet, the Cavalry Squadron motor sergeant sent me and another driver to haul the burned-out hulk back to our main firebase on the beach beside the South China Sea despite the fact that we had been in the middle of a "hooch party" and were pretty tipsy. The only real obstacle, other than our inebriation, was a rickety railroad bridge we needed to cross over the river running through a village.

We made it to the site where an M88 armored recovery vehicle was waiting. It lifted the wreck onto the long flatbed trailer hitched to our own five-ton tractor. Once it was lashed down, we turned around and headed back to the main camp.

The trip was uneventful until we were a few miles from Phan Thiet. We spotted a young woman standing beside the road with her thumb out, and watching carefully for a possible ambush, we picked her up.

We still had half a bottle of whiskey from the party with us and proceeded to renew our buzz. We also offered some to our new friend, who quickly explained that she was eager to pay for her ride with some good sex. Of course, as red-blooded American teenage soldiers, we eagerly accepted.

Once I had been "serviced" on the passenger side, we switched places so she could "pay" my buddy. I was the driver by the time we reached the old bridge. By then I was mostly seeing double. It was all I could do to line up the heavy truck on the wooden ties on either side of the steel rails. Next to me, the two "lovers" were getting pretty vigorous and kept bumping against me while I tried to steer. I managed to get the whole load—truck, trailer, and the wreck perched precariously on the flatbed—out to about the middle of the bridge when a set of rear wheels began to slip over the side. It was about fifty-foot drop to the river below.

The more I tried to be careful, the closer the inner side of the tires got to the edge, so I decided to just go for broke and jerk it back up. I stepped on the throttle and the entire apparatus, from headlights to taillights jiggled, like a belly dancer as all eighteen wheels bounced across the railroad ties.

We made it to the other side intact. Looking over at the couple, I said, "Well, how about that? We made it."

My buddy just looked back at me and said, "That felt good! Do it again."

**—1st Cavalry Regiment, II Corps, 1968**

One of the many problems we faced at Gio Linh, a base very close to the DMZ, was visiting reporters with cameras who wanted to file stories about "I've been to the DMZ and here are the photos to prove it."

As the Royal Australian Regiment's public information specialist at the base, I was assigned escort duties for any visiting journalists from back home. One afternoon, a young pup journalist with the *Sydney Morning Herald* stepped off a helicopter with a photographer in tow. He immediately announced he wanted to see this and that, including the very dangerous spots of Con Tien, Khe Sanh, and the freedom bridge over the Ben Hai. He also informed me that if I did not "smarten my footwork and make it happen immediately," I could expect some bad PR in his reporting.

I told him I would give his request serious consideration, but in the meantime he and his photographer had better learn how to get to the nearest bunker because it "rained mortars around here." As they settled in for the evening, I radioed a mate at a nearby Australian outpost and arranged for a "mortar attack." About an hour after last light, he obliged with a brace of 4.2-inch mortar rounds just outside our wire and near the journalists' bunker. We put on an act and a bit of radio traffic to no one in particular to ensure our guests were worked up.

Our "mortar attack" had the desired effect. The journalists did not leave their bunker until breakfast. They then explained they had a change in plans and boarded the next chopper south for Dong Ha—much to our relief. A friend sent me an article from the *Morning Herald* several weeks later about how the intrepid pair had spent the night under mortar fire. The reporter also remarked on how much he was impressed on the calm attitude of the Australian troops under fire.

I ran into the reporter sometime later and was tempted to tell him truth about his harrowing night under fire—but never did.

**—Royal Australian Regiment, I Corps, 1969**

While on recon patrol, a soldier in front of me let a branch fly back in my face. A thorn actually stuck in my eye. When I pulled the branch away, the thorn remained in my eye—it was stuck pretty good. I finally got it out and thought I was OK. A few days later, the pain began and soon became unbearable. A medevac helicopter was called to come get me.

On the march to the nearest the LZ, we got into a firefight. Another soldier was wounded, so now two of us needed to be evacuated. We called the incoming Dustoff and informed them that we now had two people to be picked up. The chopper came in, but the LZ was small, with some tree stumps sticking up so the pilot just hovered about shoulder high. I helped the other soldier on board and then grabbed the skids to crawl in. At that time the chopper took off. I had a split-second decision to hang on or let go. I hung on, thinking that the pilot knew I was there and that he was moving over a little to a better landing place where he could set down for me. I was wrong. The chopper continued to rise and quickly passed the point of no return. I had a full rucksack on my back and only my hands on the skids. I began to lose my grip. I fell from about a hundred feet. My first thought was my parents would soon know that I was dead. I remember hitting a large dead tree on the way down but nothing afterward, as the impact knocked me unconscious. I came to, finding myself quite entangled in a green bamboo thicket. I had hit the stand of bamboo at an angle, and it had somewhat cushioned my fall. Had I come straight down, I would have been impaled on the sharp, pole-like spikes. My fellow soldiers cut me out of the thicket, and I managed to walk back to the landing zone, where the chopper came back and landed closer to the ground to pick me up. This time they were careful to be sure I was inside before they took off.

Amazingly, I had no broken bones or major cuts, just a sore shoulder. Eventually, I was flown to Japan for surgery on my eye, but within a few weeks, I was back humping a rucksack in the jungle. Supposedly, *Stars and Stripes* did an article on the "falling grunt," but I never saw it.

**—173rd Airborne Brigade, II Corps, 1971**

If there was any highlight to a tour as an infantryman, other than R&R and the freedom bird home, it had to be "stand down." Every two months or so, we were picked up from a jungle LZ and flown to Long Binh for three days of rest and refitting. Hot showers and clean uniforms awaited us. It was also a good time to receive new equipment or get the old repaired. New maps could have acetate covers placed on them for protection and for ease of removing old marks and plans. Stand downs were one of the few, if not only, events where the infantry was treated better than the rest of the troops.

The best part of the stand down was the jeep trailers full of beer and soft drinks and the steak dinner prepared on grills served in the evenings. Filipino bands that covered all the popular songs from back home followed chow, and they closed their show with strippers. No one ever complained about the females' lack of beauty or real dancing talents. Another fun part of stand down was being welcomed into the various EM, NCO, and officer clubs at Long Binh. However, we were really not good for their business. Their regular-customer rear troops wisely avoided infantrymen who had had nothing to drink for a couple of months.

Before any of this could take place, there was one ritual that was designed to protect both the infantrymen on stand down and the REMFs that occupied Long Binh. Upon arrival in the company area, the first sergeant took charge, and the men turned in their weapons, which were locked in Conex containers next to the orderly room. He then had the men fall in platoon formations—the first time for many since leaving the States. Each man was then searched for anything he could readily use to kill anyone. Claymore mines, hand grenades, demolitions, bayonets, and all other potentially lethal items went into the Conexes. Not until then were the beer trailers rolled out and directions to the showers given.

I was concerned that everything go like clockwork for my first stand down as a company commander. However, we did not get off to a good start. The first sergeant was only about halfway through his securing lethal items when a Military Police jeep with one of my troops, still in full combat gear in the backseat, pulled up in front of the company.

I walked over to the sergeant who seemed to be in charge and asked him what was going on. He reported that the man in the jeep had somehow sneaked off from the company and gone to the Post Exchange, where he purchased several cartons of cigarettes. On his way out, he had bumped into a finance clerk wearing starched fatigues and shined boots. The startled REMF looked at my bearded, dirty, well-armed soldier in his tattered, smelly uniform and asked, "Where in the world are you from?"

My soldier had responded with a quick punch to the REMF's face that decked him. He then stepped over the REMF, saying, "I'm from the fucking jungle."

Unfortunately for my soldier, the MP had seen and heard the entire incident. The sergeant was initially very serious as he explained what had happened. However, by the time he related what my soldier had said about being from the jungle, the sergeant could not hold back a smile.

I turned to my soldier, who, looking downcast, was still firmly holding on to the cartons of cigarettes. When I asked for his side, the soldier said that his squad had been out of smokes for several days except for the few stale cigarettes from the C-rations. He said he had rushed to the PX so his squad would have some cigarettes while they went through the first sergeant's weapon and equipment drill.

The situation was something that I had overlooked. I was also a smoker and had had nothing but C-ration cigarettes myself recently. I was very happy that, on our arrival in Long

Binh, my first sergeant had given me a fresh pack of my favorite brand. We should have had some for the troops as well.

I asked the MP sergeant what he was going to do. One of my soldier's punching out an REMF was a not a good way to begin the stand down. I had no idea what legal ramifications might be hanging over my troop. The MP sergeant hesitated and then said that he, too, had been a grunt for the first six months of his tour and had reenlisted to become an MP (and get out of the field, but he did not say that). He said, "Why don't you just take care of it here in the company? No need for me to make a report."

I thanked him and invited him and his partner to join us for steaks that night. The first sergeant told the soldier to deliver his cigarettes to his squad and told me he would take care of the soldier. I understand that the man spent part of his stand down burning the latrine barrels, but I did not ask and no one told me. I did hear the first sergeant say the punishment was not for punching out a REMF, but for disobeying his order to turn in his equipment before leaving the company area. Everyone ended up happy, except perhaps the decked finance clerk—but he had been in the wrong place at the wrong time.

**—199th Light Infantry Brigade, III Corps, 1969**

Seldom do we realize when we've just had a brush with history, with an event that will change things forever. Mine happened on January 3, 1963, when I was serving with Advisory Team 27, Military Assistance Advisory Group, Vietnam. The new, aggressive commander of the Army of the Republic of Vietnam's (ARVN) 5th Infantry Division, to which our team was attached, had recently moved his headquarters from Bien Hoa to Phu Loi to be in a better position to launch operations against the Viet Cong (VC) in War Zone D.

Our advisory command post had been set up on a soccer field at the edge of the village. I was hot, and work was slow that third day of the new year. I'd been in Vietnam about ten months at that time.

A rumor began to circulate in the afternoon that there'd been a big battle somewhere in the Mekong Delta that day involving large numbers of troops. This was exciting news because big engagements were rare in those days. It sounded like this was a set-piece battle, the one we advisors had been hoping for that would demonstrate ARVN's battlefield preponderance and justify our efforts to build it into a viable fighting force. Up until that time, we Americans had been wildly optimistic about the potential of the South Vietnamese Army.

But news on this battle was scarce. I had a Zenith Trans-Oceanic Radio I'd brought with me from my previous assignment in Germany, and I tuned in to the BBC's English-language overseas broadcasting service. Faintly, tinged with static, the shocking news came through: the ARVN 7th Infantry Division had engaged a Viet Cong force at a place called Ap Bac in Dinh Tuong Province. Despite using air, artillery, and armor, the South Vietnamese troops had still been badly mauled with more than eighty men killed—and the VC force had managed to slip away mostly intact. That was an important turning point in the Vietnam War, comparable to the Ia Drang in 1965, when we realized the North Vietnamese Army would be no pushover either (and *that* was a big surprise to me too). Now we realized the VC were far from lightly armed, poorly organized guerillas who couldn't, or wouldn't, stand and fight. But that January morning I shrugged Ap Bac off. There were better days ahead; the ARVN had the best soldiers in the world—us—backing them up.

I met our Vietnamese division commander, a colonel, only once, and that was when he interrupted me horsing around in the hallway outside his office at division headquarters. I gave him a sharp salute. Later he would go on to very great things.

His name was Nguyen Van Thieu, the president of South Vietnam from 1965 until the bitter end in 1975.

**—MACV, III Corps, 1963**

★ ★ ★

In July 1967, our rifle company conducted operations near the South China Sea in II Corps. We had just come out of the Highlands farther west where we had had many intense engagements with regular NVA units. Here on the coast, it was more VC territory among the scattered villages, rice paddies, and small jungle areas.

Late one afternoon, we entered a small village of a dozen or so hooches. Apparently, stories about Americans had preceded us as the villagers seemed extremely frightened, especially the young girls. As we began to systematically search the houses, the women ran to the centrally located village chief's residence and attempted to hide inside.

As we neared the house, one of the girls ran towards us screaming and wailing. A few yards to our front, she stopped and defecated on the ground. She then picked up her own feces and began rubbing them on her face and body. Apparently, she had been molested by previous patrols and hoped to make herself as unappealing as possible.

The village women were safe from any sexual assault by us; we were better disciplined than that. We were not, however, beyond repulsion by her actions. A private picked her up, literally by the seat of her pants and the back of her neck, and threw her in one of the village's shallow wells. She came out sputtering but much cleaner. We continued our patrol.

**—25th Infantry Division, II Corps, 1967**

In August 1969, I was the leader of the recon platoon of the 1st Battalion, 506th Parachute Infantry Regiment of the 101st Airborne Division, operating in the jungles of I Corps. Late one day, I led a six-man recon on a helicopter insertion into a landing zone in the west side of the A Shau Valley near where the Battle of Hamburger Hill had taken place a few months earlier. We moved quickly off of the LZ into some thick brush and set up a position where we could watch the trails that crossed the hill. Half of the patrol slept while the others stayed alert. Sometime in the middle of the night, I suddenly awoke to the noise of what I thought was an enemy soldier walking through our small perimeter. I couldn't move to grab my rifle without revealing my position, so I just lay still, hoping he would go away. About that time, a large monkey stepped on my face and then walked down my prone body back into the jungle.

**—101st Airborne Division, I Corps, 1969**

In late 1967, our helicopter gunship fire team was providing direct fire for a 1st Infantry Division rifle company under attack northwest of Quan Loi. By early evening, the enemy had been beaten back and had withdrawn. The American wounded had been evacuated and the company had been resupplied for the night. We were preparing to leave station when the ground commander called and asked if we could transport four KIA bodies. It was not the kind of mission we usually performed; in fact, it was against company regulations. But it was doubtful another helicopter could get in until morning and the ground commander said it would be hard on his men's morale if the bodies had to remain there overnight.

I knew we were not supposed to do things like that, but we worked with the infantry every day, and I had a harder time saying "No" to them than to the straphangers back in the rear who made rules.

We had expended enough fuel and ammo that we were light enough to land in the LZ, so our flight of two went in one at a time and the infantrymen loaded two body bags on each aircraft. We called ahead to have the meat wagon from the morgue meet us at Quan Loi. When we landed, I got out to help carry the body bags and was initially surprised at the heft of the dead weight. The zipper from the waist down was broken on one of the bags and a leg flopped out. We put the bag down, and I put the leg back in. The leg was flexible, bending at the knee. It flopped out again, and we did the same thing. As I looked at the leg, I was struck by the fact he was wearing the same jungle boots and fatigues as me. Earlier in the day, he moved his leg on his own just like me. I didn't know him or had never seen his face, but I was suddenly saddened knowing he had family and friends back home who didn't even know yet that he was dead.

—**1st Infantry Division, III Corps, 1967**

It was approaching dark, and my platoon was setting up two ambushes along a trail that we were sure Charlie was using to move toward our battalion firebase a couple of kilometers away. Everything was going fine, which naturally meant Murphy would soon show up. He did. Interestingly, I had never thought of Murphy as female or as a real bitch.

I first heard the distant muffled pops followed by a series of thumps I could feel through the ground. I thought, "What the hell?" The radio immediately came to life, and I recognized the voice of my fellow platoon leader who was operating about a klick from my platoon. He was in near panic mode, his voice gripped in fear. "Cease fire! Cease fire! Cease fire, goddammit!" he was yelling over and over. "Incoming, incoming—make it stop!" he screamed into the radio. And then nothing.

Our company commander called me two minutes later with orders to get over to 2nd Platoon ASAP—they had received eight to ten mortar rounds and a ground attack was possible. I was already planning the move with or without the orders. While it meant a night march, no one questioned the risk, thinking only about getting there quickly to help our buddies. It took two hours to make our way through the dark, thick jungle and then another tenuous hour to ensure the safe entry into a shell-rattled group of men very much in shock. Our platoon immediately set security, air-evaced the critical, tended to those with minor wounds, and attempted to identify the dead. The rounds had landed throughout the platoon with deadly accuracy, and it's amazing that only four were killed.

As first light brought visibility to the carnage, it became apparent my platoon had arrived in Dante's Inferno. The dead, or at least pieces of them, were covered with ponchos but body parts—along with gear, weapons, and personal effects—still littered the ground and hung from the trees. My eighteen-year-old medic, an FNG in country for only a few weeks, stared in horror and sat motionless against a tree. I felt only slightly better, but the responsibility to sort things out remained mine. My squad leaders gathered around waiting for instructions. I told them, "Pull half your men in from security and line them up for a police call." Only this police call was for pieces of our buddies, and the litter was a part of us as much as them.

—**4th Infantry Division, II Corps, 1970**

There I was, "fat, dumb, and happy." Of course that is the way many air force stories began, but this one is a bit different, for I was fat, dumb, and happy—and sleepy. We were 16,000 feet over the South Vietnamese jungle in the fall of 1970. I was flying an EC-121R on an electronic reconnaissance mission. We flew with one pilot, one navigator, and one flight engineer in the cockpit, with another full crew off duty in an area behind the cockpit. Every two hours, we changed positions. In the back of the plane were a dozen or so technicians and specialists monitoring ground sensors, enemy radio transmissions, and providing communication assistance for other air force missions. Up front, we did not care what they were doing in the rear. The only concerns of those in back about us up front were that we "keep the plane in the air and land safely."

Most of our missions were flown after sunset and were 13.5 hours in duration. Needless to say, the nights got long. The hardest "watch" was the two-hour shift around dawn. On this mission, I was on "watch" during the hours when the sun was coming up. Since we flew at 16,000 feet and had effective air conditioning, the aircraft was reasonably comfortable. With no threat from any enemy aircraft and being too high to be in danger of ground fire, we flew a constant ten-mile-long racetrack orbit. At the end of each leg, we executed a slow 180-degree turn to reverse our course. The autopilot kept the aircraft on course with the pilot having to make only occasional minor corrections to our heading.

This morning, one of the legs took us directly into the rising sun. The sunshine warmed our dark green flight suits, making it even more difficult to keep our eyes open. When we reached the point of our turn, the autopilot reversed our direction as I leaned my head against the cockpit window to look down at the war below.

Sometime later, I jerked to an upright position realizing that I had been asleep. I turned my attention to the heading indicator and saw we were slightly off course, so I made the proper adjustment. As a first lieutenant, I was concerned that the navigator, who was a major, would have seen my lapse. I very nonchalantly looked toward him on the other side of the cockpit. To my relief, he had his head against his window and was sound asleep. I continued my look around the cockpit toward the flight engineer sitting in the back of the cockpit.

He was a senior NCO, and I didn't want to appear poorly in his sight. He had his feet propped up on the bulkhead, and he, too, was sound asleep. To this day I don't know how many times we may have gone around before I awoke.

**—554th Recon Squadron PACAF, Korat, Thailand, 1970**

Iwas new in country and stayed close to my Spec 4 squad leader to try to learn—and to stay alive. Our area of operations south of Saigon was covered in abandoned rice paddies and pineapple plantations. It was crisscrossed with canals dating back to the days of French colonialism and belts of thick nipa palm and underbrush. Most of the enemy were "farmers by day, VC by night." They rarely cared to stand and fight but rather preferred to spend their time improvising booby traps and placing them along any pathway they thought we might use.

On this particular late afternoon, the heat and humidity seemed nearly unbearable—but were because we had no other choice but to endure. On our way to our night ambush position, we crossed a small inlet to one of the canals where nipa palms and vines had nearly overgrown an old trail. My squad leader matter-of-factly told me about his experiences here a few weeks earlier in which his point man had hit a trip wire that set off a booby trap made from a dud U.S. artillery 105-millimeter shell. The explosion had blown the man to pieces. The squad picked up the various parts, tied them in a poncho, and called in an evacuation bird.

We were taking a break on the other side of the waterway when a soldier called the squad leader over to his position. I went along because I did not know better. The soldier pointed to a shriveled, mummified human hand lying under a small bush. The squad leader drug it out with the toe of his jungle boot and then picked up a stick and dug a shallow depression.

He kicked the hand into the hole and said he guessed they missed picking up a few parts after the booby trap explosion. Under his breath, he said he reckoned the funeral was long over and there was no reason to send any more parts of the body home.

No one else said anything. We were soon back humping, sweating, and hoping that we would not die and, if we did, that they would find all the pieces.

**—199th Light Infantry Brigade, III Corps, 1969**

★ ★ ★

Most folks, including many veterans, think the VC and NVA were stellar, well-disciplined soldiers. This was not always true.

We had been crossing open rice fields broken by bands of thick jungle near the coastline most of the day. We were exhausted, hungry, and more than ready to stop for the night. Word came down that the company commander wanted a recon patrol to venture eastward about a 150 meters where there was supposed to be a trail so large that it was depicted on our map sheets. Confirming the trail's location would confirm ours so the company commander and artillery forward observer could preplan artillery fires for our night defensive position.

My fire team was not happy to be assigned the mission. While the rest of the company sprawled on the ground resting and heating C-rations, we moved toward the trail. But we had no choice, and it was likely our turn. We found the trail just where the company commander said it would be. I was not surprised, as he was pretty good at land navigation. We radioed our findings to the command post.

Just as we turned to rejoin the company, we heard the faint notes of tinny, sing-song Vietnamese music drifting through the jungle. We took positions behind trees and logs and waited as the music grew louder. In a few minutes, two VC appeared. One had a transistor radio held to his ear, and he swayed to the music as he walked. A short burst from our rifles sent the two to music heaven or wherever dead dinks go. Unfortunately, the radio also took a hit. Along with their weapons, we also found a U.S. hand grenade on one of their web belts.

I am sure that somewhere in the North two mothers would eventually find out about their sons and mourn their passage. I could not help but wonder if their company commander might not be just a little happy to be rid of such losers.

**—25th Infantry Division, II Corps, 1967**

★ ★ ★

One morning we got a call from battalion that a sister company had made contact a little southwest of where the Battle of Hamburger Hill had taken place a few weeks earlier. My platoon was dispatched to assist. As we rounded Hill 996 (named for its map elevation number), we could hear the ongoing firefight. When we got closer, we began receiving small-arms and machine-gun fire from well-camouflaged bunkers.

The jungle was so thick that we were almost on top of one of the bunkers before we knew it. A steady drum of machine-gun fire with its green tracers bellowed from a small aperture. I was the nearest to the bunker and put several magazines of M16 rounds into the opening, but it had no apparent effect as the machine gun continued to fire. Because the aperture was small, I did not even risk rising up to try to toss a hand grenade.

A few meters away, I recognized one of my soldiers who carried the M79 grenade launcher. He tossed it to me along with some ammo. I fired several rounds into the bunker, but the 40mm high-explosive rounds failed to detonate. I had familiarized myself with the M79 in basic school but was not aware, or had forgotten, that the round had to go a certain number of meters before it was armed.

Despite my failed frontal assault, I must have at least distracted the two-man machine gun crew. One of my soldiers managed to work around and drop a frag grenade into the bunker, silencing the gun. Sometimes, I guess, it is just better to be lucky than good.

**—101st Airborne Division, II Corps, 1969**

March 16, 1966, started just as another day at the office. Of course, then my office was the cockpit of a U.S. Army UH-1 Huey helicopter flying over the jungle of South Vietnam.

Aboard were mermite containers of hot breakfast chow and a sling load of 400 pounds of ice intended for the 2nd Battalion of the 173rd Airborne Brigade, who were operating in War Zone D north of Binh Hoa. As a cargo helicopter, we ferried troops, ammo, food, and water, and occasionally evacuated wounded or dead troopers. This would be a good mission, I knew, because the soldiers had been humping the bush for many days living off C-rations. They would welcome hot chow and ice.

Several miles from the landing zone, we requested smoke and then confirmed the color to the ground RTO as we hovered over a small clearing surrounded by hundred-foot trees. We began to descend with our crew chief and a gunner on each skid observing to the rear to be sure we did not back our tail rotor into a tree.

Just as we began to lower into the clearing, basketball-size .51-caliber rounds passed to our front. The enemy gunner apparently thought we were continuing forward and led us just enough to miss. I kicked the manual release to drop the heavy ice and to give us more lift as we tried to gain altitude.

The NVA gunner then adjusted his sights, but he fortunately overcorrected his aim and poured rounds into our tail boom—much better than the cockpit. Unfortunately, the Huey began to spin toward the ground. I said what every helicopter pilot says at that moment: "Oh shit!"

The vegetation cushioned our fall somewhat, but the main rotor blades nearly shook the chopper to pieces as they chopped the overhanging tree branches to kindling. We finally settled on our left side on the jungle floor. We all scrambled safely from the crash, slipping on spilled eggs, orange juice, and coffee. An infantryman met us and led us to the center of the battalion's defensive position. The .51 cal had gotten quiet after we went down, but suddenly hundreds of rifles, machine guns, and grenade launchers filled the air with tracers and explosions—both outgoing and incoming.

My two door gunners joined the defenses with their M60 machine guns. Except for my pistol, I was unarmed until a sergeant handed me an M14 from the wreck. The stock was broken, but he told me that it had a light-enough recoil to fire it pistol-style "if the enemy breaks through our line." My day had gone from a routine flight in the air to a John Wayne ground fight in a couple of blinks.

For the next four hours, the battle continued. Our artillery and their mortars fell inside and outside the perimeter. Fighter aircraft strafed us as well as the NVA as they "hugged" as closely as possible to us. Finally, a sister battalion hacked their way through the jungle and fought their way through the enemy's positions to reinforce us. When the NVA finally withdrew, they left six hundred bodies behind. There is no telling how many dead and wounded they carried away. Our victory did not come without cost. Eleven Americans lay dead, and 109 were wounded.

When it came to flying helicopters, I knew what I was doing. But when it came to fierce close-quarters, gut-wrenching ground combat, I felt very obliged to the 173rd Skytroopers for "saving my bacon" when I failed to deliver their breakfast. It would be more than three decades before I had the chance to repay them.

Some thirty-six years later, the 173rd was having their
annual reunion in Fort Worth, Texas, and invited me as one of
their speakers. On the way to the hotel, I stopped by the local
McDonald's franchise headquarters and told their public-
relations director the story of that day in the jungle. That
evening, I concluded my remarks by emphasizing that their
helicopter support always delivered, even if I was a bit late.
I then passed out more than three hundred gift coupons for
Egg McMuffins good at any McDonalds.
                         **—173rd Airborne Brigade, III Corps, 1966**

Late in 1966, one of our sister infantry battalions captured a
NVA second lieutenant. A few weeks later, division intelligence circulated an analysis of his interrogation. I kept a copy
of the document that explained that the second lieutenant,
captured on December 11, 1966, was born on Khan Thien
Street, Hanoi City, Hanoi Province, North Vietnam. When captured, he was a platoon leader in the NVA 10th Regiment of
the 320th Infantry Division and had in his possession an AK-47
rifle, four magazines, and four Chicom hand grenades. Additional information followed (I have made my own comments
in brackets):

"Subject was drafted into the army at Chung My District,
Ha Dong Province, NVN in February 1964 and was immediately assigned to the 308th Division. Subject was given one
month of political before being selected to attend Luc Tion
Officers School in Chung My District. There he joined four
hundred other students in a course that lasted seven months.
Subject was taught infantry tactics, how to command troops,
and general military training. Luc Tuan is the only officer
school in North Vietnam. The school had 40 officer instructors and was commanded by a colonel. Subject graduated from
officers' school on 31 October 1964 and was commissioned a

second lieutenant and assigned to the 120th Regiment of the 308th Division as a platoon leader. During November and December of 1964, subject trained the men in his platoon to march, shoot, crawl, and other general military training.

"In early January 1965 subject was notified that he would be infiltrating south in about one month. Subject was given a ten-day leave to visit his family prior to infiltrating. Instead of sending one of the regular battalions from the 308th, subject was combined with others to form a new battalion designated K-10 [NVA units frequently changed their numerical designations prior to moves or for security reasons].

"Subject was issued the following prior to infiltration: Black uniform, one canteen, one hammock, one belt, one AK-47 rifle with 200 rounds of ammunition, two hand grenades, 750 grams of dry rice (for ten days), one kilogram of salt, one kilogram of sugar, one can of dry milk, two sets of underwear, one barracks bag, one pair sandals, one pair socks, 200 malaria pills, 20 water purification pills, one cap, one flashlight, one tent, and one mosquito net.

"Subject said he was wounded fighting an ARVN armored unit on June 1, 1965, and taken to the 10th Regiment's C-10 Hospital. Subject stated he remained in the hospital until December 1965. He later worked part time distributing rice to infantry from a jungle warehouse in the Highlands. He then returned to the 320th Division where he was told the 10th Regiment had shot down three F-105 jets and six helicopters in August 1966 with a 12.7-mm anti-air machine gun [this is not verifiable and extremely unlikely]. Two days later, the area was bombed by American B-52s. Subject stated that a U.S. or ARVN unit usually searches the area after such an attack and it is an ideal time for the NVA unit to prepare an ambush. He added that malaria was a problem when they first arrived in the South but had decreased considerably since.

"Subject stated that the 10th Regiment captured two American infantrymen in July 1966. Subject stated that American prisoners captured by the 320th are evacuated to North Vietnam. He said his battalion commander told him about the

American prisoners and that they are treated the same as NVA soldiers [the POWs cannot be verified; their treatment is not at all correct].

"Subject stated that NVA officers receive 20 South Vietnamese piasters each month for spending allowance, plus a can of dry milk, and a small amount of sugar each month. Subject stated he had heard nothing about a Christmas or New Year's truce, but that he had heard of negotiations between the North and South Vietnamese Governments for a seven to ten day truce for the lunar new year [Tet]."

**—25th Infantry Division, II Corps, 1966**

At the time, I liked the policy of burning houses, barns, baskets, etc.—anything of value—destroying all animals, wells, crops, etc. We even burned cane fields. It kept constant pressure on the VC. I am now not sure if it was all that good of a policy.

**—4th Infantry Division, II Corps, 1967**

After returning from Lam Son 719, I continued my duties as an advisor with the 5th Battalion of the ARVN Airborne Division as we refitted and rested a couple of weeks in Saigon. Our brigade then deployed back to the Tri-Border area near Dak To to defend several firebases now threatened by the NVA who were counterattacking after our venture into Laos. In early April 1971, we landed at Pleiku and then road marched to Dak To. The brigade occupied a significant portion of Dak To firebase, and my advisory team was to bunk down in the Special Forces compound. About 4:00 p.m., I met a Special

Forces lieutenant who invited me to join him in the nearby village for a beer or two—we had plenty of time because the curfew when the front gate shut was 8:00 p.m.

In a small bar, we were joined by a couple of SF NCOs. We had lost track of time and the number of beers we had consumed before we realized it was approaching 10:00 p.m. The NCOs had local girlfriends and disappeared into the night. The lieutenant and I did not know what the heck to do, but we ultimately decided to just sleep in some semi-comfortable chairs in the bar. We dozed off only to be awakened shortly after midnight by the bar owner, who informed us that VC were in the village and we needed to go. I had been in plenty of fights on the battlefield, but this was a new kind of fear.

Two women who worked at the bar told us to come with them—that they would guide us to safety. With no other apparent option, we accepted their offer. I was even less happy and more than a bit scared when our guides split us up. The remainder of the night, my guide moved me from hooch to hooch—no longer than thirty minutes in any one location. We quietly walked through back alleys and side streets. A series of families hid me in closets—nothing but bamboo curtains covering the entrance. One family placed me under a bed. About 5:00 a.m., my guide told me that the VC had left. I was exhausted from lack of sleep—and fear. My pistol had been loaded, cocked, and in my hand for five hours.

My guide led me back to the same bar where it all began. I linked up with the SF lieutenant; we had coffee and some type of Vietnamese roll, and at 6:00 a.m., we started walking back to the compound. At 7:00 a.m., when the gate opened, we marched right in as if nothing happened.

Two hours later, we moved out to confront the enemy. I realized I had been incredibly lucky.

**—MACV, I Corps, 1971**

In the late fall of 1969, we were working the rubber plantations and the jungle that surrounded the village of Cam
Tam southeast of Xuan Loc. I had been in the area as an
infantry platoon leader and was returning as a rifle company
commander.

Occasionally, we would be pulled back to the small mortar
firebase at the edge of the village for a hot meal and a little
rest. The locals kept their distance but seemed friendly
enough. A few still worked the aging rubber trees but most of
the village had been abandoned. At one time, however, Cam
Tam must have been quite prosperous. It had a rubber pro-
cessing plant, and instead of straw hooches, the locals all had
stucco houses. Most interesting were three two-story villas complete with tile roofs and stables built by the Michelin Rubber
Company for its managers back in the colonial days.

Two of the houses were long abandoned, but a one-armed
Frenchman occupied the third with his Vietnamese wife and
beautiful daughter. The old man was good for the occasional
loaf of excellent French bread and was very talkative, despite
our inability to understand him. I did have a platoon leader
who knew a smattering of French, and he translated that the
caretaker was an old soldier who had lost his arm in the Battle
of Dien Bien Phu some fifteen years or so earlier. I later heard
that he actually lost the limb in a bulldozer accident, and there
were stories that he supplied the local VC with French bread as
well as other supplies. As for his daughter, he kept her pretty
well out of our sight and informed us that she was married to
an ARVN officer. All the stories were interesting and helped
pass the day. Whatever the old man was doing to survive
seemed to be working.

One afternoon, an RTO and another soldier accompanied me on a recon of the two abandoned villas. Boredom
sometimes drives you to do silly things. We did a complete
circle around the houses and could find no sign that anyone
had been near them since the last rainfall a few days before.
The windows were partially boarded up, and the front door
was either lightly locked or jammed. My RTO said he had

a "key," stepped back, and kicked the door open with his jungle boot.

Inside, enough light came through the windows to leave sunbeams streaked with floating dust particles. A few rattan chairs and other pieces of furniture were along the walls but there was no sign of anyone being in the house for months, if not years. About the same time, we all heard something upstairs. My RTO said he thought it was just a low hanging tree branch rubbing against the roof.

We all just kind of looked at each other as I turned and began to carefully climb the stairs. I stayed as close to the wall as I could while stepping as lightly as possible so as not to make any noise myself. My RTO remained at the base of the stairway while the other soldier followed just to my rear.

At the top of the stairs, there was sufficient light for me to see that there were no tracks or other disturbance on the dust-covered floor. Again I heard the scratching sound, and it seemed to be coming from behind the door to my front. The smartest thing to do would have been to just quietly back down the stairs and return to the firebase or wait for reinforcements. We did neither.

With my right thumb, I flipped my M16 to full automatic and with the left hand began to turn the door knob. I thought about lobbing a frag grenade in but decided that might be more dangerous to us than to whatever or whoever was on the other side of the wall. When I felt the door knob click, I threw the door open and went into a crouch as I brought my rifle up to fire. To my right I saw two shadowy figures and swung the M16 in that direction. Just before I squeezed the trigger, my eyes adjusted sufficiently for me to see that I was in a well-adorned bathroom and the figures were decals of Donald Duck and Mickey Mouse on the tiled wall. I let out a sign of relief. I had damn near blown away a couple of Disney characters.

**—199th Light Infantry Brigade, III Corps, 1969**

Most ARVN commanders acquitted themselves fairly well during the long conflict, but there were exceptions. Generally, their airborne and ranger leaders were the elites, but there were exceptions there as well.

On May 22, 1968, I was the assistant advisor to the 21st Ranger Battalion when the command post, located just west of Hoi An in Quang Nam Province, came under mortar attack. The commanding officer and the senior advisor were seriously wounded, and fifty-three soldiers were killed. Two days later, the battalion, accompanied by some armored personnel carriers (APCs), moved to the west and made contact again when we received small-arms and more mortar fire. The battalion, deployed in open rice paddies, again suffered heavy casualties.

I recommended to the new battalion commander that we move forward to get out of the open area. Oddly, he denied that we had ever stopped, although we stayed in the same position until nightfall. The next day, the commanding officer locked himself in an APC and refused to open the hatch. I finally coaxed him out, but he climbed into a foxhole and refused to budge.

I continued to urge him to move the battalion, but he would no longer talk to me. He stayed in his hole even when the NVA resumed their attack. Subsequent mortar fire destroyed a medevac helicopter, killing two of its U.S. crew members. The Vietnamese officer's boss finally arrived and relieved him of command.

—**Royal Australian Regiment, I Corps, 1968**

I served two years in Vietnam with MACV and the Defense Attaché Office. My job allowed me to visit nearly half of South Vietnam's provinces. Early one morning, I stopped my jeep at a roadside coffee stand run by an ancient Vietnamese woman. Two primitive wooden tables, with an army poncho for cover from the sun and rain, made up the entire business. As I sat there drinking coffee and smoking, I read a Vietnamese newspaper in an effort to improve my grasp of the language.

A Vietnamese man hobbled up, one bum leg, supported by a crutch, maybe twenty-five years old. He sat at my table, ordered coffee, and asked if I really could read Vietnamese. I replied, "A little." Then I explained that I was trying to learn more. We continued to talk, and I determined that he was a former ARVN soldier. He had been shot through the knee. The leg was saved, but it would no longer bend. He had received a medical discharge and was looking for a job. His brother had been killed fighting the Communists, and he needed work to support his sibling's family.

I told him that I didn't know of any work but would be on the lookout. I told him that I frequently stopped here for coffee and that he should check in from time to time. I told him I would try to help. He thanked me and then awkwardly picked up his crutches and hobbled off into the village.

My anger came to a head when he left. Here I was on a rundown, crummy, pothole-filled road, with no real way of helping the veteran. I fumed with anger over the injustice of all this. I wanted to rob Jane Fonda, Tom Hayden, Dr. Spock, et al., at gunpoint—although a knife would be just fine—take all their money, and provide for people they were ready to turn their backs on and let die.

When it was time to go, I went to the old lady with a few piasters in my hand, but she waved off the payment. She explained, "The crippled guy paid for your coffee." She could have pocketed double payment and said nothing. She didn't. She was a proud woman and wouldn't. I asked her to let me know if the guy came by again. She said she would, but I never saw the disabled guy again.

But I have never forgotten him either. I'm not really religious, but I have prayed for him. What else can I do? It feels like I should do something—anything, everything. It bothers

the hell out of me to this day. I also wish it were the only
encounter like that. Unfortunately, it wasn't.

—**U.S. Defense Attaché Office, III Corps, 1972**

★ ★ ★

We were on a company patrol when a fellow marine
stepped on a booby-trapped hand grenade. Although he
suffered multiple wounds, none was life-threatening. While
the corpsman worked to bandage his numerous shrapnel
wounds, he discovered the marine was bleeding from a fragment that had struck his penis. The doc gently placed a battle
dressing on the wound and squeezed it to stop the bleeding.
The marine looked up at the corpsman, and with a smile, said,
"That feels good, Doc."

—**1st Marine Division, I Corps, 1969**

★ ★ ★

As a young cadet at West Point, I learned early on about the
"devil's bargain." One of our instructors explained that by
staying at the Academy and accepting a commission into the
armed forces that we "could look forward to a secure life . . .
never a worry about whether we would have another meal or
medical care or income. Just do your job and keep out of trouble. And the only thing our government would ever ask in
return was our life—when the time came." That was the bargain; we all knew it and accepted it.

My father served in the U.S. Army for thirty-three years,
one of the rare veterans of three wars—World War I, World War
II, and Korea. I had eleven years of service, however, and had
become a major and qualified as an army aviator before I got
called to my first conflict. I arrived in Vietnam in June 1966, to

be assigned to MACVs 224th Aviation Battalion of the 509th U.S. Army Security Agency Group (later redesignated the Army Security Agency) based in Saigon. My duties were primarily administrative as the battalion safety officer, but I did frequently fly ARDF (Airborne Radio Direction Finding) missions.

ARDF missions were flown in a twin engine RU-8D Beach Queen Air equipped with antennae that extended three feet to the front and back of each wing. The crew consisted of two pilots and an "operator" who monitored the stack of radios in the rear used to locate and identify enemy stations. The operator, qualified to read Morse Code, could not only monitor enemy conversations and movements but also could provide targeting information by locating the enemy from several of our aerial locations and then intersecting the lines drawn on his map. For this to be successful, we in the front seat had to be very careful in our navigation and ensure we knew our exact location. Many intelligence analysts claim ARDF information was some of the most accurate of the war.

Back at our base, our quarters were air conditioned, and most of our meals were sit-down, served on table cloths. I felt funny sending home my "combat pay" when my combat exposure was so little compared to the guys in the jungle. For me the tough part was being away from home and occasionally learning of a friend being killed or wounded.

Staff work was a grind and not very satisfying—certainly not like flying. There's a saying among aviators that every day of flying adds a day to your life. Flying became an important escape from the seven-day-a-week, twelve-hour-a-day routine in our super-secure building without windows. Life at 2,000 feet above the jungle, flying a twin Queen Air, was pleasant as long as one could avoid obsessing on the consequences of engine failure. Looking down at the war below, I could feel removed from it all—even the heat because of our altitude was much cooler than on the ground.

So in the air away from the office was not a bad place to be, all things considered. Ninety percent of all small-arms hits occurred below 1,500 feet, so my chance of being bothered by a bullet strike was rather remote, and it certainly wasn't something I wanted to dwell on anyway. The North Vietnamese did not have antiaircraft weapons this far south in 1966, and the Viet Cong were not well trained at hitting a moving target. Yet, on occasion, one of our planes would come back with a bullet hole in the wing or tail. We referred to these hits as "The Golden BB"—the unlikely bullet that found its way to the high-flying target.

But during my tour in Vietnam, I never heard of one of our pilots being injured by ground fire. And only once during my four hundred hours of flying over enemy territory did I even come close to being hit by a Golden BB. When a rifle bullet traveling above the speed of sound goes past you, it emits a distinctive *crack* from breaking the sound barrier. I had just started one of our 180-degree turns tracking a signal when I heard a loud *crack* from my right. I knew exactly what it meant, but the event and threat were over as quickly as they occurred. My plane, moving at nearly three miles a minute, was not available as a target for a second shot.

By early 1967, North Vietnam was sending thousands of troops and tons of supplies south down the Ho Chi Minh Trail just across the border from Vietnam in neighboring Laos and Cambodia. What had been a jungle trail in 1962 had become a veritable highway by 1967 with elaborate underground waypoints complete with vehicle maintenance and repair. It was estimated that in 1966 more than two hundred fifty troops and 60 tons of supplies moved each day down this route from North Vietnam. During this period, our air force continued their round-the-clock bombing of the trail. Many of our Airborne Direction Finding missions were dedicated to tracking NVA divisions as they moved south. At least we could track these units and learn where they were heading when they crossed the border into South Vietnam.

On one occasion, I had been in the air for over three hours in the vicinity of the Ho Chi Minh Trail when it was time to return to our airfield at Tan Son Nhut Airport in Saigon. I told my "backseater" to shut down operations because we were heading home. Just as I began a turn to the east, to my total astonishment, I found I was turning directly into what appeared to be a load of logs falling from the sky above. I veered immediately away from the long tumbling pieces. When I looked a hundred yards to my right front, it suddenly became apparent that what was falling through the air was a string of bombs that were now erupting on the earth below. Evidently, there was a B-52, probably eight miles above me, unloading on a target below and nearly taking us with it. Those air force flights, code-named "Arc Lights," were strikes on the Ho Chi Minh Trail that occurred without any prior coordination with our army units. It was the only time I ever saw a bombing run so close up and personal. It was an awesome sight!

Near the end of my tour, I moved up to group staff where I still flew but also handled numerous other administrative duties. One action I worked on was a request from the Department of the Army to determine whether the disappearance of one of our pilots should be carried as missing in action or deceased. I reviewed all the information available on the circumstance of his disappearance. His last radio transmission was made in bad weather on a heading that, if not altered, would take him directly into the side of Monkey Mountain. A search of that very precipitous mountain, north of Cam Ranh Bay, however, did not reveal any wreckage. I reasoned that he would not likely be found in that dense and inaccessible area. Further, my computations concluded that the impact at 130 mph would have resulted in a G load greater than 50, which would not be survivable.

My return teletype message to the Department of the Army listed my findings and conclusions. A few days later, I received a response that the pilot would be carried as Missing in Action. I later learned that when there was no body found, the person was always carried as MIA for at least a year. This policy not only reduced the chance of a faulty conclusion of death, but also allowed dependents to continue receiving full pay and allowances during the interim.

**—509th U.S. Army Security Agency Group, III Corps, 1966**

Lots of strange things happened in Vietnam, sometimes more than one in the same day. In 1967 my company moved from operating in the jungle Highlands to the maze of rice paddies, dikes, and canals along the South China Sea. One morning we received orders to patrol to the beach and link up with an armor unit of M-48 tanks and M-113 armored personnel carriers. Because of the likelihood of booby traps, we avoided the paths on the dikes and slogged through the muddy paddies.

Spread out in three columns, we also were to search several small villages along the way. One of my platoons engaged and killed a lone VC, capturing his U.S. M1 rifle. Another grabbed two suspected VC, including one who had several hand grenades on his person. It was a long, hot miserable day crossing the muddy paddies, but we arrived on the beach and linked up with the armor several hours before dark. We occupied a classic field manual company defensive position on a small knoll just a hundred meters from the blue water of the South China Sea. An observation post in the nearby tree line would alert us if any enemy had followed our march. We took the time to clean our weapons and equipment and get a little rest.

That evening, battalion ordered us to return inland to prepare platoon-ambush positions. A few of us had some night-movement experience, but it was not something my company, or any other, was really good at or looked forward to. Although darkness covered our movement, the sounds of the boots of a hundred men slogging through the mud certainly was not noise discipline. Again we had to avoid the dikes and trails because of booby traps and the villages where barking dogs would alert any and all to our presence. It would have been much quieter and made more sense tactically for us to move in multiple columns. However, our inexperience in night warfare prevented that. I did not want our own columns to wander off course and end up fighting each other in the confusion of the darkness.

By the time we had moved for a while, our noise and light discipline settled down. It was, in fact, so good that a VC stumbled into our lines only to be grabbed and thrown to the ground. A search revealed our detainee to be female. Although not armed, she carried documents and supplies that identified her as a VC nurse. We were in the midst of the enemy, and our prisoner kept thrashing around and making so much noise I feared she would give away our position. None of my training had given me a clue on what to do. Finally, I ordered her bound, gagged, and placed in concealed vegetation as we continued moving toward our ambush positions.

We finally reached the point where I planned to keep one platoon in place and deploy the others to each flank. A small trail to our front was our primary kill zone. While most people do not relate cactus to Vietnam, on the coast several species grow to form hedgerows that act as barriers. One of these separated us from the trail. I joined the lead squad leader to confirm our location. We found a low place in the cactus and stepped over to examine the trail. Just as I leaned down in the weak moonlight to see if there had been recent foot traffic, the night was ripped by the squad leader firing a full magazine on automatic, then reloading and repeating the fire to our left down the trail.

From my now prone position, I tried to figure out just what was going to. I heard a moan, then more M16 fire. In the muzzle flash, I saw the squad leader firing into to a pile of dinks. When the firing stopped, my men quickly searched six dead bodies and gathered five enemy weapons and a few documents. Interestingly, the enemy had been moving at sling arms. Not a one had managed to return even a single round. With our position now compromised—successfully so—we moved back toward the beach. On our way we passed the place where we had left the VC nurse. She was gone.

When we neared the beach, a fierce firefight broke out at what sounded like several klicks inland. I called battalion, and they said we had no units anywhere in the area other than us. All I could figure was that two VC units had bumped into each other in the dark and had fired at each other. I understood how their mutual panic could grow into a full-scale fight. We sat back and listened until the final shots and explosions ceased echoing in the night.

Back on the beach, I thought about all the strange things of the night before. They did nothing but confirm in my mind that only a select few—the combat infantrymen of both sides—truly experience the hardships, dangers, and thrills of the war. The rest of the folks just tag along.

**—25th Infantry Division, II Corps, 1967**

It was an unusually calm morning, the seas choppy with a few whitecaps. The temperature was its normal muggy self in the Gulf of Tonkin. The year was 1968, and I was serving as an RM2 (Radioman Second Class) onboard the USS *Horne* (DLG-30), a guided-missile frigate (later reclassified as a cruiser). *Horne* was serving on "Yankee Station." Our role there was threefold. We were operating PRIAZ (Positive Radar Identification and Zoning) to identify any aircraft flying out from the shores of Vietnam as friend or foe. We were also operating as an SAR (Search and Rescue) vessel. The last role was fire support for "the feet on the ground in Nam."

It was an exciting day—not just the normal twelve hours on and twelve hours off. The battle stations alarm began to bang, and men scrambled to get to their positions in less than sixty seconds. That in itself was a pretty amazing sight, seeing nearly 500 men running the 550-foot length of deck and up or down three levels of the vessel in under sixty seconds. The call-to-stations was triggered by an unidentified aircraft entering our airspace off the coast. The jet wasn't squawking on the IFF (Identify Friendly or Foe) frequency. The computer system recognized the aircraft as a Vietnamese MiG-21 interceptor. We had already loaded two Terrier missiles on the launchers ready for the kill. In our CIC (Combat Information Center) where the radar and fire controls were located, Capt. Stansfield

Turner (later admiral and later yet director of the Central Intelligence Agency in the Jimmy Carter administration) gave the order to fire. In a cloud of smoke so thick we could see nothing but fire leaving the bow, two Terriers were on the way to their target. I ran back to the CIC from the bridge to watch the radar. *Boom!* The MiG disappeared from the screen. It was quite a time for me and the entire *Horne* crew.

We later rescued a downed fighter pilot from the *Kitty Hawk* (CVA 63) who was stranded on a beach in North Vietnam. He said we rescued him just before his being captured by the NVA. We used our onboard SH2 helicopter to pull him out. That was an emotional moment as well. We listen to his combat stories on the mess deck before returning him to his ship.

*Horne* also shot down another MiG in 1970 and served in many theaters of action over her lifetime. I had the honor of being a Plankowner (meaning I was part of the its original commissioning detail). She was a beauty who now rests at the bottom of the Pacific Ocean near Hawaii. She was stripped and sunk in a naval exercise many years later. Such a sad end for a fine lady.

—**USS** *Horne*, **South China Sea, 1968**

My battalion commander in Vietnam once told me the following story:

> I landed by helicopter in a rice paddy in clean, starched fatigues to visit my recon platoon that was on a three-day operation in Long An Province. As I chatted with the troops, I spotted one particularly exhausted young soldier slumped against a paddy dike. Walking over to him, I signaled for him to remain seated when he began to struggle to his feet. Looking at the young man, I noted the heavily caked mud all

over his uniform, the stubble beard, the bug bites and the half-lidded, red rimmed eyes which bespoke little recent sleep.

"What can I get you, soldier?" I asked.

Looking me squarely in the eye, he responded, "Just more VC, colonel, just more VC, so we can kill the bastards and get on home."

I was too moved to respond. Instead, I simply reached down and patted the soldier's shoulder, turned, walked back to my chopper.

In my mind I thought it was indeed a tragedy of major importance that an American youngster of eighteen or nineteen years of age should be concentrating on killing anyone. I balanced this personal regret with the thought that if his country could continue to breed such young men, it would forever remain free.

To me, the statement of the colonel about this young soldier are most profound. His thoughts not only conveyed the realism of the war but also vividly portrayed the demands placed on the men who fought it. His remarks revealed that located deep inside each of us lies a dormant, vile, and disgusting animalistic instinct that only the horrors of a war like Vietnam can trigger, an instinct that supposedly separates mankind from the other living creatures found on earth. Unfortunately, only those that have come face-to-face with death will ever know the true meaning behind this horrible instinct. Yes, the meaning of the phrase, "Kill or be killed," runs deeper than most would think, and for certain, if we truly learned and understood its meaning, there would be no more wars.

**—199th Light Infantry Brigade, III Corps, 1967**

My Special Forces A Team was assigned to a small firebase near the Laotian border. Most of our time was spent training the local militia and trying to assist the nearby villagers. Late one afternoon, we got word that a regional VC leader was to meet with the village chief that evening. We made plans to abduct him—or kill him if he did not surrender peacefully.

There were only twenty or so hooches in the village, but like most in Vietnam, the chief's hooch was in its center. We would have to be careful not to wake up the dogs as well as be on the lookout for any security posted by the VC leader. About midnight, we sneaked out of our wire perimeter and slowly made our way to the village. I was on point, and just as we reached the first hooch, I spotted a VC with his rife at sling arms while he smoked a cigarette.

I signaled for the column following me to halt while I inched forward. It was time to put to use all that hand-to-hand training I had suffered in SF and Ranger schools. I silently approached the unsuspecting VC from the rear, grasped him around the neck, and pulled his head rearward with my left arm in order to cut his throat with my Ka-Bar knife—complete with leather strap wrapping around the handle so it would not slip even when blood soaked.

When I reach around to cut his throat, I realized that my left arm was blocking the way. So I went to option number two, which was to stab him in the temple. I drove the Ka-Bar almost to the hilt in the side of the man's head. Instead of going limp, he struggled even harder and broke my grip. He stared at me for a moment and then went running down the trail into the village, screaming words I could not understand. Dogs barked, lanterns were lit, and I stood there wondering how the hell the VC could run like that with a knife stuck in his head.

With everyone alert, there was nothing to do but return to our compound. A few of the guys, including the captain, occasionally asked to borrow my knife. It just did not seem as funny to me as it did to them.

**—5th Special Forces Group, I Corps, 1966**

I arrived at Phu Loi in late 1971 as a warrant office qualified to fly CH-47 Chinooks. My assignment to the 213th Assault Support Helicopter Company (Black Cats), a part of the 11th Aviation Brigade, had already been coordinated because upon my arrival, my brother, an air traffic controller at the base, would be going home under the rule that no more than one sibling at a time had to serve in the war zone.

The company operations officer met me at Binh Hoa and flew me to Phu Loi in an OH-58. I was taken immediately to meet the commanding officer. This was on a Sunday, and he was in his office in shorts and a Hawaiian shirt. The company was having a barbecue that day with water buffalo as the main course.

My first week in country started slow. In addition to my duties as a pilot, I was assigned as company avionics officer as my extra duty. I knew nothing about the job, but I met with the avionics NCO and asked him to keep me informed and to let me know if he needed anything.

There was not much flying the first few days because the missions were few with the conflict winding down. I did get selected to help out the maintenance officer and run up a couple of the helicopters after maintenance had been performed, as it always requires two pilots to start the CH-47.

Evenings were spent in the officers' club watching Armed Forces Network television and playing pool. I checked the operations board daily to see if I was scheduled to fly the next day. After a week I was still not on the board, but my roommate was. At 3:00 a.m. the next morning, a clerk came to wake my roommate for his mission. He made some excuse about not feeling well and said to take me instead. I was happy to get the opportunity to actually fly.

We took off before dawn and headed to Tay Ninh where we were to standby at the airfield there for possible missions. It took about an hour to get to the airfield, and most of our flying was in total darkness. With very few cities in that area, it was difficult to tell where the sky ended and the ground began. We arrived only to standby most of the day. Late in the afternoon, our aircraft commander called the operations center to get us released to return to Phu Loi. We were told we were released, but just as we were starting up, a jeep came driving down the runway. Its passenger came on board and told us there was mission for us. A Vietnamese unit with armored personnel carriers needed fuel—and they were surrounded by bad guys.

There were twenty-four fifty-gallon drums to be delivered by sling load under our CH-47 Chinook. Ordinarily, this would require two trips, but our aircraft commander decided to make it on one run because darkness was fast approaching. He explained that since our aircraft was fairly new, it should be able to lift the load with no problems.

We proceeded to pick up the twenty-four drums of fuel and headed toward the surrounded ARVN troops. When we were almost there, we got a call from operations that they needed an interpreter to talk to the troops on the ground. For forty-five minutes, we circled until they returned to the radio with the interpreter. By now any enemy on the ground was well aware that we were prepared to deliver our load somewhere nearby.

On our approach, bad began to happen. The aircraft commander was piloting the helicopter as I monitored the instruments. There was a lot of chatter on the radio telling us what we already knew—we were being shot at and shot at and hit. We continued our descent and somewhere below 1,000 feet, I noticed the left engine fire light came on. I performed the standard emergency procedure by pulling the handle to release the fire suppressant. The light did not go out. Not good.

We could hear pings as bullets hit the fuselage. The aircraft commander ordered our door gunners to return fire about the same time the flight engineer reported that the barrels of fuel, leaking from bullet holes, were on fire. We were still on approach when the right engine fire light came on. I again performed the emergency procedure but got the same results. Both engines were now on fire, and we could smell the smoke in the cockpit. The flight engineer recommended dropping the burning load of fuel drums and the aircraft command responded in the affirmative.

We attempted to gain altitude, but despite dropping the cargo, we were still going down. Somewhere just above the tree line, the lift in the aft rotor blades stopped. I saw the tops of the trees and then the sky. After that I felt the Chinook crash into the ground. The next thing I remember was that I was hanging upside down in my seat. I struggled to free myself and then exited the aircraft just as the helicopter became engulfed in flames.

About the time we got everyone aboard accounted for, ARVN troops arrived to lead us inside their perimeter of APCs. Everyone had cuts and scrapes, but no one had suffered serious injuries.

Our aircraft commander got on a radio and let the operations ship know that everyone was okay. Darkness was fast approaching and we would have to remain with the ARVNs overnight. We were told someone would come to get us early the next morning.

The ARVNs and their American advisors fed us Spam and water for supper and provided hammocks inside the APCs for us. Nevertheless, I remained awake all night, in part because of all the adrenaline I had pumped in the crash and mostly because of the air force C-130 circling our position, hosing down the area around the camp with mini-gun fire to keep the bad guys at bay.

Just before daylight, two UH-1H helicopters approached the perimeter with their landing lights flashing. The first landed and took aboard our crew and several wounded ARVN troops. Only when we reached altitude did I finally feel safe. Later, I learned that the second Huey was shot down and the crew had to E&E (escape and evade) for twelve hours before they were safely extracted.

Upon arrival back at Phu Loi, we were taken to the dispensary to be checked over. I had a couple of gashes on my left leg. The doctor mentioned that since I had been injured in a hostile act, a Purple Heart would be coming. I had also lost my pistol, probably from hanging upside down after we crashed.

We met with our commanding officer and debriefed. That evening in the officers' club, I was initiated into the unit by drinking flaming cognac while rolling a Chinook tire back and forth without spilling my drink. To this day, I cannot stand the stuff. The remainder of my tour was pretty boring compared to the excitement of my first week in country.

—**213th Assault Support Helicopter Company, III Corps, 1971**

You might say that this story occurred in a "very rear area"—or maybe a "rear, rear, rear area." In 1971, I was at Fort Benning, Georgia, attending the Infantry Officer Basic Course (IOBC). One day we had the mission of defending the same hill on which John Wayne had stood his ground during the filming of the movie *The Green Berets*. Ours was a mechanized infantry defense, complete with armored personnel carriers, and we kicked the shit out of the "aggressors."

Despite the victory, it was tough going because I almost ran out of Kool-Aid in my canteen, our blank ammo was getting low, and the food trucks (roach coaches) couldn't find us for the noon break.

The movie company had built a big pagoda on the hill along with several hooches and fighting positions, but all of that had been flattened by artillery after the movie was completed. It wasn't worth defending, but we did our duty. Because of Benning, I probably qualify for benefits for PTSD. The horror!!

—**IOBC, Fort Benning, Georgia, 1971**

The morning of September 3, 1969, dawned hot and cloudy over the mountainous terrain of northern I Corps in South Vietnam. Along with the other members of the infantry company of the 101st Airborne Division, in which I served as a platoon leader, I rose early and packed my gear, eagerly anticipating a helicopter extraction. There was no need for a meal break that morning because we had not received a resupply in a couple of days. Everyone was out of rations, and we were looking forward to a hot meal in the rear.

Our company had been inserted by helicopter into the mountains a week earlier. With a sizeable NVA presence in the area, we had been involved in several brief firefights in the intervening days but had suffered no casualties. Fighting the NVA was the norm, but this time out, we were challenged by Mother Nature as well. A major typhoon had swept in off the South China Sea, basically halting all offensive military operations and stranding all units, such as ours, in the field from resupply and extraction. Although we were wet, cold, hungry, and generally miserable, we knew the NVA were hunkering down just as we were. Our biggest danger was being struck by falling limbs or uprooted trees, of which there were many, from the typhoon winds.

But now all that was behind us as we waited to be extracted to LZ Sally, our base camp, where we hoped to remain overnight before starting it all over again the next day. One night in a base camp may not sound like much, but it was one less night in the mountains and another day shorter to the end of our tour. It was hot food, cold beer, and a dry place to sleep. For a grunt, it was as near to heaven as we could get.

The company arrived at the small knoll which was to be our extraction point about an hour prior to our pickup time. We were confronted by major concern. The knoll itself appeared safe enough for single helicopter landings after we cleared it of loose debris, but a serious problem remained. Downslope, in the direction the helicopters would have to depart the LZ, stood a 60- to 70-foot dead tree with a number of branches extending outward. Clearly, it would present a problem for the pilots unless it was removed.

After making extraction assignments, the other platoon leaders and I, along with our platoon sergeants, met with the company commander. I had only been with the unit for about five weeks, and since I was still on a steep learning curve, I normally kept my mouth shut in these meetings. The immediate topic of conversation was the tree and who would be assigned to take it down with C-4, a powerful explosive we carried in abundance to blow things up as well as to heat our rations. The shock was palpable when the captain denied permission to blow the tree.

A rather heated exchange followed. The captain explained that he didn't want to alert the NVA to our impending departure and that bringing the tree down would do that. I decided that it was time to earn my money, so I spoke up strongly in favor of blowing the tree. I agreed with the NCOs that the NVA were in no position to interfere with our extraction, but that the tree presented a major danger to the helicopters. The captain stood firm. We said our "Yes, sirs" and returned to our platoons. An uneasy silence settled over the LZ. I couldn't shake a feeling of dread.

The pickup time arrived, and the birds were right on schedule as we were their first lift mission of the day. Fourteen helicopters of the 158th Assault Helicopter Company had been assigned to pick us up in groups of five. My platoon went out first, and as we took off, it was clear that the pilots had to carefully maneuver around the tree, which the first seven pilots did safely by flying to one side of the tree. Then the captain, his radio operators, and the company medic loaded onto the eighth aircraft and the pilot attempted to take off to the opposite side. As he lifted off under full power, the main rotor struck the tree and the aircraft went out of control. It continued forward, losing altitude, and, in a short distance, crashed into the trees and disappeared from view.

The pickup was aborted with about half the company still on the ground. I was still in the air when the crash occurred and my aircraft crew chief told me about the crash. Someone made the decision to drop the extracted troops at the base camp, so I never returned to the crash site. The company members who remained on the ground fought their way through thick jungle to reach the downed bird. The helicopter had come to rest in a mountain stream, swollen from the recent rain. It had landed on its skids but the impact had driven the engine into the cargo and crew areas. The helicopter, nearly fully loaded with fuel, had exploded and burned. There were no survivors.

A reaction force was flown in to assist with recovering the casualties. One of their first actions was to blow down the tree. The remainder of the company was extracted later that afternoon. We remained at the base camp for several days, awaiting a new commander and grieving our lost comrades. Death took many forms in Vietnam, and the senseless tragedies such as this were by far the worse.

—**101st Airborne Division, I Corps, 1969**

In late 1971, I was visiting ARVN units in a remote hamlet in Kien Phong Province deep in the Delta near the Cambodian border. As usual, a small herd of children gathered, and I heard the little kids talking in semiwhispers, "Look, there's an American." Another asked, "Where?" The answer: "See? An American guy . . . see him? He's right there! Look . . . see him now?"

Most of the littlest kids had probably never seen an American. This was an out-of-the-way place, not much of a war going on around it, and U.S. forces hadn't been anywhere near this area in a couple of years. I turned around and saw the kids following us ("us" meaning an ARVN and one other U.S. soldier). The kids tagged along in a cluster, talking about "the Americans." Finally I turned around and said in Vietnamese, acting greatly surprised, "An American? Really? Where is he? Show me!"

It never crossed their minds that a U.S. guy could speak their language. They paused for a moment, wondering just what was going on, then they all pointed and said, "You! You! You're an American!"

I said, with mock seriousness, "Not at all! I'm Vietnamese. Can't you see? Can't you hear? I'm talking Vietnamese! And I eat with chopsticks too! And eat nuoc mam, too!" That stopped them for a second, and then they began anew, laughing, knowing the game was on. I came back and repeated, "I really am Vietnamese! I'm not an American!" Then one asked about my blond hair. I told them I dyed my hair to look like an American and that I had surgery on my nose and eyes to make them bigger.

I could see then some of the younger children really began to wonder just what the hell was going on as they stared with puzzled and comical expressions of utter disbelief. They looked like they were seeing a talking tree, or a water buffalo levitating from the rice fields. Or both. The older ones were laughing and enjoying the absurd charade. The crowd of urchins grew in size until several dozen giggling kids were swept along in the wonder of it all.

I never admitted to being an American as we walked through the entire hamlet. Their laughing parents were good indications that all was well. Our intel was apparently good in letting us know that the place was pretty much okay.

As we got to edge of the hamlet, I told the kids to be good, to study hard, and to always listen to their parents—but not to dye their hair because black hair made them handsome boys and pretty girls.

It was a funny, strange time. One of those little bits of the war that I will remember forever. I never went through that hamlet again; I often wonder how long the kids told the story of the blond-haired Vietnamese guy.

**—MACV, IV Corps, 1971**

The moon hung overhead like a big Chinese lantern, sometimes casting an eerie glow across the rice paddies outside our compound, at other times covered by dark and silent clouds that foretold of another monsoon on the way. I sat behind a big .50-caliber machine gun and scanned the rings of barbed wire surrounding our little piece of South Vietnam known as Firebase Charlie, one of several bases of the 2nd Squadron, 1st Cavalry Regiment, in Phan Thiet. The year was 1969, and I was twenty years old, on guard duty at two in the morning. I was eager to be relieved and hit the sack.

The night had been quiet, and I stayed alert by picking out objects with the big Starlight night vision scope mounted atop the gun. Every so often, I'd fire off a hand flare, watching it rocket up to hundreds of feet in the air and pop its tiny parachute. Then the bright burning light would hang over the jungle for a few minutes before it burned out and fell into the darkness. On the way down, as it lit the night like a stadium floodlight, it cast moving shadows that danced like ghosts behind the intense glare. The silence of the jungle was occasionally punctuated by the sounds of distant artillery and faraway bursts of automatic-weapons fire. It was a night of eerie, haunting images. It felt surreal, and I was in a strange mood.

The relief guard finally showed up, so I turned the position over to him. I grabbed my M16 and headed for the guards' bunker. I was the only person in that bunker since the other guards had returned to their own hooches after their final shift. I still had one more turn on guard at 4:00 a.m., so I settled into the small, dark shelter for some sleep. The bunker was simply a big box made of heavy wood, half-buried, and covered with sandbags. One end was open with a short entry space to stop shrapnel from slicing in if mortar rounds exploded nearby. The only other opening was a straight piece of three-inch drainage pipe that ran from a corner on the dirt floor out to the barbed wire. My one light source was a green army flashlight with a red filter over the lens. I hung it over my cot with a strip of parachute cord like a tiny chandelier.

Slinging my rifle over the end of the cot, I ate a couple cans of C-rations, leaving one about half-empty before deciding to get some rest. I rolled up my flak jacket for a pillow and was quickly asleep.

I awoke a while later, irritated by a tiny noise somewhere in the pitch-dark bunker. It was curious that such a small sound would arouse me when the sounds of helicopters, jet fighters, artillery shells flying overhead, and small-arms fire were always part of the local ambience. But those sounds were generally far off and infrequent.

This sound was right here, right now, with me in the bunker, and it was getting louder. From an almost inaudible scratching, it increased a little at a time and was soon joined by a vague tapping sound. Wide awake now, my mind raced with thoughts of the deadly poisonous Bamboo Viper snake, known as Two-Step because, once bitten, you died before your second stride. There were some big-ass spiders out there, too, and some really big fuzzy, fangy, dang-that-hurts tarantulas as well as centipedes.

By now the sounds had increased not only in volume and tempo but also in numbers sounding now like dozens of tiny feet pattering around me in the blackness. My heart raced. I'd made it through ten months in the war so far, and I wasn't about to get killed by some poison critter, so I slowly began to feel across the bunk towards my M16, waiting and ready with a full magazine, locked and loaded. My other hand crept toward the flashlight, since I needed to see my enemy before I could hit him . . . it . . . them.

I connected with the M16 and flashlight about the same time, running my hands along their sides until I could feel the trigger on the one and the switch on the other. As I raised the gun to the ready, just before I flicked the light on, there was a sudden, tense, dead silence. I was being watched.

In the total quiet, the little click of the flashlight switch sounded like a rifle shot. With batteries nearly dead and the bulb shined weakly, but its pathetic red glow showed dozens of pairs of tiny red eyes . . . below me on the floor . . . beside me on the walls . . . and overhead in the beams.

Rats.

I panicked at about the same moment the rodents did, squeezing the trigger in the same instant they bolted for the drain pipe like a school of herring fleeing a shark. With the rifle on full auto, the muzzle flashed in the dark like a strobe light at a rock concert and the hammering sound reverberated like a Fender Stratocaster on steroids. I didn't let up and the mass of filthy, scrambling rats soon plugged the end of the pipe, so they turned for the entrance, panic-stricken and screaming a horrid rat-herd screech of terror. Wood splinters and rat guts flew in every direction as dust and smoke filled the bunker in a violent orgasm of concentrated chaos.

And then it stopped. As the last bullet cleared the muzzle and its empty cartridge bounced off my empty helmet on the floor beside me, the last living rat jumped over the sandbags and was gone into the dark night. Around me lay squirming, wriggling shards of dead and dying rodents everywhere, especially by the drain pipe where they clumped together into a nasty pile of sticky gore. The bunker walls were perforated like a country road sign and my ears were ringing like the Liberty Bell the day it cracked.

But it wasn't over.

Just as I crawled out of the bunker, the whole firebase lit up with machine guns, grenade launchers, rifle fire, and hand flares. Everywhere I looked, my fellow soldiers were laying into their weapons and saturating the jungle outside the firebase with all the firepower they could muster.

As if we were under attack.

My best guess was that the ruckus I raised in the bunker was mistaken for enemy fire and everyone awakened by it simply jumped to their guns to fight back. So I joined in, sticking a fresh magazine into my rifle and taking a position up next to the bunker. I suppose I went through another three or four magazines before it quieted down. I went back into the bunker and cleaned up the mess the best I could, scooping the dead rats into an empty sandbag, and then I threw it onto our trash-burning pile. No one ever mentioned all the bullet holes inside the bunker—or the cot with one end all shot up. And nobody was hurt, other than a pile of rats.

But to this day, my ears are still ringing.

**—1st Cavalry Regiment, III Corps, 1969**

In October 1969, my company and a sister company were operating in the mountains west of Hue. The double- and triple-canopy jungle, combined with steep slopes, made moving extremely difficult.

One afternoon we began to come across badly deteriorated bodies—little more than bones and clothing. We counted until the final total came to more than 250. By the size of the skeletons and the clothing, we could tell that men, women, and children made up the dead. Closer inspection revealed many to have their hands tied behind their backs with communication wire. From the holes in the skulls, it appeared that many had been shot at close range. Others had broken bones and appeared to have been beaten to death.

From what we could determine, the bodies were former residents of Hue and were among the missing whom the Viet Cong had marched into the jungle and murdered during the Tet Offensive of 1968. We reported the find to higher headquarters. I don't know if anyone ever attempted to identify the bodies. We returned to our operations to try to find live enemies rather than dead allies.

**—101st Airborne Division, I Corps, 1969**

I was a C-123 navigator in the 315th Tactical Airlift Wing flying out of Phan Rang in 1970. While it was we officers who flew and navigated the aircraft, it was the enlisted crew chiefs aboard and the mechanics on the ground who kept us from falling out of the sky.

On the morning of July 4, our mission was to onload a disassembled C-123 propeller plus the propeller shop chief and several of his troops for transport to the airfield at Song Be. There they were to replace the damaged prop of a C-123 that had taxied over a mobile fire extinguisher and dinged the tips of one of the props. This caused a vibration so severe that the engine had to be shut down.

When we landed, the chief inspected the prop to find about an inch and a half on the tip of each blade was curled back. It looked like we were going to be there for some time because removing the old prop and installing the new was a long, laborious procedure. Meanwhile, the chief had been studying the prop and had an idea. He told us to chock the aircraft's wheels tight and to stack ammunition boxes in front of the damaged propeller. When that was done, he told the pilots to make sure the ignition was off, braced a pencil on the top ammunition box, held it against the prop, told his troops to pull the prop through slowly, and thus scribed all the blades.

Then he got out a hacksaw from his tool bag and began sawing off each of the blades right on the scribed line. That was a lot of work. His troops and both aircrews and I took turns on the hacksaw. Then the chief smoothed the cut-off tips with a file. Finally, he said to the pilots, "Crank it." The engine started and ran smoothly. Everyone piled aboard their aircraft and departed Song Be. Later, I was told that engine ran smoothly all the way home but that the pilots had to throttle back the engine with the damaged prop a little because it had a slightly higher RPM than the other engine.

We were soon back in the air and flew another three sorties that day, moving ARVN troops from one place to another. It was not much of an Independence Day, but one full of lessons learned nevertheless.

**—315th Tactical Airlift Command, II Corps, 1970**

We were working the Highlands in II Corps in late 1968 when we stopped midday to receive a resupply and mail by helicopter. Afterwards, those not on guard sat around eating and reading the mail. A sergeant had received a copy of *U.S. News and World Report* and promised to pass it along to me when he was finished.

While I waited I heard a private, who claimed to be from LA (Lower Alabama) accuse the sergeant of just looking at the pictures. The sergeant responded that no, he had fourteen years of education. The private laughed and said, "I dropped out of school after the seventh grade and you got fourteen years—and both of us are right here in Vietnam."

**—25th Infantry Division, II Corps, 1968**

In the late 1960s, I entered college to avoid the draft—as did many of my friends. With no scholarship, I was going at my parents' expense, which was a considerable burden for them in that dad was a carpenter and mother was a stay-at-home mom with four sons. A few guys I knew had gone to Vietnam, and some had come home in a box.

I finally came to the conclusion that even if I stayed in college, the war would last long enough for me to still get drafted. So I decided, "Shucks, all that's going to happen is that I'm going to spend a bunch of their money on college, and then still get drafted and killed in Vietnam, so why waste the time and money?" I dropped my classes and received my draft notice in a month.

The real reason I was willing to go to the war was that I didn't want my dad to have to listen to anybody saying something about his son having gone to Canada or having dodged the draft. Dad had a half-brother who had avoided the draft in World War II. He hid out in the mountains of eastern Tennessee for quite a while and his dad took him provisions for the entire time.

Earlier, my great-grandfather had gotten between some bootleggers and law officers and had ended up shooting two of the policemen. Now Pappy knew, as everyone else did, "those men needed killin'." But he figured that since they were officers of the law, and as crooked as the law was in those parts, he'd be headed for prison. So Pappy loaded up some provisions and headed into the mountains where he "scouted" for about two years. My dad spent many days in the mountains with Pappy during this time. He eventually came out and surrendered, and as the officials had cleaned up their act a little by then, they knew his actions were justifiable, so he served very little time in prison.

I relate these stories to help explain my own circumstances. When it came time for me to report to the draft board, Dad was going to drive me down to answer my "greetings from Uncle Sam." Shortly after we left home, he stopped at the end of the street on which we lived. He paused and then said very seriously and soberly, choking back tears, "Now son, I can turn left and take you down there to them people, or I can turn right and take you to the mountains and feed you 'til the day you die. Either way, I'll love you and be as proud of you as I can be. And to tell the truth, I'd rather take you to the mountains."

I hesitated to answer; I was so choked up I could hardly speak because I knew he was serious—and I was well aware of my family's past of going on scout. Finally, I answered, "I know, Dad, and I don't really understand the justifiability of this crazy war, but I don't want anyone to be able to say that I wouldn't do my part, or to tell you that your son is a coward, so let's just go on down to the draft board."

—**Johnson City, Tennessee, 1969**

I arrived in Vietnam on September 28, 1969, and was assigned to the 199th Light Infantry Brigade as a replacement for one of several men who had been killed or wounded in a fierce battle a few days prior. Over the next few months, I participated in several major contacts and skirmishes, but the most memorable occurred just after Christmas. On December 28, we flew by helicopters into an area that had been determined to have significant enemy activity. After they dropped us off the choppers in a clearing, we started walking toward the heavier jungle area. As we came to a stream just inside the jungle, we spotted some trails that had signs of recent activity.

As it was late afternoon, we stopped and set an ambush along the trail. After everyone was in position, some men stayed on guard while the rest of us sat around quietly, eating, writing, or our boots off to air out our socks and feet.

There was a new guy with us who was in the field for his first time. He was one of those on guard when he saw an enemy soldier walking toward us. He whisper-hollered, "Gook. A damn gook." Everyone instantly got into combat position and I asked, "Where?" He said, "There, right there coming down the damn trail." I queried, "Why didn't you open up on him?" He responded, "I didn't really know if that was what I was supposed to do." Needless to say, by this time the "gook" had run off down the trail, across the stream, and into the jungle.

We remained on edge and extra cautious for the remainder of the night but nothing happened. In the morning, we got up, ate our breakfast (if one can call a can of fruit cocktail and some not exactly "bottled water" a meal), and began to recon forward. What we didn't realize was that on the evening before when the enemy soldier walked up on us, he simply turned and ran back across the stream to a newly built bunker complex that he and his comrades had constructed—and, of course, prepared for our inevitable arrival. Simply put—they knew we were coming and they were ready and waiting. About 9:00 a.m., we walked right into their ambush. They opened up on us with small arms, machine guns, and rocket-propelled grenades. We returned fire the best we could as we identified most of the enemy positions. We concentrated our fire enough to suppress them until we could regroup, back out, and call in helicopter gunship fire support.

We treated our wounded and then made another assault on the bunkers. The combination of our efforts and the gunships caused the enemy to withdraw from the complex. We then went in to examine everything and to confirm that the enemy was gone. From the evidence we found, we assessed that we had killed one or two, and possibly wounded a few more, but they had taken the bodies and cleared out. We searched through everything to obtain any information that might prove helpful and then destroyed the bunker complex to render it useless for the future. We found documents, ammo, and some food—including large tins of cooking oil containers that had the "joined hands" symbol and something like "donated by the U.N. and/or citizens of the U.S.A." prominently displayed. We figured the gooks were mighty unhappy to have to leave a nice base camp that had obviously taken a lot of labor and time to construct.

There were several fresh trails out of the bunker complex and the company commander ordered us to follow one. We had only gone a few hundred meters when several well-placed machine guns and small arms opened up. The gooks had built their bunker complex with a twin a short distance away. They had simply left the one complex and taken wounded and dead to the other—where they had more troops, help, and firepower. The first one of us hit was a friend who was walking point. An AK-47 round went straight through his heart. He never knew what hit him, which is to be considered fortunate compared to others I'd seen. After we got him pulled back out of the heavy action, the medic ripped off his shirt to see if there was anything he could do to help him. But the answer was obvious. There was a hole through his chest about the size of a quarter and no pulse; he was in no pain. His war was over. Death is bad regardless how it happens, but if I had a choice for myself, this would be what I would have preferred.

My friend was dead, but the battle raged on. It was chaos for a while as the enemy had us pretty well pinned down. The other two platoons maneuvered to our flanks. There were wounded everywhere, some screaming, "Medic!" which is a most tormenting sound when you can't really do anything to help.

I was squeezed down behind a termite mound. We returned and tried to assist the wounded. I crawled over to help one of the guys who was yelling for the medic. As I got near him I could hear him yelling, "I'm hit in the back." I recognized the man as the platoon shammer—a soldier who was always complaining about some health problem so he could go to the rear and get out of the field. He had done this successfully several times over the past few months, but finally he had been forced to come out with us and do his duty. No one liked him for obvious reasons.

When I finally got to him, I calmed him down so I could examine his wound. I jerked up his shirt and looked at his back. He had indeed been hit. A hot bullet had gone through his canteen and stuck on his back, burning a small blister similar to a cigarette burn. After what I had gone through to get to him, and other more seriously wounded guys around, I was not happy. I told him to shut up, that he did not have a bad injury. I later learned he received a Purple Heart for being "wounded in action."

We called for artillery and gunships as we moved everyone backward. I stayed with my radio until everyone was clear from the enemy fire and then began crawling back myself. As I went, I gathered rucksacks and weapons left behind and drug them behind me. I didn't want to leave them for the enemy, and besides it gave me a little cover and some comfort as bullets struck the bushes and trees around me. It seemed like a mile, though it was only fifty yards or so, before I got back with the other guys and could finally find a big tree to get behind for good cover. I hadn't taken more than a few breaths, when the adrenalin slowed down and then it hit me. Man! I needed to go to the bathroom. Bad. I hope that's the only time in my life that I have to drop my pants and relieve myself while laying on my side.

An hour or so had passed by now, and we had gunship helicopters on site to help keep the enemy at bay. We began pulling back to a landing zone where we could evacuate our dead, wounded, and extra equipment. I helped move my dead friend. We laid him on a poncho and two guys carried him by his arms and I had his feet. We had to recross the stream that now had slippery banks from all the guys walking ahead of us. On the far bank the two guys in front started slipping and lost their grip. The dead soldier's body fell into me, almost as if we were hugging face to face.

While we were in the field, we always wore our jungle fatigue shirts. We would roll up our sleeves in the heat, giving us tanned faces, necks, and forearms—but our chests remained as light as our particular race permitted. As we made our way on up the bank and toward the clearing, I was aware of the hole in the dead man's clean white chest and the crimson blood that would gurgle out each time his weight shifted. This did not really bother me, as I had seen many dead and wounded before. What did bother me was that when the body slipped into me on the stream bank my friend's eyes were wide open, a beautiful brown color, looking straight at me. Bits of mud and other debris had settled in and around his eyes and I was overwhelmed with the desire to get that stuff out of his eyes. I couldn't understand how in the world he could tolerate having the stuff in his eyes and it not bother him. I thought it must be extremely painful.

I kept looking at his eyes, thinking I should clean them. We finally got him to the evacuation helicopter and, when the two guys in front lifted his body up into it, one lost his grip and the dead guy's head bumped the floor kind of hard. Again I thought, "Man, that had to hurt." The reality of the fact that he was dead and that the debris in his eyes no longer mattered finally sunk in about the time the chopper lifted off, but I can still to this day see those brown eyes with that miserable dirt in them.

**—199th Light Infantry Brigade, III Corps, 1969**

In 1970, I was the lieutenant in charge of the Division Pathfinder Detachment. A few of my men were assigned as air traffic controllers at the Dau Tieng Firebase, nicknamed "Dallas Texas." I stayed over at the firebase one evening after a visit to my troops and we passed the time drinking beer as we sat on a bunker looking into the Michelin Rubber Plantation. Suddenly we heard the sounds of "thunk, thunk" as someone yelled "Mortars incoming!"

We scrambled to get inside the bunker. I tried to be cool, but it was the first time I had been on the incoming end of a mortar attack and I was more than a bit scared. As I rushed through the bunker entrance, I forgot to duck and smacked my head on the header board, knocking myself down and nearly out. My fellow Pathfinders pulled me into the bunker by my boots just before the rounds landed. This later provided many hours of entertainment for my troops—who greatly enjoyed relating the story about their "dumb-ass lieutenant" who forgot to duck.

**—25th Infantry Division, III Corps, 1970**

In 1969, I was a rifle platoon leader in 101st Airborne Division. For several weeks, we patrolled through the mountains west of the A Shau Valley without turning up much of anything. When we came upon a creek that formed part of the Vietnam–Laos border, I decided to follow it for a while. Not only did it seem like a good place to find the enemy, but also the stream also provided a ready supply of water during our march along the hot, humid jungle floor. We followed the creek for several days, frequently refilling our canteens with the cool water, before we came across a very dead, putrid elephant lying in midstream.

**—101st Airborne Division, I Corps, 1969**

I had never been to Tan Mai Orphanage or to any of the other many orphanages in our area. With the 12th CAG's current emphasis on Civic Action projects (a derivative of earlier pacification programs), I knew that sooner or later I probably would see most of the orphanages and schools.

It was Sunday, about noon, in July 1970, and I had slept a few hours after having served as the TOC night duty officer—an additional duty to my usual job as a helicopter pilot and the brigade's public information officer (PIO). I was ambling toward the headquarters offices, noting it was a particularly hot and clear day for monsoon season, when I saw one of the clerks running down the hill toward me with that look on his face that meant somebody wanted me to do something quick.

"Sir, the colonel is going to some orphanage to distribute some clothes and he wants PIO coverage for the Civic Action article we are doing for *Hawk* magazine [the monthly morale publication of the 1st Aviation Brigade]," the clerk yelled to me. "Sir, the CO says no weapons. He does not want the kids to see weapons," the clerk said as I walked up the hill. I nodded in agreement.

Not wanting to get bogged down with the circus that surrounds the CO, I decided to travel by jeep to the orphanage. As I was attempting to scrounge a vehicle, I met the group chaplain (a lieutenant colonel) leaving in his jeep. After a cordial hello and a salute, I learned that he was going to the orphanage and would be glad to have the PIO accompany him (everyone wants to be in the news—good for advancement). On the way over, the chaplain explained that he worked with the orphanage and the people who supported it.

I had never been into Bien Hoa, the Vietnamese village for which the air base was named. I had flown over it countless times and I had driven by it—but never into it. We turned off of Highway 1 and drove under an overhead sign letting us know that we had entered the village. A transformation took place immediately. The street was still paved, but I could not see the pavement for the garbage and layer of mud that covered it. There were people everywhere. It was nearly impossible to drive through them. Between the piles of garbage were little heaps of vegetables, fruits, and fresh meats on the sidewalk. Each pile of goods was tended by an old Vietnamese woman who would haggle over the price of her wares . . . but was eager to lower the price and sell what she had.

Joining the sidewalk were rows of shops built of old wood, cardboard, tin, flattened beer and soda cans, burlap, bricks, mud, and whatever else could be nailed or pasted together. The shops opened completely across the front so that the sidewalk became an extension of each "walk in" store. In one block I saw a bicycle shop, a motorcycle shop, a Shell gasoline station, a seamstress shop, curio shops, food stores, dens for smoking pot, and, of course, the ever-present cribs of the prostitutes. Intermingled among all of the shops were the houses of the shopkeepers. It was difficult to tell the difference between a residence and a shop, and sometimes there was none. When driving along, one might be looking into a shop one instant and into the interior of a home the next. The people did not seem to mind the lack of privacy. Between the street and the sidewalk was the ever-present shallow canal that served as an open sewer.

We encountered the usual street kids (cowboys) who were hawking black market goods, wanting "American Green" money (which was illegal), hustling whatever we might want to buy, offering to sell their sisters or "number one" short timers (prostitutes), or trying to pull off our wristwatches or sunglasses.

We turned off of the street into a narrow, muddy alley. I felt for my weapon only to remember that we had been told to leave them behind. The chaplain smiled and said, "Don't worry. You are in Bien Hoa, and the locals will take care of you. This whole village was leveled in the Tet Offensive of '68. These people have seen the work of the Viet Cong." I smiled, knowing that it was our group's helicopter gunships that had leveled the village in the process of killing the Viet Cong.

Soon we were out of the heart of the village and into an area where banana trees and some sort of squash vine crowded the road. We turned a corner, and there it was, Tan Mai Orphanage. It was surrounded by a large concrete fence with a barbwire gate. My first impression from the outside was that it was a prison camp. I could not decide if the fence was to keep the orphans in or to keep other people out.

The CO's entourage pulled in just ahead of us and we joined them to form a three-vehicle convoy as we pulled through the gate. We were met immediately by two nuns who invited us onto the patio of one of the larger buildings. I looked beyond into the building to see many kids assembled and waiting for us. The two sisters explained to the colonel, with aid of an interpreter, that they and two teenage girls ran the orphanage.

There was much formality and banter, of which I had little interest. I checked over my photographic equipment and walked off the patio to look around the orphanage complex. There were four large buildings and a playground. Everything looked clean and well-kept. It was much nicer here than the village we had driven through. The chaplain, for some reason, had followed me, and I guess he sensed my thoughts. "These kids have it better than the ones on the outside," he whispered. I nodded, not yet knowing whether to agree or disagree. I had not yet seen inside any of the buildings, and I had not yet met any of the orphans.

I looked back to see that our group was moving into one of the large buildings, and I followed, anxious to get good pictures that would accentuate our *Hawk* article. I do not know what I was expecting to see inside that building, but it was not what I actually saw. The room was filled with babies. I heard the interpreter say there were 110 of them, and they were all under a year old. My first thought, "They are in cages." Actually, they were in metal cribs joined together in rows, but they sure as hell looked like cages to me. I stood stiff. I did not move for a minute. My desire for pictures and a PR story dwindled considerably.

The colonel and the sisters moved down an aisle formed between two rows of the cribs. I was still standing and looking.

I always had been uncomfortable with babies and nurseries, but this was different. This was not a nursery; it was a chicken barn. I had seen this before; my great uncle raised chickens back home.

I snapped out of it and started walking down one of the rows. I looked though my camera viewfinder, and as I focused on one of the babies, it hit me that this baby was either American or European (or at least half so). I looked around and realized that the majority were the same as the one I just photographed.

The all-knowing chaplain, still right behind me, sensed my revelation. "Don't act so surprised. Look around you. These kids are under a year old. With an exception or two, these kids' parents are not dead. These kids are abandoned because they are half-American or there is no father to help support them," he told me. Our command sergeant major interrupted the conversation, "Hell, most of these babies are black. You can see which GI is getting most of the Vietnamese goodies here." Being the old battle-hardened soldier that he was, that statement was not out of character for him, but still I had the damnedest urge to plant my new camera right in the middle of his smirking mouth.

The chaplain took the cue and continued the conversation, "There is a reason that the majority of these kids are half-black. The French have been, as you say, getting the goodies here for generations, and as a result, half-white is perfectly acceptable in most circles—unless the community knows the father is American. The Negroid child is an outcast here." He pointed out that many of the half-white, half-Vietnamese girls were strikingly beautiful and usually married rich merchants or military officers. If they didn't, many became prostitutes. He was quick to note the half-French wife of the Vietnamese vice president and commander of the Vietnamese Air Force as an example.

I had seen all of the nursery I wanted to see and I had heard all of the conversation I wanted to hear. I walked out of the building and was soon followed by the remainder of our group. We were led through a patio and into a large room where the older kids were waiting for us. They were a very impressive bunch. They were well-mannered, and contrary to the village kids outside, they were clean. They put on a show with a customary dance followed by the colonel talking to them through the interpreter. He then distributed clothing that had been collected by his son, a Boy Scout, in Colorado.

There was much picture-taking and ooh-ing and aah-ing as the kids tried on their new clothes and thanked the "good American GIs." The whole place took on the scene of Christmas with the family back home. After getting the pictures I needed, I walked outside to get shots of the grounds.

The good chaplain came out, walked to where I was standing, and volunteered some more of his free conversation, "Like I said, these kids are better off than the ones on the outside." Maybe he was right. Hell, I guess he was right, but I did not like what I had seen. The majority of those babies had American fathers, and we were going to leave them there to a fate I could not imagine. This was a side of the war I had not seen or even thought about. I knew that I would never forget Tan Mai Orphanage.

**—1st Aviation Brigade, III Corps, 1970**

In the areas south of Xuan Loc in III Corps, the enemy established bunker complexes as a base for their operations and to provide protection from artillery and air attacks. They built them near small jungle streams so they would have a water source and beneath good overhead vegetation coverage so as not to be visible to reconnaissance aircraft.

Bunkers were constructed by digging a hole in the ground about the size of a grave. It didn't have to be very deep, as the Vietnamese were generally short in stature. At each end of the hole, and at a right angle to its length, they dug a step down as an entrance/exit, which could also be used as a firing port. They cut logs six to eight inches in diameter and five or six feet long to place across the hole. A covering of two to three feet of dirt completed the bunker. Some of the bunkers were twice this size, and those on the outer perimeter were often connected with fighting trenches. Everything was so well camouflaged that we almost had to be on top to detect them.

When we hit a complex, we withdrew with our casualties and put artillery and air on them and their possible withdrawal routes. It was rare for the gooks to stand and fight. They usually fought just long enough to cover their withdrawal.

Bunker complexes always yielded lots of documents, food, medicine, ammunition, and other supplies. Once we completed a detailed search, we destroyed the bunkers so that they would be of no future use to the enemy. Every platoon seemed to have one or more "demo experts" who had usually gained his expertise on the job. If he still had all his fingers, he was considered qualified. To destroy the bunker, we dug down in its top to reach the layer of logs, placed a two-pound block of malleable C-4 on the logs, inserted a blasting cap and fuse, and then refilled the hole. We then lit the fuse and withdrew to a safe distance. The blast would drive the logs downward, filling the hole and lifting much of the dirt skyward.

One time we decided that the explosive downward force would be enhanced by placing a short log on top of the dirt-covered C-4. It did not go exactly as planned. When the charge exploded, the bunker logs went downward but the one on top of the charge went straight up—still intact—and penetrated the jungle foliage canopy. I yelled, "Heads up, there's a log up there somewhere and it's gonna be comin' down heavy." Sure enough, after what seemed to be an awfully long time, the log came crashing back down through the trees. Fortunately, no one was injured. We went back to our old method of destroying bunkers. For several days afterward someone would whisper, "Watch for VC logs."

**—199th Light Infantry Brigade, III Corps, 1970**

On my second tour in 1968–69, I was assigned to the 203rd Recon Airplane Company at Phu Hiep near Tuy Hoa as the flight operations noncommissioned officer. One of my jobs was to train artillery observers who would look for enemy targets from our O-1A Cessna's known as "birddogs." Many of the students returned from their observation training missions with a report of "negative sighting." This was the same area where I had flown during my first tour as a crewman on a UH-1B Huey gunship, so I knew there were gooks out there. My commanding officer finally allowed me to continue my instructional and operations duties in the morning while I flew observation missions in the afternoons. I also let the person in charge of duty rosters know that I was available for any night missions.

Although I was not a qualified aviator, the pilots had taught me much about flying, a way of passing the boring hours in the air. The pilots also wanted their observers to be able to land the aircraft if they were wounded or otherwise incapacitated.

One night, I was flying with a particularly aggressive lieutenant. I used a Starlight scope to penetrate the darkness but, after several hours of boring holes in the sky with no results, we returned to base. As we were landing just after midnight, we heard on the radio that the advisory team at a compound on the beach near Song Cao north of Tuy Hoa was under attack. The lieutenant asked, "Do you want to go up there?"

Never one to pass up an opportunity to fly, I told him I was ready. We refueled and headed north following the coastline. When we got in the area of the advisory team's compound, we coordinated naval fire from offshore as well as ground artillery. When the advisory team fired several parachute illumination flares, we could see so many black pajamas running on the beach that it looked like an ant hill. The lieutenant asked on the intercom if I had my backseat controls plugged in. When I answered in the affirmative, he told me to take the controls and fly down the beach fifteen to twenty meters off the sand.

When we neared the ground, the lieutenant opened the side window and began shooting with his .45-caliber pistol. I don't think he hit anyone but he sure did make them scatter. The bad guys and the advisors must have all thought that we were smoking something other than PX cigarettes.

**—1st Aviation Brigade, II Corps, 1968**

In 1972, I was a first lieutenant CH-46 pilot in Marine Medium Helicopter Squadron HMM-164 stationed aboard the USS *Okinawa*, a large helicopter carrier operating off the coast of South Vietnam. Our primary mission was to provide airlift support for the evacuation from Da Nang Air Base following the NVA's Easter Offensive. Fortunately that ended up not being necessary. Our secondary mission was to provide helicopter support to the South Vietnamese Marine Corps for their vertical assault operations. We participated in five or six of these operations, the largest being a two-squadron insertion near Quang Tri.

Most of the time, we flew admin missions as the USS *Okinawa* maintained a holding pattern off the coast where pranks often broke the monotony of shipboard life. The best one was on our squadron's flight surgeon, a great guy and, fortunately, a good sport. We had been on station for about thirty days when we were due to sail to Subic Bay for resupply. At the last minute, however, we were held on station for reasons that never reached my level of rank. While we were off the coast of Vietnam, our mail came via Da Nang. When we were back in the Philippines, our mail was directed through to Cubi Point. This last-minute change in the ship's schedule meant our mail would probably be delayed in getting to us while we remained off the coast.

One evening after chow, several of us were lounging around in the ready room when a couple of the captains, all on their second tour, began talking about getting the squadron medical officer to fall for the mail buoy joke. When lieutenant buddies and I asked, they explained that the object of the joke is to get someone to believe the navy would be delivering our mail via an airdrop at sea, and they figured the "Doc" was just the right target for the joke.

The plan was for us to be talking about the arrival of the mail buoy when the Doc came in. We did not have to wait long. As he walked to the front of the ready room, he heard the two captains trying to guess when the airplane bringing the mail buoy would be overhead. "What is a mail buoy?" he asked. He had taken the bait.

One of the captains explained that since we were delayed on station the navy would bring our mail out from Cubi Point on a C-2 aircraft and airdrop it alongside the ship. The Doc anxiously asked, "Won't it sink? How will they retrieve it from the water?"

"The mail is in a big waterproof bag attached to a buoy. The ship just sends the captain's launch over to grab hold of it and bring it back to the ship," a captain explained.

The Doc still could not understand, "But it is pitch black outside. How will they be able to find it out there?"

Patiently, the captain explained, "They drop these big flares from the plane so the ship can follow the buoy in its descent."

I could see that the Doc was not totally buying the storyline, so I ran up to the flight deck where the squadron maintained a watch officer. I told him to call down to the ready room and report an aircraft circling overhead, and to mention that this must be the plane bringing our mail. As soon as the Doc heard this, the hook was set. "Hey, you think I could get some pictures?"

"Absolutely, those flares put out a million candlepower of light. It's like daylight." So off he ran to his room to get his camera as we all climbed to the flight deck. When the Doc arrived, camera in hand, a few minutes later he saw no flares illuminating the night, but rather a bunch of helicopter pilots laughing at the joke that was just pulled on him.

**—USS *Okinawa*, HMM-164, 1972**

By May 1, 1968, it was obvious to the Special Forces at Kham Duc—an A Team and a Studies and an Observations Group (SOG) Detachment—located near the border with Laos in I Corps, that NVA troops were surrounding the camp and preparing to attack it as well as the Special Forces outpost five mile south at Ngok Tavak. Their respective headquarters at Da Nang also anticipated the attack.

On May 6, a South Vietnamese CIDG (Civilian Irregular Defense Group) patrol about four miles east of Kham Duc discovered an NVA reconnaissance position on top of a hill that overlooked the outpost and the valley. Inside the NVA camp was an accurate sand table model of the valley and Kham Duc. It was also obvious that the U.S. higher headquarters was delaying the decision on whether to defend or evacuate the camp until it was actually attacked by a major NVA unit. Some of us speculated that we were being used as bait but, of course, such decisions were way above our pay grades.

NVA patrols were moving closer to Ngok Tavak, and enemy troops around Kham Duc were conspicuously announcing their presence by shooting at approaching and departing helicopters. On April 10, a Vietnamese CH-34 helicopter from FOB 4 en route to Kham Duc was shot down about a mile north of the camp. The SOG and Mike Force troops continued to train separately in and around the camp, but the enemy situation had become too dangerous for helicopters to continue using Kham Duc as a base for their insertions and extractions of SOG's cross-border recon/commando teams.

My job was the launch officer in charge of these helicopter operations so I no longer had anything to do. Having a little more than a week remaining in country before I rotated back to the States, I returned to FOB 4 near Da Nang for out-processing. I was concerned about Kham Duc, but with my Vietnam assignment scheduled to end on May 17, I considered my part of the war virtually over.

When I volunteered for the army, I was not draft eligible. Being a schoolteacher and over twenty-six years of age made me exempt, but that had not felt right. The biggest, most important, event of my generation was going on in Southeast Asia and I was missing it as I sat in a safe classroom. My father had been a draft exempt volunteer in both World War II and Korea and I knew that Vietnam was destined to be my war. I was determined to fight it as a Special Forces Airborne Ranger officer.

My year in Vietnam had more than met my need for a chal-lenging adventure. I was ready to sit my last week out in the rear and then go home. It was not to be so, however. After the evening meal on May 6, the commander of FOB 4 told me to return to Kham Duc early the next morning to organize the SOG troops for the inevitable attack. Being given a potentially fatal mission so close to my departure date stunned me. The thought of being trapped in a virtually indefensible camp dur-ing an NVA mass attack frightened me to my core. My fear of being captured by the sadistic Vietnamese Communists was even greater than my fear of being killed.

I knew that if I objected to such a mission only ten days before I was scheduled to go home, my sympathetic CO proba-bly would not insist that I participate in the looming battle. I also knew that he did not expect me to complain or object to the order. I did not. Special Forces officers were expected to accept all the legitimate missions they were given, regardless of the circumstances or timing. I had volunteered for the army, the Special Forces, and SOG, and according to all calculations, I still owed them ten more days in Vietnam, whatever the loca-tion or possibility of survival.

If I had asked to be relieved of that mission, regardless of my justification for doing so, my CO and SF peers, and, more importantly, I myself would have seen it not as dishonorable, but as somehow less than honorable. I passionately wanted to survive the next ten days, but being forced to choose between risking an honorable death in battle or begging my CO for ten days of less-than-honorable safety, I chose to risk the battle.

For me the silent acceptance of my last mission in Vietnam at Kham Duc, knowing that it might also be the last one of my life, was not an act of courage. It was simply a stoic affirmation of my fatalistic, long-held concepts of duty, honor, and the fortunes of war. I had been unusually lucky so far, but I knew that no one's luck lasts forever.

From May 10 to 12, Kham Duc was attacked by two reinforced regiments composed of 3,500 to 4,000 troops. Kham Duc's internal defenses were negligible. The maximum effective defensive force in the SF camp on the night of May 9–10 was 141 men made up of 33 SFs and 108 indigenous troops. They were well armed, well trained, and well led, but their only hope of surviving an attack by two reinforced NVA regiments was constant, close tactical air support, which required clear weather for visual flying. At Kham Duc in May, that kind of weather was always problematic.

Most of the 266 Vietnamese troops in the three CIDG companies were totally unreliable, and the combat dependability of the 60 Mike Force trainees in the camp was questionable. The combat effectiveness of the 120 U.S. engineer troops in their isolated position across the airstrip was also up for debate. As engineers, they were good soldiers, but they were not organized or trained for infantry combat against a major NVA force, and they were not as heavily armed as the SF troops. In the SF A-Team's sector of the camp, the maximum effective defensive force was 50, 10 of whom were from the SF team, 10 from Nung mercenaries, and 30 from CIDG recon troops. In SOG's eastern third of the camp, the total defensive force was 91 men—23 SF men and 68 Nung and Montagnard troops.

The reinforcement battalion from the American Division had 577 men, including an artillery battery of 62 Redlegs. An

attached infantry company added another 98 men bringing
the total number of Americal troops at Kham Duc to approximately 675. Together with the 141 reliable fighters in the SF
camp, the total effective U.S. and indigenous defensive force
at Kham Duc was between 800 and 900 men. The total defensive force at the Special Forces outpost at Ngok Tavak,
which was attacked by a reinforced NVA battalion, was
176 men—3 Australians, 5 U.S. Special Forces men, 3 LLDB
men, 3 combat interpreters, 122 Nung mercenaries, and 41
U.S. Marine artillerymen. Several hundred Vietnamese civilians were also within the wire.

During the three-day battle, forty-three Americans were
killed at Kham Duc and its outpost at Ngok Tavak. More than a
hundred U.S. and Vietnamese were wounded but nearly all
were quickly evacuated to modern hospitals and survived.
Thirty-one Americans were listed as Missing in Action, the
most MIAs of any single battle during the long war. More than
150 of the Vietnamese civilians died when the C-130 evacuating them was shot down—the largest number of deaths in any
air crash in the history of aviation to that date.

Finally, the survivors, including myself, were evacuated. My
luck had held. The final evacuation sortie was an air force
C-123. Its pilot received the Medal of Honor for rescuing the
last three Americans at the camp under heavy fire. After
extending my tour for a few months at a SOG base in Thailand, I returned home, went to graduate school, and began a
civilian career as an international corporate executive.

Contrary to most accounts, Khan Duc was not "an American defeat," "an American disaster," "an American fiasco," or
"an unequivocal American debacle," as some reported it. Neither was it "a Khe Sanh in reverse," or "a total North Vietnamese victory." It was also not proof of a World War I type of
combat "stalemate" between military equals.

Although the battle had no strategic value for either adversary, it was a major tactical victory for the U.S. forces and a
major tactical defeat for the NVA forces for one very simple reason. Massed air power attacking in ideal flying conditions is

always tactically superior to massed infantry (and armor) repeatedly exposed to such attacks with inadequate air defenses.

The best NVA and VC fighters were as brave and skilled as the best U.S. fighters, but in 1968, they lacked most of the U.S. technological advantages. As a result, their performance in large, set-piece battles against U.S. combined-arms forces was always inferior. At Kham Duc, as at Khe Sanh, it was disastrous for them.

By inflicting enormous casualties on a major enemy force the battle was another confirmation of Gen. William Westmoreland's much-maligned attrition strategy. The fact that his big-unit tactics were often clumsy and inefficient does not imply that they were always ineffective. In large defensive battles like those at Khe Sanh and Kham Duc, the use of superior firepower to inflict mass enemy casualties was devastatingly effective for the achievement of his strategy.

During the three days of attacks and the three days of retreat, almost certainly half—and possibly up to two-thirds—of 3,500 to 4,000 troops in the two reinforced NVA regiments at Kham Duc and Ngok Tavak were killed or wounded. Ironically, they probably suffered more casualties from the three days of B-52 carpet-bombing of their retreat than they did in their futile attacks, and most of their seriously wounded probably died soon afterward.

At the cost of such appalling losses, they failed to create an American Dien Bien Phu; failed to attract much U.S. media attention; failed to divert any large U.S. military unit from a populated area; failed to kill or capture enough U.S. troops for an effective propaganda film; failed to "liberate" any forced laborers or food sources; failed to even penetrate the perimeter of the Special Forces camp while U.S. troops were there; and after it was voluntarily abandoned, failed to hold it.

All the camp's functions were soon replaced elsewhere with no loss of tactical effectiveness, and the Kham Duc area was later occupied for six weeks by a U.S. battalion and an ARVN battalion mainly to prove that they could do so. The forfeiture of another anachronistic little border camp did not

significantly damage SOG's covert operations against the Ho
Chi Minh Trail network in Laos, the SF/CIDG program in I
Corps, or the general combat predominance of U.S. conven-
tional forces in I Corps in 1968.

The NVA attacks on Kham Duc and Ngok Tavak, like their
attack on Khe Sanh, were merely another strategic gamble that
resulted in another tactical failure. Yet, because both places
were abandoned under fire, the NVA call the battle a "glorious
victory for the People's Army," and almost all published
accounts of it have either tacitly or explicitly accepted that
nonfactual Communist propaganda.

The idea that the battle was a defeat for U.S. forces erro-
neously assumes that the Americans were attempting to hold
the camp. The truth is the opposite. At 1100 hours on 11 May
1968, Westmoreland personally ordered that the camp be
abandoned. Subsequent efforts to defend the camp were only
to assist in its evacuation and abandonment. The NVA did not
want us to abandon it because they wanted to capture us. The
proof is that they fought like hell to prevent us from leaving
and giving the camp to them. If the monsoon thunderstorm
that hit the camp about twenty minutes after the last plane left
it had come a few hours earlier, it would have cancelled our
massive close-air support, which was the only thing keeping us
alive, and they would have captured or killed all of us with
their huge numerical superiority.

—**5th Special Forces Group, I Corps, 1968**

At the end of my tour of duty, I was given a week to out-
process. On the second day, an admin sergeant going
through my paperwork noticed my hometown. He said, "Are
you really from Johnson City, Tennessee? Heck, I'm from
Kingsport." So we talked about hometown stuff for a few minutes and then he asked, "What day did you come in country?"

I said, "September the 28th." He responded in a hushed, serious voice, "No, you didn't. You came in on the 25th, and don't you forget it from this point on, no matter who you talk to."

I said, "You got it! Thanks a lot." So by this little action of this previously unknown friend, I was able to come home three days earlier than I, or my family, expected.

**—199th Light Infantry Brigade, III Corps, 1970**

In 1970, I joined the 12th Combat Aviation Group as a UH-1 Huey pilot. Before the current group commander took charge, the unit was officially—or unofficially, as the case may be—nicknamed the "Blackjacks." Upon assuming command of the group, the colonel promptly decided that such a gruff name was not befitting his collection of fine aircraft and the winged warriors of the sky—the noble aviators that kept those aircraft airborne. He immediately renamed the group "Water Buffaloes." Now, for those unknowledgeable of water buffaloes, there is, in my opinion, no more ungainly animal alive.

No one was happy being called "Water Buffaloes." The call sign used by aviators in the group was to be "Buffalo," as in "Buffalo 906." Most of the 12th CAG pilots, however, retained the "Blackjack" call sign, as in "Blackjack 906." Rather amazing was the fact that the colonel himself did not use Buffalo as his call sign; rather, he went by "Corncob 6."

In mid-May 1970, II Field Forces—a unit that shared the "Plantation Compound" with 12th CAG, the 159th Medical Detachment, and the 66th Engineering Company—was scheduled to have a change of command. One lieutenant general (three stars) was to replace the current lieutenant general. Before the change of command, our colonel decided to throw a party at the 12th CAG headquarters for the outgoing general to "show the group's appreciation."

By all accounts, the party was quite a production. It was well planned by our colonel in his attempt to gain brownie points for a potential future assignment. He had one of each type of the group's aircraft flown in and parked for the ceremony. There were color guards, honor guards, banners, little decorated cocktails for all to enjoy . . . and the crowning touch—a real live water buffalo borrowed from a local village chief by the headquarters support company commanding officer. Everyone was so impressed.

After taking command of II Field Forces, the new three-star heard about the party for his predecessor. Our colonel became aware of this and decided that another gala was in order to "welcome the new commander" to the compound (can't have too many brownie points). He ordered that all of the pomp and ceremony be repeated right down to the beast of burden (a different and more magnificent one) that arrived majestically in a deuce-and-a-half truck. The water buffalo (a very large bull) was unloaded and led toward the waiting ceremony. Everyone was tense with anticipation. The general was to arrive any moment.

About this time, a dog named Rebel wandered by. This canine undoubtedly was the biggest coward that I witnessed during my Vietnam tour. As a mine and tunnel dog, he was worthless, but everyone liked him.

Rebel walked right up to the water buffalo. They stared at each other while we were all watching and laughing. Then, as cool as you please, Rebel walked to the rear of the buffalo and clamped his jaws onto its most tender part (it could have been the bull's flank, but we all thought otherwise—and it makes for a better story).

The poor animal went berserk bellowing, pawing, and spinning. There were two soldiers on the lead rope, or I should say they *were* on the lead rope. They were slung off like paper dolls.

Next, the buffalo charged everything in sight. Can you even imagine a bunch of officers, probably over a hundred from colonel to second lieutenant, not to mention an equal number of NCOs, from the various headquarters, dodging behind jeeps, trucks, and aircraft—while being pursued by a mad buffalo bull? It should not have been funny, but it was. I don't think I have ever laughed so hard. But for those who knew our colonel and who were lifers, it was not so funny; careers were on the line.

After proving that he was king of the situation at hand, the buffalo decided to exit the scene. At first everyone was glad to see him retreat to higher ground—but only for a moment. The colonel issued an order, yelling, "Catch that damned buffalo and bring him back." The chase was on.

The animal ran from our area and to an adjacent signal unit. Every time anyone got near the bull, he charged them and then he would take off in another direction. Our next strategy was to rope him from a jeep (aviators to cowboys). Immediately, the compound military police were in on the chase.

Soon thereafter, the situation looked as if it would be victorious for the good guys and bleak for the water buffalo. He was trapped on the outer compound roadway between two concertina and barbed-wire perimeters (each perimeter about thirty feet in depth). The chasers ran the bull down the road toward II Field Forces Headquarters, and they were gaining fast.

Just as they were overtaking the buffalo, a big olive green car with three stars (you guessed it) came down the road headed straight toward the roundup in progress. The general had MP escorts—front and rear. Confronted with green-clad humans on both sides, the buffalo charged the outside perimeter.

The perimeter was designed to protect us from the vicious onslaughts of Charlie—a job that it did well in Tet of '68 (198 Viet Cong died in that maze of wire in front of the group headquarters). To the dismay of the pursuers, and one awestruck lieutenant general, that animal pushed right through (and under) the barbed-wire perimeter. The last we saw of him, he was taking down fences, laundry, and anything else that got in his way as he charged through the adjoining village.

Aircraft were scrambled immediately. An intensive search lasted more than two days. The buffalo was never found (some think he went home and the owner hid him from view).

One might think the story ends here, but it does not. This prime (missing) animal belonged to the assistant province chief, a very important person in our area of operations. He decreed that he had suffered a terrible loss, and he wanted the return of his prized possession. In consolation, he would accept either a buffalo of greater stature or the equivalent of a truck load of piasters in "American Green" (about $500).

This seemed like no problem for our good commander as we were operating in Cambodia at the time (the Pentagon even admitted that we were there—to secure the weapons cache known as "The City"). He would have one of our aviation battalion commanders (12th CAG had five aviation battalions and one attached Air Cavalry Squadron) liberate a suitable NVA buffalo in Cambodia or find a suitable stray.

Soon we learned that several candidates had been found and the best one was slung back to our headquarters underneath a CH-47 Chinook helicopter. Of course, the buffalo did not meet the assistant province chief's standards. He wanted American greenbacks—an illegal transaction, of course—we had only military payment certificates (MPC). I do not know how they ultimately settled the claim because the terms were negotiated with the greatest degree of secrecy—and was far above my pay grade of first lieutenant. I am sure the assistant chief received a goodly portion of government issued items.

Regardless, the 12th CAG was now the proud owner of a one fine mascot. It was a "beautiful" animal that graced all of our ceremonies—a buffalo loved by all. And well it should be—I doubt the American taxpayers have ever paid so much for one bovine.

At the time I thought that was all of the story. I later learned that a Chinook company had found a buffalo between Tay Ninh and Cu Chi before the "liberation" of the NVA buffalo in Cambodia. The aircraft crew did not have a sling net available that was adequate for the buffalo, so they tied the animal inside the Chinook. At 3,000 feet, the buffalo got loose and charged anything and everything in the aircraft, changing the center of gravity in the process. In a panic, the crew chief lowered the rear ramp and the buffalo left the aircraft without a parachute. There was damage to the aircraft that had to be repaired. Repairs to the buffalo were not possible.

—1st Aviation Brigade, III Corps, 1970

I was assigned to the 1st Battalion, 502nd Airborne Infantry Regiment of the 101st Airborne Division, when I arrived in country. A bright red heart was the battalion's emblem and our idiot battalion commander had a standing order that the four-to-five-inch heart be painted on both sides of the helmet camouflage cover. Like a good troop, and not knowing any better, I followed orders.

When I arrived at a forward firebase to join my company, a senior NCO took my helmet and cut the red hearts off the camo cover. He said our company refused to wear them. He added that several months earlier, the company had been ambushed and that three soldiers were shot in the head in the first few seconds of the firefight. Our company commander had told the battalion CO to cram the red hearts—and had gotten away with it.

—101st Airborne Division, I Corps, 1969

* * *

Many years after returning from the war, I told my wife that I was not going to my outfit's Nam reunion. "Why?" she asked.

"Because I've closed that part of my life and most of the folks going are probably REMFs spinning war stories they dreamed up while in the rear base camp PX," I replied.

She said my objections were bogus. For six months prior to the reunion, my wife and I went back and forth with me finally putting my foot down and closing the discussion. Sometimes you have to be firm with the better halves, and I clearly knew this was one of those times.

Naturally, a few weeks later we walked into the hotel ballroom where about one hundred Nam vets mingled during the first day's activities. I guess I hadn't put my foot down as hard as I thought. I saw no one I knew, but in a strange way I knew them all. We shared some light banter about dates of tours, did the "do you remember this, or that, or who," and exchanged stories about health problems or who had died. On first day of the reunion, none of us told the real story about what Nam really was like—a survivor drill for kids whose only goal was to go home as a passenger in a freedom bird and not a metal box. Maybe someone was fighting Communism, but I never met them then or now.

The reunion concluded with a dinner. At my table were mostly vets who had been in my battalion.

Soon I struck up a conversation with a woman about my age and her son in his mid-forties seated at an adjacent table. She explained that a friend of hers had invited her and her son, who had insisted they attend.

"What is the connection?" I asked.

"My husband was a member of Alpha Company, and he was killed in November 1967," she quietly said.

"Our son Todd was born after his father was killed and only knew of him through my stories, cassette tapes, and photos," she continued.

As her story unfolded, I learned her son had wanted to be with the men at the reunion who were like his dad. He was aware that there would likely be no one there who served directly with his father, but at least he perhaps could understand a little more about his dad by meeting the kind of men with whom he spent his last days.

I thought to myself that I really should say something profound or important, but I could not think of anything. I did, however, walk over and put my arm around him and say, "Welcome home."

—**4th Infantry Division, 1st Battalion,
12th Infantry Reunion, San Antonio, TX, 2012**

As the operations noncommissioned officer for the 203rd Airplane Company at Phu Hiep, my extra duty was to also act as training sergeant. Most of the troops thought that if they were in a combat zone, there really was no need for additional training. The company commander thought differently, so I was constantly looking for class material that would be useful as well as interesting.

One evening in 1968, we received a mortar attack that, although it sent us scurrying for our bunkers, did little damage and wounded no one. The next day I learned that a Korean unit had captured one of the NVA mortar crewmen and had him available for interrogation. I gathered the troops, secured an interrupter, and brought the NVA soldier in for questions.

The soldier was polite and well mannered—although I guess he really had few other options. In response to questions, he stated he was a thirty-six-year-old rice farmer who was married with three children when he was drafted. After basic training he had gone down the Ho Chi Minh Trail to join his unit. On the night of the mortar attack, his job had been to carry ammunition forward to the mortar tubes.

A final question asked what he thought of the war. He responded that he really did not care who won or lost and that he just wanted to go home to his family.

**—1st Aviation Brigade, II Corps, 1968**

★ ★ ★

I arrived in country and was assigned to the 199th Light Infantry Brigade, where I went through training that lasted about a week. When I got my unit assignment, I was to take a chopper to the field. I had never been even close to a helicopter, let alone ridden in one. This one had no doors, and the openings looked to be about six feet on both sides. It was just me and my rucksack and there were no instructions. I got in and scooted as very close to the middle as I could. There was nothing to hold on to. Shortly after we took off, we went into a hard bank that had us practically on our side. I was certain I no longer had to worry about getting shot and killed by the VC. I was going to roll out of the helicopter and die from the fall. I was happily surprised to learn that centrifugal force would hold me in the helicopter. That was the first of many, many chopper rides during the next twelve months. I came to appreciate those open doors when we went into LZs in the choppers that didn't even stop as we quickly unloaded, when friends were medevaced out, and when we got picked up from the field for stand-down. Once, I was sitting in the door and saw the ocean far off in the distance. It was a thrill.

Shortly after I joined my unit at Firebase Blackhorse, I was assigned to a patrol and sent out on a night ambush. There were only seven of us, most greenhorns like me. Before midnight, the radio operator got a call informing us that intelligence reported approximately one thousand NVA were approaching our position. No kidding. I don't think any of us slept for hours, but we never saw anyone or made any contact.

Maybe someone was just messing with us new guys. Anyway, talk about an adrenaline flow.

I finally crawled under my poncho and slept. When I awoke, I was in water five or six inches deep. It was the monsoon season, and I was lying in a low area that filled with water fast. I quickly learned to make my bedroll on higher ground.

When I went to Vietnam, I had a lifelong morbid fear of snakes. We saw vipers in bunkers many times, and about the time I arrived in the field, one of our men got spit in the eye by a cobra. I was freaking out. But we slept on the ground with nothing but ponchos and poncho liners. We couldn't even string up hammocks. I was twenty-four and older than most of the men—including the company commander—in my unit. I had graduated from college and had worked two years before college. To some degree I think that worked to my advantage. I reasoned with myself that if I focused on, or obsessed, about snakes, I could very easily get myself shot, that I probably ought to focus on the people trying to kill me. I also reasoned that snakes would likely leave me alone if I left them alone. I'd just have to take my chances that I wouldn't inadvertently step on or lie down on one. I literally put aside my fear of snakes and that has held to the present. Today I live in a heavily wooded area and I frequently see snakes. Most are nonpoisonous, so I never kill them. For me, it's live and let live, a lesson I learned in Vietnam.

**—199th Light Infantry Brigade, III Corps, 1969**

I was new in country and had been with my infantry company for only three days. We were pulling security for a firebase perched on a high hill in I Corps. I had nothing to do so I just sat on a sand-bagged bunker trying to take it all in. About midday, a CH-47 Chinook flew in with a sling load of artillery rounds. As the Chinook took off and flew down the valley, I

saw an air force forward observer fly directly into the side of
the large helicopter. There was a big explosion—no survivors.
It was like the entire incident was in slow motion.

**—101st Airborne Division, I Corps, 1969**

My first day in the field in Vietnam was May 20, 1967. I was
among about thirty replacements who landed in a CH-47
on a beach in eastern II Corps. On the ground we met the
company commander and then the lieutenants in charge of
the platoons. The 2nd Platoon had taken the largest number
of recent casualties, so that is where I was assigned.

Later that afternoon, the company was picked up by Huey
transports and inserted into an inland rice paddy. We then
swept through a village, killing one VC, and kept moving. Seconds after we reached a Vietnamese cemetery, machine guns
and small arms exploded to our front and flank. The point
man went down KIA in the first burst. I had not been in the
company long enough to meet anyone, but I heard later that
he was a great fighter, and a good soldier who was well liked.

Our lieutenant went forward, returning fire and tossing
grenades with the platoon providing covering fire. The lieutenant took a grenade fragment but continued to fight despite
a medic trying to get him to crawl to the rear. The fighting
continued.

I tried to keep my head down as I returned fire into the
ambushers. In an instant I saw the lieutenant toss a white phosphorus grenade into an enemy trench. Just after the WP
exploded a dink rose out of the trench. Although he was
screaming from pain from the burning phosphorous that
seemed to be all over him, he continued to fire his AK-47. The
lieutenant rose to one knee and returned fire with his M16. It
was like an Old West showdown as they continued to blast away
at each other until both fell dead.

The fight continued for what seemed like an eternity—likely about five minutes or so. Two men died close to me, one on each side. I don't know how I kept from getting hit.

I would not always be as lucky as I was that first day in the field. A month later, I was hit in the leg and evacuated. After I was declared healed, I was shipped back to the company. A short time later, our new lieutenant ordered me to recon the other side of a clearing. I told him that if I went out into the open I would likely get shot. He said for me to go anyway. A few seconds later, I was shot in the same leg as my first wound. This time it was serious enough to send me home to recover. I left Vietnam with two Purple Hearts and a lot of memories.

**—25th Infantry Division, II Corps, 1967**

★ ★ ★

We were lazing around at the western end of Quang Ngai City along the railway line that had long ceased to be operational since Tet of 1968. I remember thinking that it would be a good time to take up an invitation to go to the home of one of my counterpart officers in Quang Ngai. He had a rather good-looking sister, but I digress.

Without warning, the ARVN battalion commander jumped to his feet and ran off along the line shouting and gesticulating with his swagger stick. We were all surprised, including his headquarters staff and Australian advisors. We grabbed our gear and stumbled off in pursuit, straight through the meal that our cook had just laid out for us. I quickly discovered that our battalion had unwittingly taken a lunch break on the withdrawal route of a large group of enemy.

To this day, I do not know who organized the fire support, but they had their act together. There were a couple of gunships, some artillery, and some heavy machine guns on armored personnel carriers (APCs). We met the enemy out in the open, although it was still difficult to see because of bamboo and sugar cane groves. The aircraft struck over the top of us and along one flank; the APCs were out on the other flank. I would like to say that was my advice, but it wasn't.

Frankly, we slaughtered the NVA. It was the first time that I had seen dead enemy soldiers tied to a crew-served weapon—supposedly to prevent them from running from the battlefield. Near the end of the day, I let one of the enemy retreat into a tunnel. He was wounded and even now my thoughts still haunt me. I was going to kill him for no reason, just for the sheer pleasure of it. The safety was off, my finger was on the trigger, but I let him go, turned my back, rather stupidly, and walked off. This was after advising the ARVN commanding officer to burn the sugar cane field, as that would get the bastards on the run.

**—Royal Australian Regiment, I Corps, 1968**

★ ★ ★

Our aviation group commander was a relationship builder. The unit had its own Civic Action section and it supported MEDCAP and DENTCAP operations throughout III Corps fostering cultural and social relationships with the various non-American allied units (Australian, Korean, and Thai). The group's colonel maintained a close relationship with the commander of the Thai Black Panther Division, headquartered at Camp Bear Cat. We supported the Thai ground units with various Huey companies and with Charlie Model (UH-1C) gunships.

I had learned through my various flights to Bear Cat that the Thai forces brought all of the comforts of home with them, including "hospitality ladies," cultural entertainers, and a few wives of the highest ranking officers. So it came as no surprise to me that when our command hosted a dinner reception for the commander of the Thai forces at our headquarters, we would be entertained by a Thai cultural troupe.

Our colonel invited the commanding general of II Field Forces and an air force brigadier general from Bien Hoa (whose units also supported the Thai forces) to the reception. There were about twenty-five people in the Thai delegation, including the cultural troupe composed of four males and twelve females. The Thai guests had been transported from Bear Cat by one of our assault Huey companies and it was our understanding that all of them would spend the night in II Field Forces guest quarters.

After many toasts before dinner, the male members of the cultural group demonstrated in ancient costume one of the most realistic sword fights that I could image. Six of the female troupe, in very colorful "Siamese" attire, performed several dance routines. The remaining six females did not dance but served as hostesses and greeters on behalf of the Thai commander.

After dinner, my executive officer asked, "Have you been drinking tonight?" When I replied that I had not, he told me that the Thai commander did not want the female members of the entourage remaining overnight. He wanted them flown back to Bear Cat. "Find a copilot, take one of the headquarters' Hueys, and fly them home," he ordered.

The only other nondrinking pilot that I could find in our headquarters was a newbie first lieutenant who had not yet had an in-country check ride and orientation. At least he was UH-1 rated so he could tune radios and provide another set of eyes beyond the controls. The women were small but to seat all of them in the aircraft, we had to fly without a crew chief and door gunners. I closed the doors so that none of their scarves or other pieces of their silk costumes would fly out.

Bear Cat was about a twenty-minute flight from our headquarters. I took off and flew west over Highway 1 until I picked up the Vung Tau Highway and then headed south, southeast. Camp Bear Cat, a large installation surrounded by boonies, was about two klicks east the highway. Even though it was shorter to fly direct, I did not want to be over Indian country with a newbie copilot, no gunners, and no escort—though being over a highway provided no guarantee that we would not draw fire.

The flight was uneventful and there were enough headlights on the road for navigation. Halfway there, I picked up the beacon at Bear Cat and made a call to the field controller to tell him that I would be approaching from Highway 51. He gave clearance, and I was turning final when he waived me off, saying, "Blackjack, we have incoming."

I saw the mortar rounds impacting just as he was making the radio transmission. He instructed me to overfly the active and to "hold east of Bear Cat until clear." I replied in the affirmative, cleared the active, climbed out, and started a slow circle over the dark uninhabited area east of the complex. As I was in the furthest point of my first circle, I saw tracers coming up to our front. I killed our running lights and told the controller I was receiving fire and "flying dark."

The controller said he had seen the tracers and thought the mortar fire came from the area I was circling. He said he had no other incoming aircraft but they were scrambling gunships. He instructed me to return and overfly the departing gunships and the active runway, to turn on my running lights as I reached the perimeter, and to hold over Highway 51.

As I flew back toward Bear Cat, and away from the tracers, the headline ran through my mind, "American pilots and twelve Thai women killed in helicopter crash." How in the hell would the colonel explain that to my wife and parents? The mortars and the machine gunners stopped firing when the gunships started pounding their area, my bird did not take any hits, and the Thai cultural beauties were returned to their compound. The party was still in full swing when I returned to headquarters.

**—1st Aviation Brigade, III Corps, 1970**

When we operated on the jungle floor, the thick vegetation masked observation of our location from above. In the heavy jungle foliage, the only thing that a helicopter pilot could see was the tops of dense trees. To mark our location, we would "pop smoke" (ignite a smoke-generating grenade), which would emit a heavy cloud of colored smoke for several minutes. As the smoke rose through the trees, the pilots could spot our location when we told them in what direction we were in relation to the smoke. Once the pilots knew our position, they rolled in with rockets and mini-guns.

In late 1969, we hit a series of bunker complexes. For several days we would assault the enemy, and then pull back with our casualties while artillery and air worked over the enemy. After one assault, we began pulling back, popping smoke as we went so the helicopter gunships could cover our withdrawal. The birds flew in a circle so that at least one could maintain constant fire on the bad guys. I was with rear security and tried to keep a steady flow of smoke up through the trees. Everything was chaotic, but no more so than we were accustomed to.

After a brief lull in the fire support, a gunship rolled in and began sending rockets on our side of the smoke rather than the enemy side. Before the first rounds landed, I was on the radio screaming, "Check fire! Check fire!" Only a few of the 2.75-inch rockets landed in our ranks, but that was more than enough. Several guys were wounded, one seriously. Fortunately, none were killed.

By the time we got to the LZ, we had figured out what happened. At the front of our column, some hundred meters from the rear, a new guy had gotten hung up in "wait-a-minute vine." While he was struggling to free himself, the pin on a smoke grenade that he had on his web gear caught on one of the vine's thorns. Being new, he did not realize the significance of what had just happened and just tossed the smoking canister aside. In the midst of the confusion and fear around him no one else realized what had happened. All the pilots saw was smoke that they thought marked the end of our column.

**—199th Light Infantry Brigade, III Corps, 1969**

I joined a mixed team of American and Australian advisors to South Vietnamese Region Forces (RF) in I Corps in 1965. Our operations were limited by the paramount need to defend RF headquarters, outposts, and populated areas. Within our own resources, the best we could do was lay ambushes and conduct small-scale search and destroy operations. U.S. Marines provided us with forward observers and artillery support on most of our operations. We had some success and usually managed to get a few of the enemy without losing too many of our own. One of our ambushes near Nam Hoa killed a tax collector and his escort one night and captured several weapons and a lot of cash money, causing great jubilation at all levels.

The money was supposed to be turned in, but some of it made it into the pockets of the soldiers. A few days after the ambush, two of our fine RF troops were caught gadding about on new motor scooters. Disciplinary measures were taken to recover more of the money. The motor scooters were confiscated and never seen again.

A less successful outing was conducted sometime later, just a few nights before Christmas. For reasons undisclosed to me, we changed locations twice in about three hours. Just after arriving in the third position, I was quietly counting to ten when the commander of Nam Hoa Sub-Sector, a captain, signaled me to follow him and then took off to our front. We had crawled forward for about 50 meters when I saw a dim light shining from the window of a stucco building. We crept up to the window and I peeped inside. The captain whispered, "Look, a Christmas tree." He was right! It was a Christmas tree.

Apparently our ramblings had brought us to a mission conducted by German Lutherans, just outside Hue. As we withdrew back to our perimeter I didn't say anything; I just started counting to ten again and put my grenade back in my basic pouch.

**—Royal Australian Regiment, I Corps, 1965**

There were lots of things in the jungle other than the NVA that made the life of the combat infantryman miserable. Leeches were common and revolting. About an inch long and pencil-lead thick, they looked unimpressive until they latched on us, secreted a noncoagulant substance to keep blood flowing, and began to grow. A blood-filled leach grew to the size of a little finger or even larger. The best way to remove them was to drip insect repellent on their engorged bodies. C-ration salt or a lit cigarette could also make them give up their hold.

One morning I awoke in a jungle night defensive position to find four of the blood suckers on my lips—the only area I had not rubbed with insect repellent. That was not as bad as another fellow in the company who discovered three blood-filled leeches on his testicles. His buddies enjoyed making fun of him, calling him a freak of nature because of the extra appendages.

**—101st Airborne Division, I Corps, 1969**

You know, when a bunch of long-in-the-tooth ex-soldiers get together and reminisce, they tend to tell only those stories filled with danger and adventure; the bullet that just creased the skin, the land mine that didn't go off, that kind of stuff. While those memories make great stories, the truth is war, for the most part, is more boring than a cricket game. Ah yes, I realize I may have just offended some of our British brothers in arms—but it's true!

I was assigned as an advisor to the Montagnard folks in the Central Highlands of Vietnam. Several things fascinated me about their way of life. They were primitive, self-sufficient, and yet, in some ways, much more advanced than I had expected, particularly in the area of problem solving. Their traditional attire of loin cloths for men and long black skirts without blouses for women was obviously different than what I was accustomed to. As you can imagine, the latter, at least initially, provided a lot of staring opportunities—especially for young GIs just arriving in country. Interestingly enough, after a few days, bare breasts were no longer a big deal . . . really.

And then there was their drinking and eating habits. The Montagnards crafted a mean concoction of fermented rice and river water. And when I say river water, I'm not talking about crystal-clear water from the Rockies; I'm talking about the water running under the bridge we just drove across, the one where they bathed and washed their clothes. Anyway, once the brew had properly aged (I have no idea what the time-frame was for aging), the Montagnard men would sit around a communal jug and sip the brew from a communal hollow reed. I was invited to join a local leader and his friends sharing a recent vintage. Having had the opportunity to watch a batch made and also to have already had a knock-down drag-out bout with bug-borne diarrhea a few weeks earlier, I took my turn with the hollow reed, but I did not actually drink any rice wine. I just pretended to sip a copious mouthful and then passed it on. Well, it took no time at all until one of the older, toothless guys attached a float to the hollow reed just at the high water mark. Then the reed was again passed to me with all eyes on the float. No way to fake it anymore. And yes, I was sick within twenty-four hours.

And now to their eating habits. If it swam, flew, crawled, or crept upon the face of the Earth, the Montagnards could, and would, make a meal of it. On the first day of a two-day operation, our point Montagnard came across a very large snake basking in the shade of a tree digesting what turned out to be a recently eaten critter—could have been a large rabbit or small pig. Anyway, all military operations stopped and the group immediately made plans for a feast, with the number one delicacy being the partly digested critter. Fortunately they were so excited about that delicacy that my initial "thanks but no thanks" was accepted without argument from anyone. Every scrap of critter—and the snake—were either eaten or taken back to their hamlet for some future use.

Fast forward a few months—some of the Yards invited me and my interpreter to a feast of some sort, perhaps a local holiday. Anyway, by now I'd adjusted to eating whatever they ate and drinking whatever they drank (well, at least most of the time). A big meal with lots of eating, drinking, and laughing followed. A good time was had by all. My interpreter and I returned to our base camp feeling no pain, having had a good time. I arose much later than normal (for obvious reasons) the next morning and immediately did what I did each morning. I looked for my dog, Pineapple, a small version of a German Shepherd. Well-trained, sleek coated, bright eyes, wet nosed— truly man's best friend. Anyway, the dog was nowhere to be found. I asked my interpreter if he had seen her. All I got was a short no and a sheepish exit. That should have been a clue, but I was still hung over and didn't catch on.

Later in the morning, we were once again engaged in conversation, both agreeing the previous evening had been most enjoyable. I was particularly interested in the meat—a tad sweet, definitely tender. Had it been chicken or pork? Another clue: my interpreter kept trying to change the topic to the tasks of the day, which was strange because he, like me, had no real desire to close with and destroy the enemy. He wanted the world to leave his country alone and I wanted to go back to my world as soon as possible.

Anyway, late in the afternoon, after too much whiskey, I pushed my interpreter for an answer—where's the damn dog? Maybe I pushed a tad too hard. He came over, patted my stomach, and repeated how much we had enjoyed the previous night's dinner. And no, it most definitely had not been either chicken or pork.

**—MACV, II Corps, 1970**

★ ★ ★

We were patrolling in the Central Highlands when we heard on radio that the battalion recon platoon had captured a prisoner and was bringing him to a firebase. A short time later, the recon platoon was crossing a stream and the prisoner slipped and fell into current. The platoon leader reported that they shot the prisoner—he did not want him to drown.

**—25th Infantry Division, II Corps, 1967**

★ ★ ★

Our C-123 squadron flew all over Vietnam transporting supplies, food, soldiers, and anything else the load masters could get aboard. In May 1970, we were assigned to assist in parachute qualification for members of the 101st Airborne Division who were still on jump status. Just before one sortie, while waiting for the engines to start, I heard a very small paratrooper say, "You know, my mother wouldn't want me to do this."

**—315th Tactical Air Wing, II Corps, 1970**

In the summer of 1966, I was an engineer platoon leader in Germany. As I read the news about the expanding war in Southeast Asia, I realized that I had to experience combat rather than the relative luxuries of Europe. I also felt that if I was going to fight, it should be as a member of the Queen of Battle—the infantry. So I put in a request volunteering for Vietnam and a transfer to the infantry. I soon was in Vietnam but still wearing the castle brass of the Corps of Engineers in the 35th Engineer Brigade rather than the cross rifles of the infantry.

My infantry transfer finally came through after several months and I joined the 25th Infantry Division in II Corps. Although my training had been as an engineer, the personnel officer saw that I was a graduate of the U.S. Army Ranger School and assigned me to a line company—or perhaps he was just short of infantry lieutenants.

Things went fairly well for the first few weeks while I learned from my sergeants and became acclimated to the jungle. In mid-October, our company participated in Operation Paul Revere in western II Corps. Our area of operations was described by famed military historian Gen. S. L. A. Marshall in his book *West to Cambodia* in this way: "The Plei Trap Valley is a pocket of land roughly 10 by 20 miles belonging to South Vietnam and projecting into Cambodia. The Se San River describes the boundary between the two nations on its southern side. There are mountains along the east and west borders. Although the valley proper is relatively flat, it narrows at the northern extremity to a tightly constricted pass. The floor of the valley is overgrown for most of the 20 miles north to south with triple-canopy jungle, its tallest trees standing 200 feet or more. The undergrowth is as dense as any in Southeast Asia. No nice place, but neatly named, it was never intended by nature as a freeway for maneuvering armies. For the valley was, in effect, a salient jutting into enemy-used country, which tactically gave the other camp the main advantage, only marginally offset by air mobility."

On the morning of October 28, 1966, our company moved around a hill to the north. Several times a helicopter from battalion flew over and confirmed our position. Our 3rd Platoon split off about noon for a recon to the west while my 1st Platoon and the 2nd Platoon continued with the company command group before we stopped for noon chow. We found about twenty fighting holes with overhead cover but no enemy.

After eating our C-rations we continued the march and discovered several rice fields and a hooch that we tried with limited success to burn. A hundred meters later, my point man reported hearing wood chopping to his front. I took the point squad forward to within about 25 meters of the noise. We fired on full automatic but apparently did not hit anyone. Cautiously the squad and I followed the trail of the fleeing enemy for about 300 meters. The company CO then called on the radio and told me to rejoin the remainder of my platoon.

I called my platoon sergeant and told him we were on the way. I did not want to get in a firefight with my own troops so when we neared what I thought was their position, I called and requested they make some noise. My platoon sergeant struck a tree with his machete several times. We identified the sound, he alerted the troops, and we safely reunited. While we had been chasing the NVA, my platoon sergeant had discovered a small, recently vacated base camp complete with two two-by-six-meter hooches on stilts, several chickens and eggs, water jugs, baskets, 350 pounds of rice, a few fish, and a couple of bunkers.

We destroyed everything the best we could and then moved to unite with the rest of the company. About 1800, we joined the company minus the 3rd Platoon that was still some distance to our west. The company commander established his CP in the middle with my platoon on the east half and the 2nd Platoon on the opposite side. A light rain was now falling so we hastily put up some poncho tents low to the ground to protect our radios and other equipment. We had just begun digging our foxholes when we received heavy small-arms and machine gun fire from our northeast. Everyone dove for the shallow holes that they had just started digging. The hole I jumped into, meant for two when completed, already had four soldiers in it.

The initial fire killed my 3rd Squad leader with a shot in his lower back. Several other soldiers fell wounded. One of the wounded near me asked me to contact his mother if he died and tell her that he had been a good soldier. My RTO crawled out of the hole we were sharing to retrieve his radio. Only when he returned did he tell me he had taken a round in his right thigh in the initial burst of firing. My men returned fire as the company medic joined my platoon doc to tend the wounded. We had more wounded than holes to place them in for their protection. So we placed their torsos in the depression and left their legs on the surface so we could get more wounded in each hole. Nearly all of the enemy fire remained concentrated on my side of the perimeter. The 2nd Platoon on the other side began sending us additional machine gun ammunition as the NVA attack continued.

One of my platoon's problem soldiers had "lost" several entrenching tools over the past weeks so that he would not have to carry the extra weight. He now came running to the platoon sergeant seeking a shovel so he could dig in with the rest of the troops. Not surprisingly, he survived the battle. It seemed to me that it was always the good men that were the first to fall.

Every infantryman has a particular wound they fear the most. For many it is taking a round in the groin. Others fear bullets to the face, chest, or back. Mine was a fear of being struck in the top of the head as I lay prone returning fire. I kept thinking about a bullet penetrating my helmet and then my skull, and then deep into my brain. In the midst of the firefight, I took my entrenching tool, sat it on its edge, and placed it in front of my head—another quarter inch of steel protection.

The enemy continued their attack and on several occasions rose from the jungle and attempted to physically overrun our positions. One NVA managed to make it to one of the shallow foxholes only to be beaten to death with fists, rifle butts, and machetes. The victors took from the dead NVA his only weapon—a Soviet-made pistol with six rounds of ammunition. He had been either a very brave or a very foolish individual. Now he was just very dead.

My soldiers grabbed, tied up, and made prisoner of another enemy soldier. Other NVA got near enough to throw hand grenades at us. Some went off, causing more wounds. At least one was a dud that we found at the bottom of one of our occupied holes the next morning.

The company forward artillery observer finally got some support fires coming in, allowing me to crawl around our small part of the perimeter to check on the wounded. I also passed along the order from the company CO for everyone to stop shooting their M16s on full automatic and to fire on semi to conserve ammunition.

We had been out in the jungle for several weeks with no opportunity to change clothes and my uniform pants were wearing out. My trousers split more and more as I moved around. I guess it might have been funny under different circumstances, but it was not then.

The fight was still ongoing at 2100 hours. Our 3rd Platoon tried to come to help us, but they were cut off and became engaged in their own fight. Contact finally was broken at 2245 hours, and a U.S. Air Force Huskey flew in to extract the wounded. Just why we got an air force bird and not an army medevac, I do not know—nor did I care. We took help from any available source.

The Huskey hovered over our perimeter. There was no room to land so they lowered a stretcher for us to strap in the wounded. Slowly three men were wrenched aboard the hovering chopper and we had a fourth on the way when I had just turned to my RTO, whose leg wound was not as severe as those on the medevac and who was not yet in line to be hoisted out, observing to him that it was taking too long to complete the evacuation. I was afraid that the NVA would renew their attack. Just then a rocket-propelled grenade and a recoilless rifle round screamed through the darkness and struck the helicopter. The pilot tried to ascend but it did no good. His tail section broke away as the chopper crashed into our perimeter.

Everyone ran to get out from under the burning Huskey. My RTO, who a few minutes ago could barely move because of his wound, ran at my side until we reached a large tree to get behind. It would have been a good time for the enemy to resume their ground attack, but other than spraying our perimeter with a few automatic burst, they held off. The helicopter continued to burn, illuminating the entire area.

Despite the incoming fire, soldiers grabbed axes out of the chopper and pulled the air force pilot and copilot from the wreckage. They remained in the perimeter moaning for most of the rest of the night before we got them evacuated. I later heard that the copilot died.

In the early morning hours, we evacuated the remaining wounded and began to recover our dead. About dawn a single NVA wandered near our perimeter and quickly fell to our small-arms fire. An air force F-4 flew some close air support, dropping bombs and napalm just outside our positions. Unfortunately, they delivered some of the napalm too close, burning three of my soldiers.

Our company, mostly from my platoon, suffered six killed and nine wounded. Additionally the air force crew had one dead and two wounded. The NVA body count officially totaled seven dead and one captured, but there were likely more lying out there in the jungle or drug off by their comrades. We had picked up six AK-47s, three pistols, two SKSs, and a RPG launcher off the battlefield.

One of our dead was on the helicopter when it crashed and burned. His wound had not been serious, but he had made his way to the front of the line for evacuation. Despite his squad leader telling him that he was not hurt badly enough to be evacuated and that the chopper might get shot down, the man had gotten aboard only to die in the crash. If he had stayed on the ground, he would have survived.

I later learned that the interrogation of the POW revealed that we had been attacked by least two companies of the 2nd

Battalion, 95th NVA Regiment—and it was possible that the remainder of the battalion joined the attacked before it was over. The prisoner, a private first class, said his battalion had a base camp about a day's march to the west. The battalion had sent out recon elements looking for Americans.

Sometime that morning, we got a resupply, and I finally got a new pair of trousers. No effort had yet been made to recover the four bodies from the helicopter. I got my entrenching tool, some ponchos, and dug through the ashes and debris until I found their bodies. They were badly burned but there was sufficient evidence, such as dog tags, to identify the bodies. I guess it really made no difference since I later heard that the bodies got mixed up once they got to the morgue in Pleiku. From the condition of the bodies I am sure there were no open casket funerals back home so I suppose it was not all that important.

S. L. A. Marshall did a good job of describing the terrain in his book—but I'm not too sure about the reliability of his description of my first big fight. In his *West to Cambodia*, General Marshall includes direct quotes from me. This is noteworthy because I never had a conversation with, or even met, the writer.

**—25th Infantry Division, II Corps, 1966**

It was Christmas Eve 1969, and I was assigned as the flight operation noncommissioned officer of the 203rd Recon Airplane Company at Phu Hiep. The company was required to fly two recon missions a day minimum over Phu Yen Province in our O-1A Birddogs. I suggested to my operations officer that he and I take one mission and another captain and my clerk take the other so everyone else could have Christmas Day off. He agreed and said we would take off early and then drop in at a Special Forces camp up the river for breakfast after we flew our missions. My call sign at the time was "Hawkeye 3 Bravo," but because I had taken a break in service between enlistment and Vietnam tours and while I worked as a deputy sheriff, all the pilots called me "Deputy Dog," even on the radio.

I called MACV in Tuy Hoa and asked them to inform the camp that Deputy Dog would be there for breakfast. We loaded as much food as we could to take up to them, items like eggs, bacon, oranges, etc., but there isn't that much room behind the seat in the 0-1A Birddog.

The next morning we flew our missions and then rendezvoused over the river and flew to the SF camp. Both captains were aware of my telling them "Deputy Dog" was en route so they made it look like one plane was escorting the other. As we were going in to land my pilot said in the intercom, "Oh, shit! Look at that."

There was a jeep waiting for us and a major standing at attention next to it. After we taxied to a parking area and got out, my captain saluted the major and said, "Sir, I would like you to meet 'Deputy Dog.' After we shook hands, I took off my flak vest and the major saw my SSG chevrons. He said, "Captain, you better have a damn good explanation for this."

He then laughed, saying that it was a good thing we brought food. We still had to face his communications sergeant who had spent half the night going through the Signal Operating Instructions (SOI) trying to identify Deputy Dog.

**—1st Aviation Brigade, II Corps, 1969**

Everyone who ever spent any time in Vietnam has stories about C-rations. Those in country in the early years talk about their love, or more often hate, for ham and lima beans while those who arrived later hail the virtues of beans and wieners and tuna fish. Nearly everyone agrees that peaches with pound cake rivaled even their mother's finest desserts. Of course, there is always a holdout claiming the pecan nut roll to be the tastiest.

No matter what their opinion of individual rations, those army infantrymen and marines who sustained themselves with the canned rations for weeks at a time collectively have little good to say about Cs. They laugh about how they used the barrels of their M16s to open the wire wrapped cases. Platoon sergeants always turned the C-rations cases upside down so no one could read the ingredients of each of the dozen boxes. The old-timers just smiled and took advantage of having memorized the location of each meal, however the case was situated.

After rations were broken down, the troops traded for their favorites. Nonsmokers had an advantage because they could usually get something in return for the four-pack of stale cigarettes. Then the rejected items and punctured cans were placed with the paper cases and boxes to build fires to destroy any remaining rations so they could not be scrounged by the enemy. Everyone kept their distance from the fire because inevitably someone failed to put a hole in a can and the heat and pressure made it explode. A common warning was, "Spread out you guys. A peanut butter grenade could get you all."

Every case of twelve rations came with four P-38s, or U.S. Army Pocket Can Opener, Hand, Folding Type I. About an inch and half long, it consisted of a short metal handle with a small hinge that folded out to pierce a can lid. A notch on the handle just under the hinge point kept the opener hooked to the can. The P-38 may very well be the most rugged, efficient piece of equipment the army has ever fielded. Developed in 1942, the P-38 was a part of every veteran's life in Vietnam and was the subject of many a debate by bored infantrymen. Most figured the name came from the thirty-eight strokes it took to go around a C-rat can. A few more erudite grunts, and that description could only be placed on a few, said that it came from the opener being thirty-eight millimeters in length.

I heard that the marines called their P-38s John Wayne openers because the actor once made a film on how to use them. I'm not for sure about that story, and after all, we army grunts reserved John Wayne's name for those dry chocolate bars that came in some of the rations.

What the arguments got really serious about was just what P-38 was the superior. Two brands, their names stamped on the handle, prevailed—Speaker and Shelby, both manufactured by an Ohio hardware firm. Some openers made their way through the system with no markings, and I've heard that there were a few labeled Androck, but I never saw one.

GIs with nothing else to do would argue for hours over which was best, fastest, easiest to use, etc. In fact, I don't think there was any difference other than their markings, but that did not deter loyalties. I can't really say which I thought was best, but I guess I preferred the Speaker if for no other reason than they were not as many of them. Scarcity seemed positive to me. Actually, it made little difference. While some soldiers put a P-38 on their dog tag chains or in their pockets, I never could keep up with one of the little things. If I could not get one out of a new case of C-rations, I could always borrow one from one of the other guys.

Each individual C-ration also came with a plastic spoon in its own sanitary plastic wrapping. I threw extra spoons into the reject pile to be burned. I cannot really explain why, but I used the same spoon often for weeks at a time. I would finish a meal, wipe the spoon on my trousers, and put it in my fatigue shirt pocket. When I needed it again, I took it out, rubbed it again on my trousers, and ate my meal. Of course we often wore the same uniforms for weeks without a change so they were not exactly clean. Wiping the spoon on the fabric was as much habit as an effort for cleanliness. With the passage of days, my spoon yellowed and then turned a shade of brown. Finally, it would crack, or I would lose it, and have to give another spoon a try.

As I said, I have no explanation for my far less than sanitary repeated use of C-ration spoons except maybe in a world where we all wore the same things, ate the same things, and carried the same things, it was nice to have something that was uniquely mine. Even if it was just a dirty spoon.

**—199th Light Infantry Brigade, III Corps, 1969**

★ ★ ★

I had been in country only a few weeks when our company received an alert that we would be airlifted from Camp Eagle in I Corps and inserted into an unsecured landing zone with reported NVA activity. My platoon was chosen to be the lead platoon, which meant I would be in the lead chopper on the LZ. Immediately stories of second lieutenants lasting only a few minutes in combat flashed through my mind. I felt the greatest fear that I've ever experienced. It all but paralyzed me, as I envisioned my potential death on landing. I finally suppressed my panic, clinched my trembling hands, and accepted my fate as one of the responsibilities demanded of platoon command.

I had to decide who to take with me in the lead chopper, as well as who would go in the other two that would land in the first wave. The sobering aspect of this act was that I was potentially putting the troops in the same danger as myself. I also had to plan what we would do when we landed on the LZ. All of this somewhat took my mind off of my fear.

On the flight to the LZ, my thoughts were tied up with reading the map to be sure we were landing where we were supposed to, planning what actions to take upon arriving, and what to do if we started taking fire. The insertion plan called for us to travel in a parallel direction to the LZ and then make a hard left turn into the LZ to confuse the enemy about where we were heading. As we banked toward the LZ, I could see artillery rounds hitting with a ferocious intensity. As the artillery ceased, the gunships accompanying us plastered our destination with rocket fire, and the chopper crew on our Huey raked the perimeters with rounds from their door guns.

All of this action just increased the intensity of the situation and my trepidation of what was to come as we dropped down to the landing zone. My fears now were not of losing my life, but of not performing my duties well and endangering not only my platoon, but also the rest of the company that would be landing in later waves.

When we landed, we immediately exited the LZ and set up a defense perimeter. I threw a green smoke grenade to signify a noncontested landing and radioed the CO about the situation. As the rest of my platoon and company landed, my fear had been replaced by a realization that I could perform well under extreme conditions.

This lesson give me confidence that I could live with whatever came my way, including later firefights and loss of some of my platoon. Not much good came from the Vietnam War, but those of us who experienced it firsthand know things about ourselves that the civilians of the world will never learn.

**—101st Airborne Division, I Corps, 1971**

Anyone who ventured more than a foot or two into the Vietnam jungle or rice paddies came across the various "Safe Conduct Passes." These propaganda leaflets, distributed by aircraft and artillery shells, promised safety for Viet Cong or North Vietnamese soldiers who wanted to rally to the Government of South Vietnam. This "Chieu Hoi" program, loosely translated as "open arms," ultimately removed as many as one hundred thousand soldiers from the Communist ranks—although the actual status of these "Hoi Chanhs," as they became known, before their surrender was debated and never fully defined.

The most common leaflet, and the one that made its way into many a GIs letters home, contained a picture of the South Vietnamese flag surrounded by flags of each of their primary

allies—the U.S., South Korea, Thailand, Australian, New
Zealand, and Nationalist China. Along the lower portion of
the leaflet, printed in each country's language appeared were
these words, "Safe-conduct pass to be honored by all Vietnamese government agencies and Allied Forces." On the back
in Vietnamese were promises of safe passage as well as rewards
for weapons surrendered.

Like most everyone else, I picked up one of these leaflets
and put it with the journal I kept of my tour. What was unusual
was that I also accumulated several leaflets aimed at
us Americans by the enemy. The first I found on a jungle trail
in II Corps near the South China Sea. Reproduced on very
thin paper and poorly printed horizontally, the three-by-five-
inch leaflet stated on its front:

**U.S. Colored Armymen**
You are committing the same ignominious crimes in
South Vietnam as what the K.K.K. cliques are
    perpetrating
against your family at home.
Those who are killing and shooting at our people and
those who have caused bloody repression against
    Negro
people in the U.S.A. are the same.
They are U.S. imprialists [*sic*].
How can you stand on their side against our people!
The S.V.N. National Front for Liberation

On the back, in all caps, it said:

DEMAND PEACE IN VIETNAM AND YOUR
OWN REPATRIATION TO YOUR FAMILIES

I have no idea if any of the black soldiers read the leaflets.
If they did, they made no comment. Near this leaflet were two
more printed on the same type of flimsy paper. The first
stated:

THE IS THE PEOPLE'S AIR
AND CANNON SHELTER. DON'T FIRE AT
AND SPRAY SUFFOCATING GAS
NOXIOUS CHEMICAL INTO IT.

The second also appeared to have been written by someone with only a basic grasp of the English language. Perhaps
the author was using the ageless soldier trick of convincing his
commander that he had a special talent that should keep him
off the front lines:

DON'T MASSACRE INNOCENT CHILDREN WAK
[sic] WOMEN.

BURNING HOUSES, KILLING HONEST PEOPLES
DOES IT BRING TO

YOU VERY INTEREST, OR IT ONLY GIVES RISE TO
HATRED.

A short time later, we killed several NVA soldiers and in one
of their packs was a bundle of more leaflets. These were much
more professionally prepared. The first was printed vertically in
blue ink on an four-by-six-inch off-white paper. The same message was on the back of the document in Vietnamese. Spelling
and punctuation is as it appears in the document:

**U.S. Servicemen**
You have been sent to South Vietnam by Johnson-
Westmoreland to carry out the aggressive war against
our country to massacre our people and patriots and
to make profits for the U.S. monopolist capitalists and
weapons dealers headed by Johnson-Westmoreland
who have highly profits.

Your enemy is really Johnson-Westmoreland who
have thrown you to the unjustic aggressive war and not
the Vietnamese people.

We have known that the most of U.S. officers and
men had known these mention and hated the Vietnam
war but have been forced to fight against the Vietnamese people who are struggling to defend the independence of their country.

What are you doing now? We call on you:

—Oppose the Johnson-Westmoreland's dirty aggressive
war.
—Oppose decidedly to your being sent to the battle-
front to massacre the Vietnamese people and to
destroy their villages. Let the Vietnamese people to
settle their own affairs by themselves.

The U.S. officers and men who cross over to the liberation area will be well treated. The SVNNFL will
carefully help these who want to live in neutrality country or come back to United States.

Hold this handbill you will be helped by our compa-
triots to lead to the Front.

We will well receive and look you as the friends of
the Vietnamese people.

SOUTH VIETNAM NATIONAL FRONT FOR
LIBERATION

The second four-by-twelve-inch leaflet was folded horizontally to allow four pages of black print on an off-white background. This one's author had much better understanding of
the English language and spelling. The leaflet also emphasized
that it was an internal conflict between South Vietnamese and
that despite the fact that the leaflet was likely published in
1966, the Communists were already well aware of their supporters back in the United States.

## AMERICAN SOLDIERS IN SOUTH VIETNAM

The U.S. Government has brazenly sabotaged the international 1954 Geneva Agreements and waged a war of aggression in South Vietnam.

The South Vietnamese people, led by the South Vietnam National Front for Liberation and enjoying the sympathy and strong support of peace-and-justice-loving people all over the world including America, are determined to make every sacrifice to win victory in their just struggle in pursuit of independence, democracy, peace, and neutrality.

Washington has played all its cards in a desperate gamble. Despite changing their stooges so often and sending additional U.S. fighting units, military advisors, and modern war equipment, the U.S. Government will not be able to win this game and will finally suffer a gambler's shameful defeat.

Page 2:

In fact, the past few years, thousands of American officers and men have lost their lives or been wounded uselessly and nonsensically—not for their own interests but for their warlike rulers and the arms dealers. Their happiness has been shattered. Their families have had to endure mourning and suffering.

It is clear that you have been forced to go to South Vietnam to serve as cannon-fodder for American war profiteers. Moreover, as you have to fight in the very hard conditions of a tropical land and climate, you will not only die because of guns but also of wretched diseases such as malaria, dysentery, typhoid, etc., which are threatening your lives every passing hour and day.

It is not only absurd but dangerous to continue to serving the munitions' makers interests in South Vietnam.

Page 3: [Considered important enough to merit mostly capital letters]

Therefore we appeal to you to:

—DEMAND THAT THE U.S. GOVERNMENT STOP ITS AGGRESSIVE WAR IN SOUTH VIETNAM, WITHDRAW ALL TROOPS AND WEAPONS BELOGING (*sic*) TO THE UNITED STATES AND ITS SATELLITES FROM SOUTH VIETNAM, AND LET THE VIETNAMESE PEOPLE SETTLE THEMSELVES THEIR OWN INTERNAL AFFAIRS.

—REFUSE TO OBEY ALL ORDERS TO CARRY OUT MOPPING-UP OPERATIONS AND MASSACRE THE VIETNAMESE PEOPLE.

—REFUSE TO ATTACK THE VIETNAM PEOPLE'S ARMED FORCES.

—SYMPATHIZE WITH AND SUPPORT THE JUST STRUGGLE OF THE SOUTH VIETNAMESE PEOPLE FOR INDEPENDENCE, DEMOCRACY, PEACE, AND NEUTRALITY.

The South Vietnam National Front for Liberation

Page 4 (back of the leaflet) displays a picture of an American Marine being assisted by two buddies. The captions states, "Just after landing at Danang, a number of U.S. Marines were killed or put out of action by South Vietnamese guerillas."

The third leaflet was also folded to allow four vertical sheets. This leaflet was specifically aimed at the 3rd Marine Division and the Army's 1st Infantry Division. I have no idea what they were doing in our 25th Division area of operations. The black printing on white paper began with a picture of a grieving GI with the caption, "In Danang hell, the nerves broke down." The photo credit is to *Paris Match* magazine. I found it interesting that a Viet Cong propaganda officer using a jungle printing press would be concerned about giving picture credit. I really doubt if the magazine or anyone else was going to sue him. Page 1 continued below the photo:

> Nowadays is there any place in South Vietnam which is not Hell to you? Especially after the throwing of tens of thousands American troops from the 3rd Marine Division and the 1st Infantry Division, etc. into this US dirty, cruel aggressive war.

Page 2 began:

It's a Hell of a life

*Inside the base:*
—Tropical heat!
—Over-strain!
—Disease!

*Outside the base:*
—Mosquitoes, ants, leeches, poisonous snakes infest the forest.
—Spike traps, mines and sniper's fire are your inseparable companions.
—A hand grenade may be tossed at you when you are driving a car or sitting in a café, who knows?
—Even your reluctant "allies"—the South Vietnamese soldiers—will turn on you at times as happened near Danang.

After a day of tension comes those dreaded lonely minutes, when you long for your dear ones and realize the distance dividing you . . . when the shadows of night fall and you sense the horror of disasters which may catch you unawares.

Page 3 focused on the marines with exaggerated or out-and-out false claims:

What happened to the 3rd Marine Division in its first days in South Vietnam?

—On Thanh Hill (South of Danang) on the night of May 24, 1965, attacked by a hand grenade and bayonet charge, 139 US Marines died right at their position.
—At Chu-Lai Airfield, on the night of June 5, 1965, the Liberation fighters made their way into the US Marines' camp and wiped out 75 of them.
—The Danang Airbase is by no means impenetrable: on the night of June 30, 1965, the Liberation Army and Guerrillas penetrated into it, destroyed 47 aircraft and 3 rocket launching pads, and inflicted 193 casualties to US troops etc.

There is no safe place for you!

Because:

—You are being forced to fight an unjust war against the South Vietnamese people who are resolved to fight through to the end for national liberation. You are being besieged by a whole nation. It is the same in all American bases.
—The American troops are fighting a guerrilla war in a foreign land with no experience in this type of war.

The fourth and back page clearly showed that the Vietnamese Communists already were well aware in 1965 that they had many friends and supporters back on the streets of America. The page began:

Meanwhile the American people who gain nothing in this war are demanding:

—An end to the war in South Vietnam!
—Withdrawal of US troops from South Vietnam!

In the middle of the page was a photo of what appears to be the flag-draped casket of an American soldier surrounded by grieving relatives. One is in uniform, but it appears to be more of the World War II era than Vietnam. Unlike the cover photo, no credit is given to its origins. The leaflet concludes with a question and some demands:

Why should you die in Vietnam?

Demand your repatriation!

Refuse to fight!

When attacked, preserve your lives by crossing over to the side of the liberation army, or by offering no resistance and surrendering!

SOUTH VIETNAM NATIONAL FRONT FOR LIBERATION

During the remainder of my tour, I never saw any more National Liberation Front leaflets. I suppose it did not take them long to figure out that propaganda efforts in support of their cause went over much better on the streets and campuses of the United States than on the battlefields of Vietnam.

**—25th Infantry Division, II Corps, 1966**

During the late spring and summer of 1966, I was a corporal in a Marine Combined Action Platoon (CAP) in Ky Hoa village, on the coast several miles to the north of Chu Lai. We were a combat outpost-type CAP; two understrength rifle squads and a combined-arms weapons squad. Every night we put out three patrols, each of which had a Marine fire team and anywhere from three to eight South Vietnamese Popular Forces (PFs).

Our area of operation included a small, deserted hamlet maybe two kilometers across tidal flats to the west of our Marine compound. At high tide the flats were covered with six feet or more of water. The hamlet, whose name I can't remember, was a suspected resting place for local VC, and we were supposed to patrol through it every second or third night. We never encountered anybody when we went there, but the suspicions might have been true because sometimes the PFs patrolling with us refused to go there.

One moonless night we decided to end VC use of the hamlet as a rest spot. Without telling anyone not directly involved in the mission, we cancelled two of our patrols and combined them, along with the PF commander and his four or five best men. Taking advantage of shadows from passing clouds, we crossed the tidal flats to a cemetery to the south end of the hamlet's island. We flitted through the grave mounds until we reached the southernmost hooches.

The hamlet only had eight or nine buildings, half of them masonry, the other half bamboo and thatch. Our plan of action was to throw a Willy Pete (white phosphorous) grenade into each of the masonry hooches and a fragmentation grenade into each of the others—and then shoot anybody who ran out.

There was one problem with the plan. One of the masonry hooches was across an open area separated from the others and our position by at least seventy-five meters. We'd have to have somebody run across the open expanse to get close enough to throw a Willy Pete into the hooch, or, if we just attacked the others, it would give anyone inside the isolated hooch time to get away or to prepare a defense.

Our solution was to initiate the attack by hitting the far building with a rifle grenade. I had a rifle grenade adaptor, and my M14 had a sight mount on its stock. I was to start the proceedings even though I did not have an actual grenade sight.

The night was moonless, but the stars rained down enough light to read a newspaper. I had two options to use to put a

Willy Pete inside: a window and the door. The window was almost straight on to me, but the door was at an acute angle. I knew that if I had the elevation correct, I could easily put the grenade through the window. The door was tougher because of its visual narrowness, but I didn't have to worry about elevation. That was the deciding factor. Using Kentucky windage, I took careful aim on that door and fired my crimp cartilage that propelled the grenade. *Bang!* The grenade sailed through the door and the hooch belched white phosphorus smoke from all openings. It was a good thing I chose the door because my elevation was off and the grenade would have hit the wall under the window had I shot at it.

As soon as I fired, everybody began throwing grenades and firing. We raced through the hamlet, shooting and throwing grenades. One of my fellow marines spotted figures in the vegetation line to the north and we all began firing in that direction. We ran to the trees, but found no one. On the other side of the trees was a stream with scrub forest beginning on its other bank. The stream also marked the northern boundary of our area of operations. Since nobody was in sight, we didn't pursue. When dawn broke, we found a blood trail, so we knew we'd hit someone.

After that night, even the most timid of our PFs never again refused to patrol through that hamlet, and we heard no more rumors of VC resting there.

In boot camp, I qualified as an Expert Rifleman, but that shot of a rifle grenade at seventy-five meters at night without sights is the single shot I'm most proud of.

**—1st Marine Division, I Corps, 1966**

I went to Vietnam and then came back home 365 days later. During my tour, I sang "I Left My Heart in San Francisco" and "We Gotta Get Outta This Place" with no fewer than seven

Filipino stripper bands and went on R&R to Hawaii to meet a PanAm stewardess. It must have been a great experience for her because I never heard from her again. I heard my first B-40 rocket in Tay Ninh—if I had been wearing drawers, I would have had to change 'em. Our O-Club had better food than the mess hall, but the rusty Falstaff cans made bad beer taste like warm piss. I hated ham and eggs C-rats, but liked lima beans and ham. Malaria pills gave me the runs, but pound cake clogged me up. Soc Trang had a great steam bath but charged too much.

The only rockets I shot from my helicopter didn't come within two kilometers of the target (they wouldn't let me shoot rockets after that). I did get the 40mm Pooper and 20mm in the targeted grid square. The best aircraft I flew was the OH-6A (Loach); the worst was the OH-58A (Kiowa). They only let me fly in the front seat of Cobras with strict instructions not to touch anything.

My greatest achievement was throwing a damned spider monkey out of my aircraft from 2,000 feet because the stupid thing bit me. That was after I had dropped its owner off at Bien Hoa for his freedom flight home, promising to take care of his stupid monkey . . . I did "take care of it!"

Thank God for flight pay or I wouldn't have been able to enjoy my all-expense-paid trip to Southeast Asia as much!

**—1st Aviation Brigade, III Corps, 1970**

☆ ☆ ☆

It was not difficult to hate the enemy. Just his presence in the field required us to look for him as we endured heat, thirst, and loneliness. We liked the dinks even less when they killed or maimed our friends and fellow soldiers.

Occasionally, something happened that solidified our disdain for our enemy. One of our platoons was caught moving across a rice paddy by a VC ambush. The platoon managed to withdraw to the safety of several rice dikes, but their wounded point man remained exposed in the middle of the paddy.

Nearby, an innocent farmer accompanied by what appeared to be his two young daughters, watched. When the firing ceased, the man saw the plight of the wounded soldier and began to walk over to help. The VC opened up, killing him and the two little girls.

**—25th Infantry Division, II Corps, 1967**

My duties of flying Cobra gunships with an Assault Helicopter Company mostly meant either sitting around waiting for something to happen or flying escort for Huey's on assault missions.

One morning we left Tay Ninh and flew to a firebase near the Parrot's Beak in III Corps. The slicks picked up a company of grunts and we followed them to a cold LZ and then went back to the firebase to standby. Sitting around with nothing to occupy our time, we decided to shoot up the earthen berm that surrounded the firebase with our .38-caliber pistols. We shot for a while before we got a hot call for the guns. We jumped into our birds and took off. The slicks, calling from another LZ, were taking fire. They dropped a red smoke grenade on the source of the enemy fire so I rolled in hot on the smoke. As I got to the bottom of the rocket run and started to pull out, I heard and felt a thud in the tail boom area of my Cobra. I continued to pull out of the dive. Everything seemed OK, so I rolled back in for another run on the target.

As I started my second rocket run, the aircraft began turning to the left with no input or control from me because it had taken a .51-caliber machine gun round through the tail rotor driveshaft that finally sheared off when I started the dive. I immediately cut the power, entered autorotation, and started looking for a place to land. I could see nothing but trees and bomb craters full of water.

I chose the nearest bomb crater and headed for it. Before long I could see that I wasn't going to make it to the crater, so I braced for a crash landing into the trees. That worked out okay. My copilot and I jumped out of the Cobra. We had no idea if the VC were near, but we were well aware that they were within machine gun range. We looked at each other and realized about the same time that neither of us had reloaded our .38 revolvers after our target shooting. We both had to stop and reload our pistols before we headed to an opening where one of the slicks could pick us up.

Fortunately, there was a large bomb crater only seventy-five meters away. We were extracted and soon back in Tay Ninh.

A Ch-47 Chinook later came and picked up the Cobra to bring it in by hook. It was sent back across the world for a rebuild. When I returned home I was in Corpus Christi, Texas, where I saw my old Cobra on a barge waiting for restoration at the ARDMAC docks.

**—187th Attack Helicopter Company, III Corps, 1971**

In 1972, I was working in the intelligence section of MACV Headquarters in Saigon but spent much of my time in the provinces of IV Corps. It had not been a good year. In the NVA Easter Offensive, an American helicopter pilot who was a great buddy of mine was killed in action. An ARVN Airborne friend was missing in action, and I had the gut-wrenching experience of seeing his fiancée's red, tear-swollen eyes. I also had had to console a thirteen-year-old kid who'd witnessed the VC put a bullet in his father's head. I had dysentery that cramped and bent me over in pain and had me popping various medicinal remedies like candy. To say I was in a foul mood, mentally and physically, was a gross understatement.

Then I learned that a U.S. mess sergeant, new on the job at our team compound, was telling some of Vietnamese kitchen help that their future employment would be guaranteed if they provided him sexual favors. All the women were war widows—their husbands had been killed fighting the Communists. That was the reason they had been given their jobs.

I had been in the army and Vietnam long enough to know that I had to backtrack this story to ensure that someone was just not trying to burn the sergeant. I soon found the accusations were true and requested an investigation. What followed was a sick joke. The captain and warrant officer undertaking the "investigation" apparently cared little for Vietnamese, or women in general for that matter. They suggested that a little roll in the hay never hurt anyone. Snicker, snicker.

I exploded and told both of them, using many obscenities, that they were a putrid disgrace to the uniform and that their incompetence would be made known to their superiors. The captain could have locked my heels and played the rank game, but he didn't. He just sat there looking stupid and gutless. Perhaps he finally realized just how wrong he was. Regardless, nothing happened to rekindle the investigation.

It was time for Plan B. I'd recently spent many days flying over the Mekong Delta in a chopper, looking out the open door and being scared shitless I'd see the deadly spiral smoke trail of a VC/NVA heat-seeking Soviet SA-7 missile that would send me to my grave, though likely leaving little or nothing to put in a coffin. I began scheming in own mind on how to get the creepy, fat, slug bastard mess sergeant taken out—permanently. Why the hell not? Why should he live when so many good men lay dying? Why not send the vile wretch to his greater reward? The world would be a better place for it . . . or at least less shitty.

I spoke Vietnamese, got along well with the locals, and figured that if I found the right element, they'd be glad to do the guy in for, say, $25.00. My only concern was tactical: how to pull it off leaving no tracks, which might be hard to do given my outburst against the captain and warrant officer had been

witnessed by five or six people. My display of volcanic anger
had definitely established a motive. I lay on my rack, ponder-
ing "tactics," and then realized that I was planning a terminal
hit on a fellow American with all the moral reservations one
might apply to selecting a mechanic to do a brake job on his
automobile. All I cared about was not getting caught. I wanted
to have a guy killed, and I had no more remorse than having a
wart removed. What the hell had happened to me? And, perhaps worse (or better?), why didn't I even give a shit? Finally I
decided I didn't care that I didn't give a shit.

Fortunately, another officer found out about the mess sergeant, launched a new investigation, and carried it all the way
through. As none of the war widows had actually been forced
to submit to the cook, the slime-bucket pig fucker got off with
a severe reprimand, which went into his file and no doubt
(one hopes) ruined, or at least slowed, his career.

He probably never realized how easily he got off.

**—MACV, III Corps, 1972**

★ ★ ★

I was flying trail in a UH-1 Light Fire Team at night. We had
been shooting for the Special Forces Compound at Song Be
which had come under attack, and were heading to our
remain overnight (RON) location at Lai Khe. It was like flying
in an ink bottle—pitch black in the sky and with hardly any
light on the ground. As the trail ship, I was responsible for
securing artillery clearance, so I called on the radio and
learned that a battery of 155s were shooting flare rounds. It
appeared that we were flying right through the projected gun
target line, so I requested a check fire. My copilot was at the
controls while I looked at my map to figure out the best way to
get out of the way of the artillery.

Suddenly, a blinding ball of fire in front of us lit up the
whole cockpit. Next came a loud *ka-rump* and the shudder of

the aircraft—and then total darkness. We couldn't see out of our constricted pupils, but I could feel that we were still flying. However, we had loud banging noises coming from the side of the aircraft.

My eyesight soon returned and I could see that an artillery flare was attached to our helicopter. Fortunately, it was no longer burning. I quickly figured out that the flare's parachute had hooked on the pilot's right bottom door hinge. We slowed down, I stretched as far out the window I could, but I couldn't reach it to unhook it. I slowed the helicopter as much as I dared and the door gunner, trusting his monkey strap, stepped out on the skid, but he couldn't reach it either.

We flew into Lai Khe with the flare banging the bottom of the ship the whole way. It was still attached when we landed. When we unhooked the flare, we were astonished at its weight, well over fifty pounds. The bottom of the helicopter had been beaten to shit.

Fortunately the impact had knocked the fire out of the flare casing. If it had continued to burn, we would have had to find a place to land in the murky jungle before the intense flare heat started our aircraft on fire. Or if the flare would have hit just a few feet higher, it likely would have taken out our rotor blades, the only thing keeping us in the air. And helicopter crews don't wear parachutes!

**—1st Infantry Division, III Corps, 1968**

After I arrived in Vietnam, I was assigned the 199th Light Infantry Brigade where, after a week-long orientation and training, I reported to my platoon at Firebase Elvira southwest of Saigon. Elvira was kind of the poster child of bad places to be as it was surrounded on three sides by abandoned rice paddies full of water, mud, and booby traps and on the other by a French Colonial–era canal. The only way in and out—other than by foot—was by water or air because there were no roads.

I arrived by helicopter and soon got in the routine of setting up ambushes at night and sleeping during the day time. One afternoon a couple of weeks after I arrived at Elvira, I awoke to hear an incoming chopper that delivered actor Greg Morrison to our isolated base. Morrison was a pioneering black actor who had earned a role on the popular TV series *Mission Impossible.* I liked the show and was impressed by meeting the actor. He was very cordial, shaking hands with everyone at Elvira. He stayed awhile to talk to several troops who gathered around him, but I did not try to take up any of his time. I was a new guy, and I figured that the old-timers were much more deserving of his attention than me.

Anyway, I thought to myself, there will be many entertainers and famous people visiting the company over the remainder of my tour. I was wrong. I never saw another famous visitor while I was in Vietnam.

I did have one more chance. I had seen the TV shows of the annual Bob Hope Christmas visits to military installations around the world. Soldiers joining in the singing of "Silent Night" never failed to raise a lump in my throat. The witty Hope and the bevy of beautiful women who accompanied him would be great to see. When word spread that Hope's 1969 Christmas tour was coming to the brigade main base in Long Binh, everyone got excited about seeing the comedian and his special guests Connie Stevens and astronaut Neil Armstrong, who only a few months earlier had walked on the moon.

By this time, we had put Elvira and the Mekong Delta far in our past, operating now in the jungles and rubber plantations south of Xuan Loc. Rumors kept circulating that helicopters were going to pick us up and fly us directly to the Hope show. We should have known better. We finally received word that the allocations for our battalion for the show was one, yes one, man per company. On the radio I could hear the other company commanders ordering that one of their men in the rear area could see Hope—along with words that the Federal Communications Commission frowns upon on public airways.

Our company commander did not go along with the others. He left it up to the platoon leaders to select a man, by lottery I think, and then we humped several kilometers through the jungle to the nearest LZ. Our one man made the show. I felt foolish for thinking that those in high-ranking positions would ever let the majority of us out of the meat grinder even for one day. After all, we could not deliver body counts sitting in Long Binh watching the Hope show.

When the soldier returned, he talked about how good Connie Stevens looked, about his theory that walking on the moon was likely safer than walking in the jungle, and about how the show venue was filled almost entirely with Long Binh warriors—REMFs who had never gone outside the wire.

Few of us had any good thoughts about REMFs in general or Bob Hope in particular. I am sure than Hope was good for the morale of those fortunate enough to see him, and he certainly deserved credit for being one of the few celebrities who came to Vietnam, seemingly to care about servicemen. However, I later did a bit of research and found that the 1969 show was Hope's sixth in Vietnam and his nineteenth to military bases around the world. The military, or the USO, picked up all the transportation and other expenses. Hope, infamous for his pursuit of his show's females, rarely, if ever remained in country overnight, preferring to fly to the luxury hotels in Bangkok, Manila, and elsewhere. The real rub came when I discovered that all of the Hope shows were filmed. These were then edited and sold to TV networks for airing during the Christmas season. Copies were further merchandized through catalogues and other promotions.

Just another lesson learned in Vietnam—but I'm not sure exactly what it was. Something about the grunts getting the worst of everything, that making money while doing good was

good—at least for Bob Hope—and a lingering respect for
Greg Morrison.

**—199th Light Infantry Brigade, III Corps, 1969**

One morning, we were preparing an LZ for extraction
from the jungle to Firebase Jack in I Corps. Everyone was
in a pretty good mood because we were getting out of the jungle for a while. A hot meal awaited us.

First we had to clear the LZ. We used C-4 to blow down the
trees until only two about eight inches in diameter remained.
Since we had already made so much noise, a little more would
not hurt. Our two best M60 machine gunners came forward
and proceeded to "chop" the two remaining trees down with
their bursts of bullets. Everyone cheered them.

**—101st Airborne Division, I Corps, 1969**

By the spring of 1970, most MACV Military Assistance
Teams (MATs) were no longer searching for and fighting
the enemy; instead they were building schools, helping farmers, and performing other "hearts and minds" kind of work.
I'm pretty sure our MAT was the last in the Mekong Delta still
actually fighting the war.

In March 1970, my team was in an ambush—and we were
not the ambushers. I was shot high on my thigh, well to be
honest it was my ass, and the bullet came out very near my
"family jewels" in front.

By the time I was evacuated to a hospital, the pain was so
severe that I was not sure what I said or did. I was later told

that I was in shock and that I spurted out verbiage not fit to be heard by even a sailor or Marine. I do recall that there was an ER nurse who had the prettiest eyes I have ever seen, even to this day. I still regret that I never got the chance to apologize to her for my profanities.

But what really pissed me off was that before they gave me a shot that put me into la-la land, I realized that the scissor-equipped nurse was going to cut off my fatigue trousers. I was not concerned that I, like everyone else who worked in the wet, humid Delta, was not wearing underwear. What did concern me was the simple fact that I was wearing the first set of "new" jungle pants that I had been issued in months. The goddamn supply shitheads and everyone in else in the rear always had good-looking, fresh uniforms. My previous pair of pants had become bleached out almost white. And now they were going to cut these new ones off of me and there was nothing I could do about it. It was a sad day in my life; those pants deserved better than an AK hole in them and then some nurse cutting them off. But she did have beautiful eyes.

**—MACV, IV Corps, 1970**

★ ★ ★

There are two distinct faces of armed warfare because combat is like a whore. On one side, it is exotic, alluring, and exciting beyond words. On the other side, it is painful, sinful, immoral, and horrible. Despite these latter characteristics, I was drawn to combat at the same time I was afraid of it. I volunteered twice for infantry tours—and they were vastly different in the composition of infantry units with the passage of years.

The Vietnam War differed greatly for the infantrymen who shouldered the greatest burdens and real dangers depending on just when they were in country. My experience serves as a good example as I basically served in two different armies.

In 1966, I joined the 1st Cavalry Division as a second lieutenant. Our captains, who commanded our companies, had
from eight to ten years of service. The big difference, however,
was in the NCOs. From squad leader to first sergeant, they had
from ten to twenty years in uniform and several were veterans
of the Korean War and even World War II. The Cav was a good
place to be a green second lieutenant.

When I returned for my second tour in 1969 and assumed
command of an infantry company in the 101st Airborne Division, I had been in the army for four years. Only four of my
NCOs had more than six years of service—and many companies had even fewer experienced NCOs. Most of my sergeants
had gone to Noncommissioned Officer Candidate School
(NCOC) upon graduation from basic and advanced individual
training. Upon successful graduation from NCOIC, the former
privates became buck sergeants—and several who excelled in
each class were promoted to staff sergeants. These instant
NCOs were known derisively as "shake and bakes," but they
well-acquitted themselves on the battlefield.

Despite the pumping out of instant NCOs by Fort Benning, we were always short of sergeants, regardless of their
experience. Squads were frequently led by Sp4s with E-5s or
E-6 performing the duties of platoon sergeant. During the
months of my company command, I remember only one week
that I had a full complement of lieutenants. This meant that at
any one time at least one platoon was led by a NCO.

In short, the company was a unit of young men being led
by young men. Nevertheless, the company performed well for
the simple reason that combat is relatively simple compared
with the mired of regulations and over-supervision in stateside
units. My company would have never passed muster in a peacetime setting, but in the jungle, we kicked ass.

**—1st Cavalry Division, I Corps, 1966;**
**101st Airborne Division, I Corps, 1969**

After nearly sixty days on the line in the Gulf of Tonkin, where I was a RM2 (Radioman Second Class) aboard the USS *Horne*, we received notice that we would take some time off. Fifteen days to be exact. The really good news was we would spend the time in Hong Kong. Wow! Hong Kong. I had seen it in the movies but never dreamed I would one day put my feet on the ground there. I could feel the excitement building as we headed off station toward the island city.

When we arrived in Hong Kong harbor, the USS *Providence* was already in port for her crew's R&R. So we had to tie up on her port side and cross over her to get to the pier. It was no big deal for any of us, except we never considered the harassment our stewards would receive from the *Providence* sailors. Our stewards, like many of the time, were from the Philippines. The deal with the U.S. government was that they could serve eight years active duty as a navy steward to earn U.S. citizenship. Onboard the *Horne*, we really like our stewards. They worked in the galley and served the officers in all capacities— laundry, food, shoe shining, etc. They also handed out cakes and pies to enlisted crewmen anytime they thought they could get away it. They were good shipmates.

The first night in port, one of *Providence*'s sailors had had a bit too much to drink in town and jumped one of our stewards. They fought, and our steward got the best of him.

The pier was about a half-mile long and if we cut across a field alongside the pier we could save about half that distance on the way to town. On the second night, our stewards (different group) headed for town with nothing but a good time on their minds. They decided to take the short cut. This proved to be a bad decision. Some *Providence* sailors were waiting in the dark. A fight broke out, and one of our stewards was knocked to the ground. Where he fell was a piece of window glass about one foot by two feet in size. He picked it up and swung it in the direction of a *Providence* sailor. It hit the sailor in the throat, cutting everything except the spine. No one knew what to do, so they all ran.

The next day, the news circulated without either side coming forward to acknowledge their deeds. Finally, at midday, we found one of our stewards dead by suicide. A note lay beside him with a confession and prayer for forgiveness. He was one of the friendliest and most softspoken stewards on the ship.

I didn't feel much like participating in the R&R any longer. However, I had an E-9 chief who had never married and had spent most of his career in the Western Pacific. He took a group of us to the other side of the island to a place that sounded like "Repulse Bay." The chief, who had been in Hong Kong many times before, had rented a house near the water from a longtime friend (Chinese lady) who owned several bars on the island. The beautiful house came completely stocked with everything we needed—liquor, food, and women. We spent four days there getting our heads around what had occurred back on the pier and just having a good time.

This was maybe the best, most meaningful four days of my life. We sailors left there with an undying friendship which has lasted a lifetime. Sadly, it already has outlasted four of us.

**—USS *Horne*, South China Sea and Hong Kong, 1968**

We had a soldier who had worked in a restaurant as a cook in civilian life. He was not happy to be an infantryman. He was always asking his sergeant, "Wouldn't it be better for the army to make me a cook since I already have training in cooking?"

The sergeant finally looked him straight in the eyes and said, "Young man, you are assigned to the infantry. You will stay in the infantry. By the way, how many of the men that come through here have had any prior training in 'killing people?'"

**—25th Infantry Division, II Corps, 1967**

In the autumn of 1969, Blackhorse was the forward operating base for my battalion of the 199th Light Infantry Brigade. The firebase had been built by the 11th Armored Cavalry Regiment before they moved further north, and we now shared the vast installation with elements of the ARVN 18th Infantry Division. Located northeast of Saigon in an area of jungle, rubber plantations, and farmland, the area was stunningly beautiful.

My unit—the recon platoon of Echo Company, 2nd Battalion, 3rd Infantry, the 199th Light Infantry Brigade—operated in the jungle searching out elements of the North Vietnamese Army. The young are immortal in their own eyes—and I was young. I had begun my tour as a crewman in the battalion 4.2-inch mortar platoon. It was a relative safe position but I wrote a letter to the battalion commander asking to be reassigned to the field. He, of course, was happy to oblige. He put in a call to the company commander, who was none too happy, and I was reassigned to the recon platoon. At least one other guy I knew of had asked for reassignment to the field. I don't know if he regretted it. I guess we wanted the experience of real combat in our young, restless, and boring lives.

Between missions, which could last anywhere from three days to more than a week, we often returned to Blackhorse to rest and refit for the next mission.

In the wooden sandbagged main mess hall at Blackhorse, the officers and enlisted men sat in separate sections. I recall that once I inadvertently sat down in the officers' section only to be summarily shooed away. I learn quickly. So I was sitting in the EM section, alone at a table, when a lieutenant approached and sat down with a friendly greeting. He was new to the platoon—I recall him on just two short missions before this—and I was not sure I even recognized him at first. I did take note of the black bar on his lapel and used "sir" liberally. He clearly knew I was one of his men, but he conversed with me more like a friend than a subordinate. At the time, I was very shy, somewhat downcast, and immature. I would have thought the lieutenant was at least ten years older than I was, though he was, in fact, at twenty-two, two months younger.

The lieutenant was handsome, of average height, with short black hair and glasses, broad shoulders, and sinewy arms. As we chatted, he exuded a good humor—but that was characteristic of him. One would say he was solid, at ease with himself.

That he had graduated from West Point was scarcely a matter of notice among the men. I only became aware of this detail from one of the other guys as word filtered through the platoon. The lieutenant certainly didn't make an issue of it.

In fact, I didn't even recall the lieutenant's arrival in the recon platoon when he sat down to eat with me. I had not recorded it in my journal. There must have been a brief speech of introduction, probably out in the jungle before setting off on a mission straightaway. One day he was just there— friendly, good-natured, and in command as naturally as a man breathes. That was the salient feature of the lieutenant as a soldier—his leadership was smooth, effortless, and utterly beyond question. To the best of my memory, he had the utmost respect of his men and no one would think to question his ability as a soldier. But beyond that, there was an easy relationship between the lieutenant and the men of recon. To my knowledge, everyone liked him.

"Well," the lieutenant said at one point in our mess hall chat, "I guess we'll go out on another mission, crash through the jungle for a few days again, find nothing, and come back in."

"Yes, sir," I said, finally figuring out whom he was, "that's the way it's been going. But we'll give it a try, anyway."

When the lieutenant had arrived, we had been going through a dry spell for four or five weeks in terms of contact with the enemy. Though we had threaded our way through the jungles of Phuoc Long Province day after day, our luck had not been good (or had been very good, as we grunts saw it). The jungle was a big place, and we had been missing the enemy somehow.

Our battalion commander at the time was a tall, thin, ramrod-straight soldier's soldier on his third or fourth tour in

Vietnam. We came to learn that he expected soldiers to look the part. Once, I forgot my jungle hat on the way to the mess hall, but I didn't return for it. As luck would have it, I encountered the battalion commander, his look of displeasure was quite intense, as if I had somehow insulted him. I can recall another time he approached a man and motioned for him to button his shirt—"So the mosquitoes don't get at you," he said. I heard that the battalion commander had taught at West Point and had even had our lieutenant in one of his classes.

The thing about the battalion commander that got the attention of all of us right away was that he spent much of his time actually on the ground in the field. We all marveled at him for this. He would walk on a mission with a platoon in the jungle. Once I sat on squad ambush with him on a rainy night.

The battalion commander was such a traditional soldier that now I can see how the draftee army must have been hard on him. He took the war personally. He chased the enemy with relentless passion. At one point during our dry spell, before the arrival of the lieutenant, the battalion commander had gathered the men of recon around him and said, "The contacts aren't happening, are they?" His eyes swept the men. "I don't know why." The tone of voice was, as I recall, troubled. "I'm trying to put you in the right places, and I know you are all professionals."

I am certain that to a man—other than the platoon leader we had at the time, of course—that no one was the least disappointed in the lack of contact, quite the contrary.

The day after my lunch with the lieutenant, we were back in the jungle. But we didn't make contact with the enemy on that mission, or the next one, or the next. A growing air of discontent was weighing on the lieutenant. He wanted action and his frustration of not making contact was building inside him. The closest we came to contact on those missions happened when the point man opened fire at a fleeing shadow.

There is a proper way of getting on the ground with a heavy pack—a three-step maneuver. My inclination was only to get there—as fast as possible. On this occasion, in falling to the ground, I banged my face on the rear sight of my M16. I had cuts on my nose and above my left eye. I recall clearly that the lieutenant watched intently as the medic cleaned the cuts and applied bandages. It wasn't a firefight—the point man had opened up on a large animal of some kind—but apparently from the lieutenant's point of view, it would do—at least for a few minutes. Soon he gave the order to move on.

The lieutenant's sense of humor was irrepressible and somewhat irreverent. Once, after eating a C-ration meal, he belched loudly and proclaimed, "From a West Point graduate. One of the best. By Act of Congress." Another time, sitting in the jungle, he read aloud a letter from his father. Apparently, he found it lighthearted. In the letter, his father asked what he wanted for Christmas. The lieutenant commented, "As for what I want for Christmas—the army doesn't authorize that."

But the aggravation was growing. On one mission, we sat in a small jungle clearing beneath a hot sun for most of the day. I don't recall what we were waiting for, but the wait was oppressive. At one point, long into the day, an element of perhaps four armored vehicles came bursting through the jungle. The lieutenant talked briefly to the armored commander, who asked, "Do you want to come with us?"

"Sir, don't volunteer us," someone said.

"No, I've got to wait here," the lieutenant said. He sounded disconsolate.

I recall clearly that the lieutenant then walked off a little ways by himself, and lingered, looking into the jungle. I knew then—we all did—that the lack of contact was wearing on him. The lieutenant seemed to transcend the figment of war as a matter of glory and bragging rights. I never heard a word from him about the six months he was in country as an infantry platoon leader before he joined recon. In my mind, he was not out to prove that he could stand up to combat—of that he was sure—and he didn't want to amass war stories, either. He wanted to be a soldier, in function, not just training and stature. He wanted to encounter the enemy and lead men against them under fire. In the absence of that, what was trekking through the jungle but an extended camping trip at taxpayer expense?

The recon platoon had seventeen men on the mission during which the lieutenant was killed. We had spent much of the day, November 11, 1969, chasing around in the jungle, almost frenetic, going from one set of coordinates given to us by headquarters to another. Apparently, there was intelligence of enemy activity in the area. But we couldn't make contact. As I recall, on one of the recons, we fairly dashed to the coordinates. The lieutenant's exasperation was growing, and things were getting a little out of hand. No one said anything about it being Veterans Day.

I overheard one radio exchange between the lieutenant and the battalion tactical operations center that I recorded in my journal. "Okay, we just finished a mad dash through the jungle," the lieutenant said, "which accomplished nothing. Now what are we supposed to do?" He listened for a time. "Okay, we'll make another mad dash through the jungle to those coordinates. What do you want us to do when we get there? Assuming we find nothing, which is likely what will happen. Do you want us to walk in circles, do push-ups, or what?"

"Check out the area," was the return message.

"Oh, yes, of course, we'll just fuck around some more," the lieutenant said and ended the transmission. He then said, "Let's go, guys."

So we set off again through the jungle, which was fairly sparse in ground cover in that area. I was near the back of the file. We were moving fast.

We hadn't moved far when a sudden avalanche of sound crashed through the jungle. The lead men had made contact and opened up. We dodged forward to get on line. The lieutenant pulled us back, formed a front, and moved us forward again. Another contact exploded on the lead guys. Two guys were wounded. The enemy was not running away. We were facing, as it turned out, an unknown number of NVA in bunkers.

I was providing rear security. The lieutenant, his RTO, a machine gunner, and a couple other guys lay on the jungle floor just in front of me. Up front the men were laying down a volume of fire, and I could hear the distinctive popping sound of AK-47s returning fire. Our machine gun rattled as an M79 thumped out explosive rounds. There was a lot of shouting.

Right away, the lieutenant got on the radio to call in artillery fire. He dropped the rounds as close to the bunkers as he could to hold the enemy in place, a technique called blocking fire. The whoosh, whistle, and roaring slams continued for some time. The artillery landed so close to us that the ground shook and chunks of spent shrapnel crashed through the trees overhead, dropping on top of us, spent, like steel hailstones.

At one point, the artillery lifted and Cobra gunships the lieutenant had called for swooped in overhead. They circled the area of contact, like eagles or vultures, firing rockets and grenades, their mini-guns rattling like buzz saws.

We responded to the barrage of artillery and Cobra fire with delighted shouts, until the lieutenant yelled, "Shut up! Everybody shut up! If there's any shouting to do," the lieutenant yelled, "I'll do it."

As the fight continued, an evac chopper arrived, hovering overhead, and dropped a basket at the end of cables to haul out the wounded. One man had a shrapnel wound to the head; another was in convulsions from being been grazed in the head by an AK round.

Finally, the lieutenant shouted, "Okay. Hold your fire. We're going to check out the area."

The lieutenant went forward with a sergeant beside him. In a short time, they came upon a lone NVA soldier. The lieutenant shoved the sergeant out of the way and tried to draw his rifle on the enemy soldier. But he lost the duel, fatally shot. The sergeant scrambled back to cover.

The next thing I heard was someone yelling, "Sergeant, is the lieutenant dead?"

"Yeah, he's dead," was the downcast reply.

We resumed firing. Another soldier was hit in the arm, smashing the bone, which protruded from the flesh.

The platoon sergeant, now the acting platoon leader, called for the gunships to resume fire. He must have been a little incoherent because the Cobra pilot said, in a very calm voice, "All right, bub, just tell me where you want it, and I'll put it there."

After the gunships worked for a time, we called for artillery fire, but the enemy fire did not let up. With more than a quarter of our platoon dead or wounded, we pulled back, a sad straggle of men. We had to leave the lieutenant behind.

One soldier, his arm wrapped and trussed to his side, followed behind me. He was glassy-eyed from two shots of morphine. When we got to the LZ, I fed him a half-canteen of water.

In a short while, the battalion commander joined us and used the recon platoon as his forward headquarters as he supervised a battalion-sized operation directed at the bunker complex. He talked frequently to the brigade commander who flew in a chopper overhead. He called in airstrikes of bombs and napalm. I remember the slam of the bombs and the soft thud of the napalm explosions.

Ultimately, it took two days to get back to where the lieutenant had fallen. When we got to the area, I was again providing rear security. The others found some thirty-three enemy bodies. Most had been killed by artillery fire. We discovered some seventy bunkers there.

We found the lieutenant buried in a shallow grave, were he fell. His body had not been mutilated, though someone had taken his West Point ring. There's no way of knowing if they knew they had killed an elite soldier.

A group of army engineers came in to blow the bunkers. I remember so clearly how the jungle shuttered with each explosion. Soon we had a new platoon leader and were back humping the jungle looking for the elusive enemy.

**—199th Light Infantry Brigade, III Corps, 1969**

As an OH-58 pilot with the 1st Aviation Brigade, I flew all kinds of missions from LZ Plantation and the adjacent LZ Red Carpet. The latter LZ was so named because it supported many VIP flights, civilian and military, for USARV Headquarters.

The OH-58 required only one pilot and no crew so there was extra room for passengers. One of my frequent passengers was the Vietnamese Assistant Minister of Health in President Thieu's cabinet (the only female to hold such a position). Her husband was a full minister in the cabinet. She was a medical doctor schooled at Johns Hopkins Medical School back in the States; she spoke perfect English; and she was a joy to fly with. One of her responsibilities was to supervise nurses in Vietnamese military hospitals and field medical units.

I also flew many news reporters, including Morton Dean and Greg Cook; and entertainers from Red Carpet including singers Roy Acuff and Sammy Davis Jr.; numerous beauty contest winners from back home, professional sports cheerleaders, and more small bands than I could count. I heard "Proud Mary" performed with every accent imaginable (Thai, Korean, Australian, British, Vietnamese, Cambodian, American—to name a few). I missed being involved in the Bob Hope USO mission because I was on R&R in Hawaii during Christmas. I flew the "decoy" aircraft when Vice President Agnew visited the area in August 1970. I did not have enough years or hours flying to qualify for the real mission.

I also flew several Donut Dolly missions. These young female Red Cross volunteers visited the troops, bringing gifts, games, treats—including donuts—and, most of all, the opportunity for the soldiers to talk to "round eye" girls from back home.

One morning, I got a Red Carpet call to fly three Dollies in an OH-58 to some remote locations, a mission coordinated with mail delivery and resupply. Normally, a UH-1 was used for Dolly missions so that everything and everyone was on one bird. Because the places we were visiting were small support posts, three Dollies were sufficient, which was good because I could only take three passengers in the OH-58 and the loaded Huey had no room for them. We coordinated the flights so that if we could not both land (some places only had one pad), the Huey would go in first and unload and then I would come in with the Dollies. The Huey would go on to the next stop and wait for us. Each Dolly visit was to last about two hours.

Our last stop was to the top of Nui Ba Den (Black Virgin), the 3,268-foot mountain jutting out of a flat plane near Tay Ninh City, a few kilometers from the Cambodian border where the Ho Chi Minh Trail terminated. The French and then later the Americans had vied for control of the mountain. In 1964, Special Forces troops assaulted the top of the mountain and installed a signal relay station. Throughout the remainder of the war, Americans controlled the peak, but the VC and NVA controlled the base and most of the remainder of the mountain. In 1968, the station was overrun by VC who killed all twenty-three Americans at the signal station. The Americans retook the peak and retained control until the U.S. pullout from Tay Ninh Province.

I had flown to the peak of Black Virgin a few times, delivering mail and radio equipment, and had accomplished the tricky, windy landings that greeted arriving helicopters. The peak was often covered in fog. Clouds could form with no notice, stay for hours, and just as quickly blow away. Because the VC were always at the base and on the sides, steep approaches and max performance takeoffs were mandatory.

We arrived with room to land both aircraft. The Huey went in first, touched down, and reduced lift. I followed and made a shaky but safe landing. The troops knew the Dollies were arriving, so we had an enthusiastic, cheering greeting party. Since this was the last trip of the day, the supply chopper unloaded and departed. Before getting in his bird, the Huey pilot pointed to a cloud layer beginning to form below the peak and told me to either get out ahead of it or wait until it cleared. "Do not try an instrument max performance take off from this peak in that thing," the pilot said as he pointed to my OH-58, an aircraft not rated for instrument flying.

While the Dollies were entertaining the guys, I made small talk with the detachment CO, warily watching the clouds come up and cover the peak. We had only been there an hour and had only a couple more before dark. The unit commander told me the clouds usually cleared right before sundown. When they did not disperse, he warned, "Do not take off until morning. The VC hole up during the day and work their tunnels and supply paths at night. We usually don't have aircraft arriving or leaving here at night. If we do, the VC think they are being attacked and they shoot at the aircraft," he emphasized. He saw the look of concern on my face and quickly added, "Don't worry, we've had a deal going here for the past year or so. We don't shoot down at them, and they leave us alone."

The troops were thrilled to have the Dollies stay though I was less than thrilled to be stuck on top of the Black Virgin. I declined the friendly offer of a beer from the CO, but the Dollies accepted—and the party was on. I climbed into the aircraft through a relay via a bird in the air near Tay Ninh and reported to flight ops that the Red Cross Dollies would not be back until the following morning.

The unit commander walked me to the edge of a rock cliff where we watched a procession of lanterns along the sides of the mountain. "VC," he said.

I carried a .38 revolver side arm and I had an M16 mounted behind my seat in the OH-58. That night was the only time I ever took the M16 out of the aircraft while on a mission. I sat on a rock until daylight watching those lanterns and keeping the perimeter guards company. I got no sleep, the Dollies got no sleep, and the troops got no sleep. Everyone had fun but me. At the crack of dawn, with no cloud cover, three tired Donut Dollies and I had a quiet flight back to Long Binh.

**—1st Aviation Brigade, III Corps, 1969**

✯ ✯ ✯

Back in the stateside army, accounting for equipment was a top priority. A missing weapon, radio, or other "sensitive item" might cause the lockdown of a unit, a detailed search, and an investigation. If the equipment was not discovered, the soldier responsible for it—the one who had signed a hand receipt—would be the subject of a Report of Survey. If found liable, the soldier had to pay for the items with monthly pay deductions. Vietnam was different—as it well should have been. After all, it was a war zone.

When I arrived in country in early 1969, I was on my second tour and had been promised the command of a rifle company. When I reported to my unit, the battalion commander said he wanted the current line company commanders to remain in place for another month. He said that in the meantime he wanted me to take over Echo Company, a unit that contained the battalion mortars, recon platoon, ground radar equipment, and other ash and trash attachments. He added that Echo had some significant equipment problems and my main job over the next month was to get it all accounted for. Not really having any choice, I saluted smartly and said, "Yes, sir."

When I inventoried the company, I discovered that fifteen M16s, two M60 machine guns, three radios, a couple of Starlight scopes, and host of smaller items were missing. The company commander I was replacing, a lieutenant, signed the papers acknowledging the missing items just before he left for his freedom bird to go back home. He did not give a shit and I really did not blame him.

I began my task of accounting for everything. To make up for lost equipment, I took the easy course of action and looked in the battalion logs to see when the mortar and recon platoons had been in contact. While doing this, I also learned that part of the battalion firebase had been overrun in the Tet Offensive of 1968. Easy write-offs.

Some of the equipment I found in other units in the battalion. For others, I had to get the proper forms, have someone sign that they remembered losing the equipment in a subsequent battle. Then that particular item was written off our accounts. The final two missing radios showed up just before I left the company when a supply warrant officer dropped them off with an explanation that he had heard I was looking for them. They did not work, but that was not important. Just their existing was what counted.

During my search and paperwork drill, I heard several other stories on how to make up for lost equipment or to replace items that did not work properly. The first method was simple: if a radio did not work properly and the supply chain was reluctant to replace it, all you had to do was put a couple of bullets through it after the next firefight. DXing (direct exchange) of battle-damaged equipment was fast and easy.

The second method was a little more complicated and iffy. In this process one would wait until a helicopter that had recently transported or resupplied the unit crashed and then claim that the missing equipment was aboard and destroyed. There was a story that went around that a helicopter that had just completed resupplying each of the battalion's four line companies crashed on its way back to base. Each of the four companies immediately reported that they had a radio or two, a couple of weapons, and other miscellaneous gear on the bird that crashed and burned. The investigating officer later reported that the cause of the crash was obvious—it was overloaded with nearly a ton of equipment.

Back in the States, a single missing piece of sensitive equipment might end the career of a commander or empty the pocketbook of a soldier. In Vietnam, it was just a part of doing business, and usually business was good.

**—101st Airborne Division, I Corps, 1969**

I arrived in Vietnam in 1969 as an infantry lieutenant, but I was not sent to a regular unit. The replacement folks had reviewed my records and, because I had a master's degree in agriculture, they forwarded my file around to various head-quarters. The legendary John Paul Vann, who ran the war in the Delta, took a look at my records and instead of humping a rucksack as an infantry platoon leader, I was assigned to MACV's Civil Operations/Revolutionary Development Support (CORDS) to introduce new varieties of rice seeds that would increase production for the South Vietnamese farmers.

As a reserve officer who had no plans to remain in the military after my minimal obligation, I accepted the assignment—of course I really had no choice. I had a few regrets about not serving in the infantry, but looked forward to putting some of my agricultural background to work as well as a desire to help the South Vietnamese people.

CORDs assigned me to Chuong Thien, the only province in the Mekong Delta at the time that did not have an agricultural advisor. There were fewer than 170 Americans in the entire province and only 30 to 40 advisors actually worked outside the small army compound at the provincial headquarters in Vi Thanh. At one time during my tour, the U.S. military and the CIA classified Chuong Thien as the least-secure province in Vietnam. Conversely, of course, that meant that the VC considered it their most secured province.

My duties were to distribute the high-yielding IR8 rice seeds to the local farmers. Even though The International Rice Research Institute (IRRI) in the Philippines had first introduced IR8 in late 1966 throughout Southeast Asia to launch the Green Revolution, by the time I arrived in the Delta in July 1969, the farmers of Chuong Thien had only about four square miles of the crop in the entire province.

In my initial overflights of the province, I quickly learned to spot the semidwarf IR8 variety. It had short, stiff stems that held it erect while the traditional tall varieties toppled over, losing their grain. Instead of stalk, IR8 converted soil nutrients and water into heavy heads of rice and held them upright.

For centuries Asian farmers had produced about one to one-and-a-half tons of rice per hectare. IR8 increased this production to five or six tons per hectare. The international press called IR8 the "miracle rice." Its official Vietnamese name was Lua Than Nong—"Rice of the Farming God." The Vietnamese farmers had the simpler and more descriptive name of Lua Honda—because one IR8 crop paid for a coveted new motorbike. The North Vietnamese were aware of the rice variety, but without sources for it called it Nong Nghiep 8 or "Agricultural 8."

Our compound received the occasional rocket or mortar round, but we were mostly safe. American advisors who led South Vietnamese Regional Forces into the countryside were not so much so. Several were killed in ambushes or in brief firefight during my tour. Other than a working shift in the compound tactical operations center at night where I coordinated B-52 and other air strikes, I had little to do with the "fighting war." I spent most of my days in a jeep, in a sampan, or on foot delivering seeds to farmers and checking on their progress. Other than for an interpreter and a part-time security guard, I ventured into the countryside alone. I did carry my M16 and a bandoleer of ammo, but I usually wore civilian clothes. In the villages I met with local and South Vietnamese agricultural officials.

My not wearing a uniform and working fairly much on my own raised the curiosity of my fellow Americans. Several were convinced that I was CIA and that CORDs was just my cover job. Fortunately, the Viet Cong in the province did not share that opinion.

So I spent my entire tour spreading rice seed across the Delta—something like a modern Johnny Appleseed. By the time my year had come to an end, I felt good about what I had accomplished and hoped that it would have some far-reaching effects. There was a personal impact as well that would influence the rest of my life. Not long after I completed my tour, IRRI offered me a job and I would work for that organization for the next two decades.

In 1988, IRRI sent me to what had been South Vietnam to see how the rice production was progressing and to discuss new varieties with the Communist officials. In Chuong Thien, my host was Tran Van Rang, the vicechairman of the Vi Thanh Province People's Committee. Two decades earlier, he explained, he had been the Viet Cong political officer for the area. I was aware that political officers had the ultimate power over regular military leaders and could give them orders.

Rang told me that he remembered me, saying that I was in his territory when I went out into the province. He said that all local farmers supported the Viet Cong and that they reported on my movements. Rang added that he was often only a kilometer or away from me when I traversed the canals in a sampan and that my civilian clothes did not fool him at all.

He then really got my attention when he told me that he had many opportunities to kill me, but he had let me live because of the new rice seeds. Rice had not only become my vocation, but also had literally saved my life those many years before in the Mekong Delta.

—MACV, IV Corps, 1969

★ ★ ★

I was a FAC, a Forward Air Controller, in Vietnam from 1967 to 1968. As an air force officer I was assigned to the 505th Tactical Control Group but was attached to the 25th Infantry Division at Cu Chi. This was as short distance north of Saigon, the South Vietnamese capital. In between were farms, some small and some enormous. The larger farms were typically orange plantations with great mansions and well-kept grounds. It was a beautiful country from the air.

My job was to direct air strikes usually delivered by F-100 fighters carrying 500-pound bombs and/or napalm. These planes could not release their ordinance without specific direction from a FAC who coordinated with a ground commander, if one was present; some missions were conducted in enemy-controlled territory where no friendly forces were on the ground. Almost always we delineated the target with smoke rockets. We would dive low, fire the rockets, using best guess aiming and pulling up quickly since we usually drew ground fire. It was not uncommon to bring home a plane riddled with bullet holes.

At 3:00 a.m. on May 9, 1968, in the dormitory-style barracks at the 25th Infantry Division Headquarters, a hand on my shoulder brought me awake. An FAC mission was required. I quickly donned my flight suit and boots, headed out into the moonless and starless night for a short jeep ride to the flight line. The crew had my gray, single engine O-1 ready. I did a quick preflight and then strapped in to the high wing FAC plane. I pushed both side windows up until they locked under the wings so I could put my arms out each side of the plane and channel air up the sleeves of my flight suit. This would dry the sweat that was already flowing down my back.

Once in the air, I turned as directed toward the mission area. A reinforced infantry battalion was under devastating attack by the Viet Cong and NVA. The battalion was dug into flat farmland about twenty miles southwest of Cu Chi. Their armored vehicles had been positioned in a 150-meter circle, and each was placed in a hole dug by bulldozers. Only the cannons and guns were visible above the encircling earthen berm. There were several large artillery pieces—155mm and 175mm—inside the perimeter.

When I arrived above the scene, a Spooky C-47 gattling gunship had the entire area illuminated with flares, but the encampment would have been clearly visible in any event. Many vehicles and guns were on fire, delineating the circular perimeter. Two army helicopter gunships were doing their best around the perimeter; they reported their actions to me. I tuned into the ground commander's radio frequency to discover that the artillery commander had been killed and many others were dead or wounded. The perimeter had been breached in several places and the troops were engaged in fierce hand-to-hand combat. The commander's voice was grim, and behind his voice I could hear, through his microphone, a steady cacophony of small-arms fire and people screaming and yelling. I flew about 600 feet above the ground to get a better view of the battle.

Three flights of fighters had already been launched and were due on station within moments. All were armed with napalm. It was important to get the Spooky and two army gunships clear of the area to enable easy access for the fighters. When I radioed them, they pulled back immediately and the first flight, Buzzard 15, reported in on the fighter channel at 0410. It was necessary to keep three radios tuned in at all times to properly coordinate among all the forces in the area. Buzzard reported that they could see the area, but we spent a moment on the formality of confirming orientation since I would not be marking the site with smoke rockets.

The ground commander reported an enemy penetration of the south perimeter and I directed an east-to-west bombing run. Because of the emergency situation, I requested a strike within fifty meters of the perimeter, a dangerously close drop, especially on a dark night with considerable smoke rising from the battle site. Any farther away would probably do little good. The fighter pilots, four of them, in succeeding runs, dropped their ordnance beautifully. The ground commander reported that the unit had a few minor burns because the splash of napalm came within fifteen meters of his troops. He said the run was perfect and another just like it would help.

The second flight, Buzzard 07, was available as soon as the first flight's ordnance was expended. We continued to hammer the southern perimeter. By the time the third flight, Dice 05, was working. I began to receive heavier ground fire. The staccato AK-47 fire was easily recognizable and I could see some tracers from a .51-caliber gun. None of the fire was accurate enough to force a change in my position, but I did turn off my running lights and, occasionally, I flew with one rudder pushed in as far as I could comfortably hold it, on the off-chance that the enemy gunners could see my plane in the glare of the ground fires. This illusion was intended to mislead ground gunners by suggesting a false flight path.

The ground commander suddenly reported that they were now being overrun on the northern perimeter. I ordered a fighter about to drop napalm on the southern end of the perimeter to make a dry run and save his napalm for the north perimeter. The fighters were able to orient easily for an east-west run, and the next plane dropped napalm very close to the northern perimeter. After four more drops, the commander reported that this had stopped the attack. In fact, he reported that all enemy activity had ceased, so I directed the last fast-movers to make their napalm runs out from the perimeter and along a tree line that seemed the likely enemy retreat route. No sooner had the last fighter left the area than the Spooky and gunships reported in, ready to follow up.

The Spooky gattling gun used many tracers and its fire looked like waves of northern lights as it shredded the trees on the escape route. The gunships went in low looking for survivors and operated until out of ammunition. The attack had been costly, but the enemy had been repelled. The mission lasted for some three hours and morning light was beginning to glow when I returned to Cu Chi. The reliable O-1 had sustained several hits; the ground crew was always ready to point these out.

At division headquarters the next day, several large and burly men approached and openly hugged me as they thanked me for the mission. They said that the napalm saved their lives; they were sure they would have been overrun and killed if the fighters had not arrived when they did. Within a few days a mass grave was found west of the site containing many enemy dead.

**—505th TCG, 25th Infantry Division, III Corps, 1968**

There was a two-month period early in 1970 when we were not finding the enemy, or least not in force. Our area of operation was usually not too far away from Xuan Loc. When the enemy became scarce, our AO was moved further east.

On patrol we would stay off the trails, hacking our way through triple-canopy jungle with machetes, because the trails were often booby trapped. We felt much safer cutting our own pathway even though at times we slowed to a snail's pace. During the frequent stops, we would bend over at the waist to provide some relief to our lower backs after the strain of carrying 80-pound rucksacks. Making our own trail also made it less likely that our movement would alert the locals to our presence, although I am sure that the noise of our machetes carried for quite a distance. We stayed a thousand meters or more away from all villages, again to try to keep the locals guessing as to our location.

The jungle was no-man's-land, and it was assumed that anyone we encountered in the area was Viet Cong or NVA. The locals, for the most part, used the available roads and stayed away from the jungle pathways. So when we found a jungle trail, we would look for footprints. If we found recent activity, we would usually set up an ambush.

The primary focus of the ambush was three or more Claymore antipersonnel mines. The M-18 Claymore had seven hundred or more steel balls embedded in epoxy in the shape of an arc, backed by a couple of pounds of C-4 plastic explosive. It was very effective at penetrating through the jungle undergrowth to blast the steel balls into whoever was within range (usually about twenty yards). With the ambush we would set up a trip wire across the trail, hooked to a flare—or maybe trip wires in series—so that if Victor Charlie tripped the first flare and took off running down the trail, he would trip the second and third flares as well, lighting up our fields of fire.

We detonated the Claymores with electricity. First, we would aim the mines in different locations on the trail, and run a wire from each mine back to our night watch position. We hooked the wire from each mine to its own detonator. The detonator had a small palm-size lever to push that would generate an electrical current to detonate the mine. Typically, we would set up the ambush in a linear or L-shape pattern with fields of fire converging on the kill zone. We then set up watches of one hour to two hours in duration for each group of two to four soldiers.

On watch, the guard faced the trail, with the Claymore detonators within easy reach. When a trip flare went off, it was the responsibility of those on watch to immediate blow the Claymores.

On May 2, 1970, operating east of Firebase Blackhorse my unit—the 3rd Platoon, Bravo Company, 2nd Battalion, 3rd Infantry, 199th Light Infantry Brigade—set up an ambush under triple-canopy jungle, along a muddy trail that had footprints that were less than a day old. Just before dawn, a trip flare went off. Not being on guard, I was asleep when the concussion of three Claymore mines lifted me off the ground. Then I heard the ear-splitting chatter of the M60 machine gun spraying 7.62mm bullets up and down the trail, joined by a cacophony of M16 5.56mm rounds. I rolled over on my stomach, very much wide awake, looking for human shapes in the dim light cast by the trip flare. I emptied three M16 magazines in short bursts, shooting at shadows in the eerie light.

There was no return fire that I could see or hear. The platoon leader called a cease-fire after a couple of minutes of free-fire mayhem. We watched the tripped flare dwindle to a flame and then puff out leaving us in utter darkness once again. I lay in my firing position, pumped full of adrenalin, listening and watching for any movement in the darkness in front of me. How many VC were out there? A few or a few dozen? Did we just surprise the lead element of an enemy unit? Racing through my mind were all the possibilities about what tripped the ambush. Like my buddies around me, I pushed those thoughts aside and concentrated instead on the darkness. I could hear no movement, no sound at all other than the constant buzz of dozens of mosquitoes around my sweating head and neck. After an hour or so at full alert, the grey of dawn lit up the few patches of sky in the jungle canopy overhead.

When the sun arose, my squad crept forward to investigate. None of us had seen a human in the light of the flare, and for all we knew, the flare could have been tripped by a deer or some other large animal.

But it was no deer. Out on the trail, we found three rucksacks stitched with Claymore fragments and bullet holes. There was one heavy blood trail apparently left by a wounded Viet Cong making a getaway.

We opened up the rucksacks to see if we could find any enemy documents. Much to our surprise, the first rucksack contained women's garments—black pajamas and underclothing—as well as a sizeable quantity of drugs in vials, some surgical tools, a diary written in Vietnamese, and a French medical journal. The other two rucksacks contained rice, 7.62mm ammunition, and men's clothing.

We had captured a lot of male uniforms and equipment in the past, but this was the first female clothing we had seen in the jungle. Considering most of the GIs were eighteen or nineteen years old, the conversations that followed were predictable.

"I wonder if she was a babe?" asked a soldier who hailed from somewhere in California.

"Yeah," mused another from New Jersey, "She could be traipsing around the jungle with no blouse on, since we got it here."

"Yeah, and no pants, either," another added.

Each of the glass vials was topped with a metal band that secured a rubber membrane so that the needle on a syringe could pierce the top and the drug could be drawn into the syringe without opening the vial. All of the writing on the vials was in French, and we had no clue as to what clear liquid each contained. "Wow, man, maybe these are some good drugs," said our street-wise machine gunner who hailed from Philly. "Maybe there're bennies or speed. Speed comes in vials."

"No, these are some kind of hospital drugs," said our platoon medic. "Probably something they use for surgery since they were in a rucksack with scalpels and stuff."

We followed the blood trail only a short distance to see if there was a body to go with it, but there was none. We stopped finding blood twenty meters or so down the trail.

The platoon leader reported our find to battalion and they relayed the information on up the chain of command. Brigade intelligence was interested in the diary so they sent out a chopper to retrieve the medical rucksack and drop off a fresh supply of Claymores and ammo.

After a quick delayed breakfast of C-rations, we were off to another suspected infiltration trail, a good day's hump from the one we'd blasted the night before.

As we moved off into the jungle, a native of Tennessee took the point. The California soldier yelled to him, "Hey, let us know if you see that topless mamasan running around the jungle. I want a good look."

—**199th Light Infantry Brigade, III Corps, 1970**

On the afternoon of March 21, 1967, I was listening in to radio traffic in the Tactical Operations Center (TOC) of the 2nd Battalion, 35th Infantry, 25th Infantry Division. I drifted off into a catnap before being awakened by heavy message traffic about C Company being in severe contact. I had been in country for nearly a year and had been a platoon leader in C Company from July to December 1966, before joining the TOC in the S-3 Operations section. In the meantime, I had been promoted to captain. I was seriously thinking about extending for six more months in country in order to be able take command of a rifle company. Before the day was over, the decision had been made for me.

Since the first of the year, the battalion, as well as the rest of the brigade, had been working the wild, unpopulated jungle of western II Corps from a series of artillery fire support bases perched on the cleared tops of several hills. The battalion was experienced but tired. Only a week before the battalion's A, B, and C Companies had been in a fight with an estimated battalion of NVA. It was surmised that the NVA had recently infiltrated into South Vietnam as their uniforms, equipment, and weapons were nearly new.

In the battle that lasted from March 11 to 12, 14 Americans were killed and another 46 wounded. Enemy body count numbered 55 with an estimate of another 150 killed and their bodies removed from the battlefield.

Among the American KIA was a young second lieutenant in B Company who had only been in the field for a few weeks. Although inexperienced, he had proven his valor in a very short time. Early in the fight he dashed into an open space under intense fire to throw smoke grenades to mark friendly positions for the attack helicopters. He then moved among his men, directing their fires and forcing the enemy to withdraw. In the midst of the battle, an enemy sniper shot the lieutenant in the chest just above his heart. He refused aid from his medic, placed his finger in the bullet hole to stop the bleeding, and continued to lead his platoon.

The lieutenant directed his men into a defensive position just before the enemy reorganized and resumed their attack. After several hours of exchanging fire, an NVA crept to the edge of the American perimeter and tossed a hand grenade between the lieutenant and two wounded soldiers. Although the lieutenant was in a protected position, he leaped from his cover and placed his helmet over the exploding grenade. His action saved the lives of the two wounded soldiers but added wounds to his own legs. Despite the chest and leg wounds the lieutenant continued to direct the actions of his platoon before he died several hours later. I guess they presented his Medal of Honor to his family—but I did not hear about it until much time and many more battles had passed.

Now less than week later after a brief rest at Fire Support Base Dragon, the battalion was once again committed back into the meat grinder known as infantry combat. The dead lieutenant had been replaced along with some of the other casualties. C Company had sustained fewer casualties, five wounded and none dead, in the previous fight so they were the focus of the next operation.

On March 17, 1967, C Company air-assaulted into a landing zone northeast of the battalion fire support base. Led by a company commander who was a highly decorated enlisted veteran of the Korean War and now a captain, the unit was somewhat undermanned with a total of ninety-nine soldiers. From the LZ the company proceeded westward through thick jungle and mountainous terrain toward a river to block possible NVA infiltration and exfiltration routes. After three days with no contact, the company turned back southward and moved toward the battalion FSB.

The company commander split the company into two columns about 600 meters apart with the 1st and 2nd Platoons to the east and the 3rd Platoon and the headquarters element (company minus) to the west. This separation allowed sufficient maneuver space while also permitting rapid reinforcement. Before moving out, the company fire support team plotted preplanned fires along the route of march. These preplanned targets placed fires on likely danger areas along the route from which the platoon leaders or company forward observer could rapidly adjust the fire if needed. The fires also provided known points from which the two columns could calculate their current positions.

At about 1550 hours, the 1st and 2nd Platoons came upon a bunker complex. While searching the area, they briefly took fire from a small enemy element that fled to the southeast. As the platoons continued their search of the bunkers, they again received fire, this time by at least five automatic weapons and various small arms. After receiving the report from the 1st and 2nd Platoons, the company commander reported the contact to battalion and requested that A Company, operating several kilometers to the northwest, move toward him. He then began maneuvering the company minus toward the two platoons that were in contact.

The company minus moved as rapidly as possible toward its other two platoons. About halfway to reaching the ongoing contact, the company minus came across a well-used trail. Despite precautions to secure a crossing of the trail, the company minus came under fire from an undetermined size enemy force at 1620 hours. The 3rd Platoon maneuvered to develop the situation while the headquarters section provided rear and flank security.

No sooner had the maneuver begun than the 3rd Platoon began receiving intense fire from the east. The company commander moved his command group to secure the flank and gain the top of a small hill. The good news was that they now occupied the high ground; the bad was that they could now observe at least a NVA battalion, later determined to be a part of the 66th Regiment, maneuvering against them.

The commander consolidated his headquarters and the 3rd Platoon, a force of only about forty men, on the hilltop just before the NVA began the first of three "human wave" attacks against the small command. Air support could not identify the ground positions so were of no help. The small command did have the advantage of two 106mm recoilless rifle teams. Assisted by artillery, the beleaguered Americans managed to repulse each attack, but the costs were high. At 1630 hours, the NVA attacked from three directions. In seconds the forward support team were all casualties and the company commander seriously wounded. He would lapse into periods of unconsciousness for the remainder of the battle. For much of this time, the company RTO, a SP4, took over the company's communication and coordination. Only one radio remained operational, and he used it to report to battalion, coordinate additional artillery, and to request help from the 1st and 2nd Platoons. That was not possible because the two platoons, although only 200 meters away, remained in a significant battle of their own.

During the fight by the 1st and 2nd Platoons, an RTO from the 1st Platoon was in contact with the TOC. In the midst of a message, he said, "I've got to put this radio down now and shoot." He left the radio mike open and M16 fire could be heard followed by the distinct sound of several AK-47s. The mike went silent.

It was about this time that the battalion commander, a veteran of the Korean War, ordered me to take his helicopter, the company executive officer, and several RTOs to attempt to join C Company and to assume command while he remained in the TOC to coordinate supporting fires and the other two rifle companies. I grabbed my rifle and rucksack and headed for the chopper pad. There was no fancy change of command ceremony to worry about—my greatest concern was just how I was going to find the company in the gathering darkness. A great sense of excitement and apprehension, mixed with more than a little fear, nearly overpowered me.

We finally found a small landing zone near the contact area, but we could not make radio contact with what remained of C Company. I recalled the helicopter and we headed back to the TOC.

Finally, at about 1730 hours, helicopters from the 170th Aviation Company spotted the 1st and 2nd Platoons and their supporting fires finally broke the enemy's primary attack. Back on the hilltop, however, the company minus continued to take sniper and mortar fire.

A Company, commanded by a Cuban refugee who was a veteran of the disastrous Bay of Pigs Operation, reached the 1st and 2nd Platoons at 1825 hours. After consolidating the perimeter, they cleared an LZ to evacuate the wounded. A Dustoff arrived at 2000 hours only to be shot down as it hovered above the clearing. This ended any further evacuation attempts from that LZ. Following directions from the battalion commander, they began to move 500 meters to the south to a larger clearing.

It was already well past sundown when we—the battalion S-3, the battalion surgeon, the C Company executive officer, several RTOs, and myself—once again mounted the battalion command helicopter to go looking for C Company. While A Company was linking up with the two platoons, we found a small LZ and then moved through the darkness to the C Company minus group. The jungle was ink black. As we moved, we could hear what we thought were enemy soldiers also moving through the jungle. At one point I bumped into a shadow. Thinking it was a member of our party, I was about to identity myself when I saw in the dim starlight the profile of an NVA. He must have recognized me at the same time. Neither of us made any attempt to fire our weapon. He turned and moved away as quickly as possible—I suspect every bit as frightened as I.

We finally linked up with the company minus about 2030. A half hour later a platoon from A Company joined us. The 3rd Platoon leader, although wounded, supervised the construction of poncho litters. The NVA had booby trapped several of the bodies of men killed outside the perimeter with their own grenades, adding to the wounded count. The walking wounded of the company minus then carried the more seriously wounded to the new extraction LZ while the platoon from A Company provided security. By 2230 hours the remainder of A and C companies joined us on the LZ where the battalion S-3 took charge of evacuating the wounded, including the former C Company commander, and then the dead. This was completed by 0130 hours on March 22.

B Company air assaulted into an LZ to our south at 1030 hours the next morning. C Company was extracted and returned to the battalion FSB to refit and reorganize.

Over the next several days A and B Companies found more than sixty enemy bodies. It was estimated that three times more were killed but not found. Our casualties totaled twenty-four dead and fifty-five wounded, nearly all from C Company. On March 25, 1967, Easter Sunday, the battalion chaplain conducted memorial services.

I had replaced the wounded company commander. The only officers in the company still able to perform their duties were the 2nd Platoon leader and the executive officer. Within days two new platoon leaders and an artillery forward observer reported for duty. We also received forty-one E-2s and E-3s from the week-long in-country training course. Less than two weeks earlier, these men had been on the predeployment leaves back home with their loved ones and family. Now they had joined the meat grinder.

An interesting paradox of war occurred when the truck loads of replacements arrived. My first sergeant, whose company clerk had recently finished his tour and returned home, asked, "How many of you know how to type?"

A single hand went up and the new soldier became the company clerk—just one of the examples of the inequalities in a combat zone. Men with skills such as mechanics, cooks, medical, etc. were pulled out of the system and assigned to support units. Those without ended up in the infantry. In this case the rudimentary skill of operating a typewriter was the variable that would keep one soldier off the front lines and in the relatively safe confines of a the company orderly room in a FSB.

Some of the wounded trickled back in from the evacuation hospitals; others we would never see again. We promoted several SP4s to sergeants or acting sergeants and we quickly began to at least resemble a rifle company. Despite losing half the company, we were back in the field within two weeks. Training was "on the job," and generally the response from the soldiers was good—they were well aware that their lives depended upon each other.

The first of April we returned to normal operations—whatever that was. The company field strength grew to over one hundred. The battle of March 21 had made me a company commander. My decision a short time later to extend my tour by six months ensured that I would remain in command.

**—25th Infantry Division, II Corps, 1967**

I did not come from a military family. My mother's grandparents immigrated to America from Germany and Italy to allow their sons to avoid conscription into their country's army in the latter part of the nineteenth century. My father's only remark about family military history was that we had seven relatives who served in the Civil War. He made no mention that they fought on the losing side. He was of the right age to be drafted in World War II but received a critical occupation deferment because he farmed and ranched. It was a pretty good indication of the ranch's success, and our finances, that we could not afford horses. We herded the cattle the old-fashioned way—on foot.

I once heard my father say that he would not have hesitated to serve if called upon, but he never was. That was a good thing. I don't know what my mother and older brother, who was an infant at the time, would have done by themselves on the remote West Texas spread that was five miles from the closest neighbor and twelve miles from the post office and nearest telephone.

My father never made any comment about producing beef, wheat, and cotton for the war effort. He did say that perhaps his greatest contribution was to serve as a target to be buzzed by the women pilots training at nearby Avenger Field in Sweetwater while he plowed his fields on a bright orange tractor.

The house we grew up in was four rooms, no running water or central air and heat. In fact, we did not even get electricity until shortly after my birth in 1946. Neither my brother nor I had any desire to remain on the ranch. During our formative years, from 1950 to 1957, the Great Southwest Drought was the center of our world. For seven years there were little rain and no crops. My father divided his cow herd in half, and then in half again, and then again until he had only a few head remaining. Dad selling cattle and Mom pinching pennies, combined with mortgaging the land, got us through the drought, but it left my brother and me both looking forward to seeing what was over the horizon.

My brother and I came of draft age in the late 1960s, and the U.S. Army appeared to be the fastest, furthest ticket out of West Texas. Times had improved some with drought-ending rains that allowed my father to rebuild his herd and produce an annual cash crop of cotton. My father told my brother and me that the ranch was not big enough to support two families, much less three, so we should not anticipate marrying and moving back home. There was no chance of that: we were off to see the world and all the fun, travel, and adventure that the army promised.

Part of that travel and adventure, if not fun, ended up being orders for Vietnam. I was still at home when my brother went off to war. Shortly after his departure, my mother secured a three-by-five-foot map of South Vietnam on the living room wall—nearly covering its entire surface. I don't know where she got the map, but I doubt if my frugal mother put out any money for it. Likely, it came with a newspaper or magazine. Each time my brother wrote home from a new place in country, my mother studied the map to find it and then placed a pin in the location. She had some kind of color system for current and past locations, but I never paid all that much attention.

My brother ended up extending and did not return home until eighteen months later. By that time mother's map had pins all over II Corps and adjacent areas. Mom did not take the map down. It remained on her wall. She said nothing, but I was well aware that she knew that I would soon be in country. During my twelve months in Vietnam, my mother added more pins, this time in the III Corps part of her map.

I don't know what my dad did during my brother's tour. I was too busy growing up and having a good time to really notice. Not until I got home did I learn from mother and several neighboring farmers how my dad passed the time.

Shortly before I left for Southeast Asia, I purchased a pocket-size transistor radio for dad. They had just become small enough and cheap enough to be really desirable. I never saw him listen to it while I was home, but after I left, he spent the late spring and summer in his cotton field hoeing out the weeds and Johnson grass from among his cotton stalks. This was a job at the time that migrant workers usually performed. I never heard of my father before or after my time in Vietnam hoeing cotton, but that how he spent much of my tour. As he went down the long rows, he kept the transistor radio in his shirt pocket. The top of each row, he would stop, turn on the radio, and listen to see if there was any war news from far, far way.

After my return and the war wound down so neither my brother nor I was in danger of going back, my parents resumed their previous way of life. Mother finally took down her map. Dad put his radio in as desk drawer. After they passed away a couple of decades later, I looked for mother's map in her effects. I was not surprised not to find it. She did not keep anything that was no longer useful. My brother read this story and said he thought he had the map. I paid him no attention—my story is better.

I did find my father's radio, its insides so corroded by the old batteries that it no longer worked. I really did not care because I knew how important the map and radio had been in helping get my parents though two and a half years of having their sons in the infantry in Vietnam. We had come home; that is all they cared about.

—**West Texas, 1966–70**

We had a tall, skinny guy from an Iowa corn farm in our company. He told us that just before he left for Vietnam he had gotten a great buy on a motorcycle and was looking forward to riding it when he got home. He had only been in country for a brief time before he got a letter from his parents explaining that the county sheriff had been out to the farm and had confiscated the bike. The reason it had been so cheap was that it was stolen. So he lost his money and his motorcycle.

During those long days and nights in the jungle, the Iowa farm boy also revealed a bit more of his past. When he graduated from high school, he was not really interested in college. He did not want to be drafted and have no choice about his specialty assignment so he went to his army recruiter and volunteered. By doing this he incurred a three-year commitment rather than the two years of a draftee. The extra year was worth it, however, as he would get to select his military occupation specialty and avoid frontline combat and perhaps not be sent to Vietnam at all. He should have read the fine print.

He finally settled on the specialty of refrigeration repair. Working on air conditioners and refrigerators would surely be better than humping a rucksack in the jungle. Everything went according to plan in his training until one morning when he was not feeling so good and gave some back talk to one of his sergeants. I don't know what he said, but it was enough to get him kicked out of refrigeration repair school.

The small print of his enlistment contract stated that if he did not successfully complete his training that the army could reassign him according to the needs of the service. The biggest need of the service at the time was, of course, infantry. After eight weeks of advanced infantry training, he joined us in the boonies—with not an air conditioner or refrigerator anywhere near.

One time he showed me a letter he was writing to his mother telling her we were back in the jungle after a great stand down. He wrote her that during the break we had seen a Filipino band complete with a stripper. He added, "But I didn't look, Mom."

Despite losing his motorcycle and becoming a grunt, he remained in good spirits and became an outstanding soldier. After several months and many firefights had passed, he was promoted to sergeant and took the leadership of one of the squads. One morning just after we had moved out of our night defensive perimeter, we got in a brief firefight. In less than a minute, the Iowa farm boy lay dead on the jungle floor. I don't think that would have happened if he had been fixing air conditioners.

**—199th Light Infantry Brigade, III Corps, 1969**

In 1969, one of our missions in the 101st Airborne Division was to patrol Rocket Ridge. This range of mountains ran along the coastal plain in I Corps and overlooked Camp Evans, which contained the brigade headquarters. The high ground had received its name because it offered excellent terrain from which the NVA could fire rockets, mostly 122mm, into the compound. The rockets rarely did any damage to the base, but they worried the hell out of the brass who never left the safety of the circle of concertina wire.

After humping up and down and across the ridge, I came to a realization. With no more than twenty men and a mobile rocket launcher or two, the NVA kept an entire infantry battalion of nine hundred men effectively tied up and limited our search for major enemy units—all to keep the folks at the brigade headquarters feeling secure.

**—101st Airborne Division, I Corps, 1969**

It was a dark and stormy night. Or it was a night like all the others, but not like the others. It was monsoon season in South Vietnam. I was flying an EC-121R, call sign Bat Cat, on an all-night electronic reconnaissance mission.

I was in contact with a radar intercept controller for the area on the ground at the Pleiku air field. There was very little happening that night. Because the weather was so bad, no interdiction flights were in the air and no forward air controllers were flying either. We were just boring holes in the sky and the guy on the ground was just bored.

The EC-121R (Lockheed Super Constellation) is known for its oil consumption. A pilot preflighting his aircraft who did not find the bottom of the fuselage coated in oil knew that it had either just come from the wash rack, or something was badly wrong. I had flown flights where the mission was terminated early because of high oil consumption.

The radar controller, well aware of the Connie's oil problems and likely bored from his night duties, called on the radio and asked, "Hey, Bat Cat, why don't you just go home?"

I responded, "I would be very happy to go home, but I'm wondering why you are so anxious to get rid of me."

He replied, "I'm tired of you helping Charlie!"

"And how am I helping Charlie?" I asked.

The controller responded, "You are putting out so much oil that all Charlie has to do is just slide down the Ho Chi Minh Trail!"

**—553rd Recon Wing PACAF, Korat, Thailand, 1970**

Bob Hope gave his 1967 Christmas Show to 1st Infantry Division at Lai Khe. Only two men from my helicopter gunship platoon were allotted to attend, one pilot and one enlisted crewman. So we drew straws, and as with all the pilots except one, I didn't get to go. However, four of our helicopter gunships were assigned to fly cover and rocket-and-mortar watch. There were about a dozen helicopter gunships flying around the perimeter of Lai Khe during the show to discourage Charlie from trying to disrupt it. The operation was well organized with a sector assigned to each fire team, and we were cleared to immediately fire if necessary. As a young twenty-year-old Nebraska farm boy, I felt extremely honored to play an active role in protecting Bob Hope, Raquel Welch, and the rest of the troupe. To this day, I look back at that mission and feel a sense of pride and purpose, more so than if I had gone to the show.

**—1st Infantry Division, III Corps, 1967**

Other than the end of your tour, one of the few things to look forward to in the boonies was the resupply bird. Sometimes it came every two or three days; at other it was a week between resupplies. When we were in the midst of a firefight, there might be an emergency resupply of ammo, grenades, etc., but no creature comforts. During my two tours as an infantryman in Vietnam, I saw many changes, including what was contained in the resupply packages.

During my first tour in 1966 with the 1st Cav, resupplies, no matter how often, consisted of C-rations, cigarettes, and pieces of uniforms for those who had worn theirs out. Incoming mail was, of course, the most looked-forward-to item of resupply. Outgoing mail to let family and friends know we were okay was also important. Soldiers coming and going on R&R were also a staple of resupply.

By my second tour with the 101st Airborne in 1969, resupply missions had become much better. In addition to mail and C-rations, there was an SP pack designed to be issued to one hundred men. It contained cigarettes, chewing tobacco, writing paper and envelopes, boot laces (always in demand to help in making poncho hooches), toothbrushes and toothpaste, shaving gear, and half a dozen kinds of candy. The only thing I ever heard anyone complain about concerning the SP packs was that there were too many unfiltered cigarettes (Luckies, Camels, and Pall Mall) compared to the brands (Winston and Marlboros) more popular with the young troops.

—**1st Cavalry Division and 101st Airborne Division,**
**I Corps, 1966 and 1969**

Depending upon which figures you take a look at, from 2.5 to 3.9 million Americans served in Vietnam or its surrounding countries and waters. The most widely accepted number is 2.9 million. It is interesting to note that the Department of Defense never kept definitive figures of how many soldiers, sailors, airmen, marines, and coasties went to Southeast Asia. In part this may have been because the numbers of service members who were there for only a day or two on passing aircraft or on ships that briefly cruised nearby could not be tracked.

At the height of the war, half a million Americans were in Southeast Asia. With that huge number, one might think that there were a lot of strangers in country who had never met. A dead soldier might be known and mourned by only a few, mostly from his own unit. Such was not the case. Those who served in Vietnam were a small community and those who actually fought the war were even smaller.

Fewer than one in ten young Americans eligible for Selective Service were ever actually drafted or volunteered to serve in uniform. There were education and job exemptions and every city, town, or village had a sympathetic or antiwar doctor who would provide medical reports saying an old football knee injury or other malady made a potential draftee physically ineligible. Still other young men claimed mental problems or declared themselves homosexuals to avoid the draft. The ultimate dodge of the draft was simply to move to Canada, Sweden, or another country that refused extradition.

Many of those who did serve were those who did not have the connections or finances to take the route of their brothers who did not want to be "in arms." Others saw military service as a duty to their country that, while it might be inconvenient and dangerous, was something they had to do. A large group also came forward to serve because they recognized the Vietnam was the most significant event of their generation, and they did not want to miss it.

The result was inductees from the farms of the south, the mines of Appalachia, the ghettos of the big cities, and small towns across the country. These young men went through basic and advanced individual training together and they ended up in Vietnam together. The community got even smaller when the new arrivals reached the infantry units that sustained the vast majority of the casualties. In fact, only 20 to 30 percent of those who served in Vietnam ever experienced any amount of sustained combat.

All of this became very obvious to me when we returned to Firebase Blackhorse south of Xuan Loc in early July of 1969. We had had a difficult couple of weeks with several major fire-fights in which we had taken a number of killed and wounded. Everyone was sad about losing their buddies but were happy to be alive and have the opportunity to get a shower, a clean uniform, and a mess hall hot meal. Stacks of mail also awaited us, including several weekly magazines from the States that came to the company. I don't know if they were gratis or if some fund paid for the subscriptions.

On the top of the stack of magazines was the June 27, 1969, edition of *Life*. A black-and-white picture of a young GI stared from the cover with the caption, "The Faces of American Dead in Vietnam: One Week's Toll." Inside were the portraits of most of the 242 young men killed in Vietnam from May 28 to June 3. *Life* presented the pictures of the dead in a high-school yearbook format, listing the name, age, service, rank, and hometown of each.

The article about the pictures began with an explanation that there was no significance in the week selected other than it included Memorial Day and that the numbers of dead were average for any week for the current stage of the war. Following the pictures was a brief article about a few of the pictured dead.

The edition of *Life* sold a lot of copies back home and around the world. There was pseudo angst on the part of the war protestors about the loss of life. Those that supported the war, or at least its warriors, expressed outrage that the article and pictures backed the antiwar folks. Those dodging the draft back home or hiding in Canada must have felt relieved that they had not inconvenienced themselves and risked their lives with military service—and perhaps a bit of shame that they had not.

Our dead from the previous few days had been too recent to make the list. But almost every soldier in the company recognized someone. Some of the men expressed anger about the article in words only a soldier, or possibly a sailor, is familiar. Mostly, however, they just commented about recognizing the face of a friend or neighbor. I overheard men say, "Hey, I was in basic with that guy," or "Wow, we went to high school together," or even "Damn, he grew up right down street." We band of warriors were indeed a small community.

Personally, I felt *Life* had invaded our private world and gone where they had no right to go. They were our dead, and only we and their families could fully understand and feel for their loss.

I looked through the many pages and 242 names and pictures and felt fortunate that I did not recognize a single person. I guess it just was not my week, for the war took many of my friends away, including a best friend from high school who was killed with the 3rd Marine Division near the DMZ in July 1967. He had been seriously wounded the previous December and had just returned to his unit. One of my best friends in college died on May 28, 1970, as he led one of the point companies in the Invasion of Cambodia. He had also been my Ranger Buddy during that difficult training and once had placed my feet under his field jacket in the winter mountain phase to prevent frostbite. My best friend in Vietnam was killed on Veterans Day, November 11, 1969, as he led the battalion recon platoon in a fight against an NVA bunker complex where he earned a Distinguished Service Cross and a posthumous Purple Heart. He had replaced me as the reconnaissance platoon leader two weeks earlier.

Yes, we band of brothers were, and are, a small community. A saying that has recently been far overused is nonetheless no less accurate, "All gave some, some gave all."
**—199ths Light Infantry Brigade, III Corps, 1969**

I arrived in Vietnam in July 1967 and was assigned to the 116th Transportation Company in Cam Rahn Bay. At that time in the war only the infantry branch had more officers in Vietnam than the Transportation Corps.

My company was responsible for terminal services—in other words we unloaded incoming ships. The hours were long and the days very hot, but it was a very secure area and a safe place to sit out a year in Vietnam.

After several months, I got bored and decided that I wanted to get a better look at the war. It was not an easy process. My fellow officers and enlisted men in the 116th thought I had lost my mind to want to go "down range." My company and battalion commanders rejected my request but according to regulations it had to continue forward to U.S. Army Vietnam (USARV)—where it was approved.

Soon I joined the 1st Cavalry Division as a Movement Control Officer in the 1st Forward Support Element that supported the 1st Brigade. My duties included supervision of an enlisted soldier who worked at the LZ English airfield and another who worked with the riggers to sling supplies to field units by CH-47s. I also assisted in working up movement plans to transport the 1st Brigade anywhere in country.

LZ English was much closer to the real war than Cam Ranh Bay. The VC were mostly ineffective in their frequent mortaring of the firebase—but close enough for me to learn the locations of the nearest bunkers. The most difficult mission that I was involved in was assisting in the entire brigade's movement from LZ English to Camp Evans near Quang Tri. We had plenty of helicopters of our own and access to air force C-130s to move the brigade, but almost no trucks to disperse the men and equipment from their arrival airfields. We tried unsuccessfully to borrow some wheeled transportation from marine units in the area before finally a couple of truck battalions arrived from the south.

Before we could disperse the units, the NVA took advantage of the concentration of Americans to fire multiple 122mm rockets into the compound. One struck an infantry battalion tactical operations center, killing its commander and many of its staff. Later we heard small-arms fire along the perimeter. Rumors of being overrun swept the base. One of my men suggested that we drink up all of our beer to prevent it from being captured.

From my post at the Quang Tri Airfield, I frequently coordinated transportation for officers and troops to their units. On one occasion a captain, who had volunteered to be transferred from Europe to Vietnam, arrived too late in the day to be transported forward. I found him a place to sleep in my bunker. Early the next morning I put him on a helicopter for LZ Jackrabbit.

Another of my duties was to transport bodies of the dead brought to Quang Tri from the airfield to the morgue in Danang. About 1600 hours in the afternoon after I had put the captain on his chopper, an ambulance of dead arrived for transport. Among the dead was the captain; he had not survived his first day of combat.

By the outbreak of the Tet Offensive in early 1968, we had all of our units dispersed across I Corps. The Cav acquitted itself well in the month-long battle. I kept busy directing incoming and outgoing aircraft. Tet disrupted a lot of our activities, including in country administrative air sorties. Ultimately, we ended up with a fairly large contingent of GIs who had finished their one-year tours and were due to go home. Many of this group had also completed their overall service commitment and were only an official discharge away from being civilians.

When a C-130 delivered a new unit to the airfield, I learned that the plane did not have a further mission. I loaded as many of the completed-tour soldiers on the plane as I could and sent them south to the relative safety of Cam Ranh Bay. I later got some calls from higher headquarters with some comments about my unauthorized initiative, but at least I had got the soldiers closer to home.

Getting my own self around was also difficult during Tet. Near the end of the offensive, I was due to go on R&R to Australia but there was no transportation to Cam Ranh Bay. I finally hitched a ride on a Huey going to Danang but nothing was going south there. I began to think I was going to miss my R&R.

About that time, Gen. William C. Westmoreland flew in on his converted C-123, called the White Whale to visit with some USMC commanders. The plane's pilot said he would be happy to drop me off in Cam Ranh when they headed back south.

I arrived in Cam Ranh Bay with no civilian clothes, no khaki uniform for the flight, and no money. Fortunately, a friend assigned there found me some clothes and lent me some money. I was soon on the way down under.

Back in country, things fell into fairly much of a routine. There were always reminders, however, that death was never far away. Near the end of my tour, an air force OV-2 pilot asked if I would like to accompany him on a flight to Danang to pick up some beer and steaks for a unit party. I thought about it and then turned him down. There was going to be a Filipino Country and Western band at the club, and I decided to stay and watch the show. Late that evening I learned on his way back, the pilot had been asked to do a recon of the A Shau Valley. He had been shot down and killed.

My last job in Vietnam was to act as an official courier on the way back to the United States. It was my duty to ensure that 2,200 bolt-action rifles (Russian made M-144s) that had been captured made it back home as trophies for the Division Support Command. To transport the rifles, I had to go to Saigon and have the Provost Marshall stamp an individual piece of paper for the export of each rifle. This took several days, but they were well spent on my part as it gave me a chance to tour Saigon. Soon after returning to Quang Tri, I, with rifles in the plane's cargo hole, was on my way home.

**—1st Cavalry Division, I and III Corps, 1967–68**

Things could change quickly in Vietnam. In 1968, I was the commander of Headquarters Battery, 6th Battalion, 71st Artillery, a Hawk missile outfit stationed in the safe confines of the massive Cam Ranh Bay complex. Our mission was to serve as an antiaircraft screen for the area.

Late in the year, the Department of the Army came to two conclusions. First, it was unlikely that North Vietnamese MIGs or bombers were going to wander far from Hanoi. Second, the army, which was restricted in the numbers of soldiers it could have in country, was more in the need of infantrymen than air defenders. As a result, our battalion was ordered back to its home at Fort Bliss, Texas, allowing an additional infantry battalion to be sent to Vietnam.

Those with enough time in country had flown back to Fort Bliss the previous day. Those of us who did not were transferred to other units in Vietnam. I had orders assigning me to 1st Field Force Artillery. Early in the morning, my first sergeant dropped me off at Cam Ranh Air Base and took our last vehicle to be turned in at the shipping dock.

I flew to Nha Trang Air Base where I found my way to 1st Field Force Headquarters and presented my orders. I waited for a short time and then was received instructions to report to the 6th Battalion, 32nd Artillery, a 175mm gun/8-inch howitzer unit at Tuy Hoa. I was told that there was a 2:00 p.m. flight and that, if I hurried, I might be able to catch it, which I did. En route to Bien Hoa, we stopped briefly at Phu Cat, and then on to Tuy Hoa. By the time I arrived, it was early evening. At the airfield I encountered an NCO with a 1st Field Force patch who offered me a ride to the unit headquarters. I arrived after dusk and was immediately taken to see the battalion executive officer who told me that I was the now the battalion maintenance officer. In less than twelve hours, I had gone from a secure area in an air-defense unit with no targets to an artillery battalion supporting U.S. and Korean infantry troops in regular contact with the NVA and VC on the central coast of Vietnam. This was a new world for me; the adventure had begun.

**—1st Field Force Artillery, II Corps, 1968**

Those of us who flew in Vietnam were quite familiar with a wide assortment of white and blue fixed and rotary wing aircraft that also flew in-country. They were operated by Air America, a civilian airline that everyone knew was a front for the CIA. I had been around Air America pilots at Tan Son Nhut Airport, Bien Hoa Air Field, and Vung Tau. They were distinctive with their crisp white shirts, dark blue pants, neatly cut hair and sunglasses. I had flown a few special missions where I had received packages from, or delivered packages to, Air America pilots or crew. Most Air America pilots were former military pilots who "changed jobs" or assignments without leaving Southeast Asia. I was soon to learn just how much they were "like us."

One of my missions was to fly some operations personnel to Can Tho for a meeting. We were on short final with my copilot, who had only been in country for only a few days. when I heard a field controller order an Air America aircraft, "Do not land to the taxiway. Use the active runway." Just as I heard that transmission, a fixed-wing aircraft (a PC-6 Pilatus Turbo Porter) came right over the top of our Huey and touched down in front of us. Both of us were headed toward buildings at the end of the taxiway. I knew the short landing capability of the Turbo Porter, but I could not imagine that the pilot could stop that aircraft in such a short space.

I grabbed the controls and flared our Huey to stop our forward flight, resulting in a high hover. Just as I was flaring, the PC-6 stopped and did a rudder turn to the left. My rotor wash got under his left wing and nearly flipped the long-wing plane. It was balancing on its right gear with its left wing in the air. I could not see its right wing tip, but I presumed it was resting on the ground. I immediately set the Huey down to relieve the rotor wash, very relieved to see the PC-6 sit back down on both gears.

I was less than relieved though to see the white-shirted and sunglass-wearing pilot jump from his aircraft waiving a pistol in the air. He took a few steps toward us, then suddenly stopped, lowered his pistol, and put his other hand into the air. It was not until he put his hand up that I realized my left door gunner had his M60 machine gun aimed right at the pilot.

I looked back at the pilot and started laughing—my tense crew thought I had lost it, especially my newbie copilot. The Air America pilot was an old college friend. I motioned for him to approach the Huey and he reluctantly complied because my gunner was still trained on him and I was wearing a helmet with the visor down. I told the gunner to swing away from the pilot. As he approached I pulled off my helmet and pointed at my name tag.

We exchanged greetings and "what the hell are you up to" comments. I asked him if I could buy him a Coke (no booze while flying) after I parked the Huey off of the taxiway. He declined, saying he landed at the flight operations shack's front door because he had to grab a package and run. I asked if he thought his aircraft was OK. He replied, "Yes, that bird is a tough bitch."

He walked away and I never saw him again. He survived Vietnam but was killed in a car wreck soon after he got home. We never had the opportunity to retell that war story over something much stronger than a Coke.

**—1st Aviation Brigade, IV Corps, 1969**

In August 1967, I was the RTO for my company commander in the 4th Infantry Division. The job offered a good opportunity to hear and see what I might have missed if I had stayed in a regular squad—and I didn't have to walk point.

One afternoon our resupply helicopter landed in a very small LZ. A soldier, who I mistook for a staff sergeant, was the replacement artillery forward observer and, I learned later, a lieutenant, jumped off the bird and hurried to the nearby jungle. I had been in the army long enough to get used to the usual profanities, but this guy spewed a stream of cuss words from the time he got on the ground.

He came over to where our command group was standing and dropped to the ground next to a clump of bamboo. As he leaned back, he triggered a hand grenade booby trap that just tore his body all to hell. Small pieces of shrapnel hit me and the company commander but did little more than break the skin. The new FO and my radio had taken most of the blast.

We called for the chopper to return and loaded the FO's body aboard. He had been on the ground only a few minutes before he was killed. It must have been the shortest field tour of the Vietnam War.

—**4th Infantry Division, II Corps, 1967**

I had been in the army for only about six months—basic training, advance infantry training, and a thirty-day home leave—before I arrived in Vietnam. After a week of in-country training and orientation at the 199th Light Infantry Brigade's rear area, I reported to Bravo Company, 2nd Battalion, 3rd Infantry. Soon on a helicopter on the way to join the company in the jungle, I was already homesick, apprehensive about being the new guy, and scared of what the next twelve months would bring.

The helicopter landed in a small clearing between the jungle and a rubber plantation. A buck sergeant took charge of me and several other replacements, leading us into the straight rows of rubber trees. Along the way I spotted several two-man observation posts providing security and early warning. Inside the perimeter things were much more relaxed as men ate C-rations, smoked, or napped. My new, clean jungle fatigues and boots stood out among the absolutely filthy men on the ground. It was the rainy season, and mud covered uniforms as well as faces.

The sergeant took us over to what I could see from the multiple radio antennas was the company command post. We sat down for a few minutes before we quickly stood when the sergeant approached with a tall, thin man and said, "This is the company commander."

I had heard the men in the rear refer to the company commander, even though he was a first lieutenant rather than the usual captain, with the traditional title of "the old man." There were also stories that despite his youth, he had been in the field longer than any officer in the battalion. He sure did not look old to me, in fact he looked way too young to be a company commander.

The "old man" introduced himself and shook the hand of each of us as he asked where we were from. Before he told us to take a seat next to a rubber tree, I noticed that he had his boots and socks off as he aired his feet out from the rains earlier that morning. His feet gleamed white compared to his suntanned face and arms. I also noticed he had several running sores on his arms and even one on his jaw.

In my brief time in the army, my conversations with officers had been brief with me standing at attention. Sitting on the ground with the company commander talking about hometowns and what was going on back in the world seemed strange but was welcoming and even somewhat comforting.

After a few minutes, the lieutenant got serious and said that he had been in the field as a platoon leader for six months and had been in command of Bravo for two more. He then said something I have never forgotten. "All I ask is that you be careful, pay attention, and listen to your NCOs. If you do, you and the rest of us will survive this year—and then you can go home and fuck off for the next fifty years or so. One year for the rest of your life is really not asking for much."

—**199th Light Infantry Brigade, III Corps, 1969**

We had a brief firefight in July 1967 with some VC near a village. One of the dinks tried to hide in a bunker but we killed him with a hand grenade. The platoon sergeant ordered one of the new troops into the bunker to recover the body.

He went in with a dim flashlight and a .45 pistol. A few seconds later he dragged the torn-apart carcass of the VC out of the bunker. Only then did the soldier reveal that the VC was the first dead body he had ever seen. It would not be his last.

**—25th Infantry Division, II Corps, 1967**

I served in Vietnam in 1971 in the Corps of Engineers as a real estate officer. Pretty cushy job, right? That's what I thought, too. I was assigned to the Corps of Engineers branch after completing ROTC in college, presumably based on my agriculture economics degree. During branch selection, the cadet in line in front of me had an engineering degree so they put him in the infantry. I offered to go to the infantry in his place so he could be in the engineers. The NCO told me to get my butt in gear and move out. It all made sense at the time.

The real estate division in Vietnam had its headquarters in Long Binh with offices in each of the four corps areas. I was in charge of the branch in the Delta (IV Corps) with the office located in Can Tho, the biggest city in the area. Although only a lieutenant, I was a commander by virtue of my position, and, thus, automatically was a member of the State Department Club that contained a restaurant and bar where all the hot-shots hung out. In addition to the military, we had lots of civilians, State Department people, CIA, and other assorted folks because Can Tho was the major center of operations. People, regardless of assignment or rank, were nice to me because I was in charge of where everyone lived. Life was good.

Of course, I resided in the nicest place in town. It was a three-story duplex with an open courtyard in the middle. All stairs were situated in the courtyard. Our offices, kitchen, utility rooms, lounge, etc., were on the first floor. The second floor consisted of several bedrooms and baths. The third floor was a penthouse-type arrangement with a bedroom/bath suite, windows facing the front, and a balcony on the back with a ladder to the roof. I lived in the penthouse. Hey, I was in charge of real estate. No air conditioning or hot water but then no one had that.

My staff consisted of an interpreter, a secretary, a jeep driver, a body guard, an NCO who mainly scrounged around for anything we needed since we weren't assigned to a local unit for supplies, and assorted mamasans who cooked and cleaned. I had another NCO who was in charge of local Vietnamese security for our various properties around town. I never was sure where he got those guys. My personal security soldiers lived on the second floor. I had drilled them to run upstairs in case of attack. We could then fire down the stairwells into the courtyard until help came. An American military police station was only a few blocks away.

The folks on the other side of the duplex wouldn't tell me what they did, but it was pretty clear that they were CIA and Department of Defense Intelligence. I mean who else won't tell you what they are doing and are always talking about the alert category. They were nice enough but we didn't visit much.

So how can anything go wrong?

Because of the heat, I would sleep at night without any clothes on, covered only by a sheet which I soaked in water. I had a fan blowing across the sheet, which made it very cool and comfortable. I kept my M16 and .45-caliber pistol nearby but without clips in them. The street in front of my building was fairly major; occasionally there was sporadic gunfire, but not much.

I was sound asleep when the shooting started. I heard automatic rifle fire, pistol rounds, and people yelling like mad. Motorcycles roared back and forth. Most of the noise came from the street in front, but there was also a lot of commotion downstairs. Were the enemy already in the house? I was terrified, and when you are really scared, it is hard to pull a wet sheet off your body. When you finally get it off, it is even more difficult to pull on your pants because everything is wet and you are shaking like mad and your heart is pounding. I finally gave up on getting dressed and grabbed my weapons to head for the roof.

It is nothing to shove a clip into your weapon and take it off safety. I had done it hundreds of times. However, if you have one in each hand and unsure which clip is where, it is a little more difficult. I was also distracted because none of my people were coming up the stairs, and the gunfire was becoming more intense. I saw someone out of the corner of my eye and yelled "get up the ladder and go to the roof!" Nothing happened. So I yell again, "Did you hear me soldier? Get your butt on the roof and see what's happening." When I heard his response, I think the first thing that occurred to me was how silly I must look buck naked.

"Lieutenant," the soldier said, "this is Major Anderson, military intelligence. You get your butt up the ladder."

He looked like he had done this type of thing before and I was pretty sure he wasn't impressed with the fact that I was a real estate officer. So up I went. It is not that easy to climb a ladder with a weapon in each hand—especially when you are naked. It got even more complicated when the major told me that there was an armed Vietnamese security guy on the roof but that he really didn't know much about him. He suggested that maybe I should subdue him before doing anything else. Great!

The security guy was very surprised to see me pointing a gun at his face and yelled, "No shoot—*tungwi, ti ti VC* (No shoot, lieutenant, very few VC)." Having gotten that straight, we crawled to the front of the roof to see what is happening. The crawling reminded me that I didn't have anything on. There was still a lot of shooting and yelling going on so we crouched and observed. His assessment regarding the Viet Cong was almost correct. There weren't any.

In this late stage of the war, a lot of ARVN deserters operated as petty thieves, harassing the populace, and generally being a dangerous nuisance. Everyone hated them. We referred to these guys as cowboys. Apparently some cowboys had made the mistake of ripping off an ARVN military police officer when he was in civilian clothes. The MP had found some of his buddies and returned. The police and the cowboys had battled it out right in front of my house. Most of the gunfire that night had been from the military police, and it was pretty clear the cowboys had lost the fight.

I returned to my room and dressed. Then I went downstairs to find my staff and security. All of them were behind a bed in one room. Relieved that they hadn't seen me without any clothes, I made them go through the drill of running upstairs with their weapons over and over and over again. It felt great. Once again, I was a commander.

**—USARV, IV Corps, 1971**

A tour in Vietnam for soldiers was twelve months. Many did not stay around for anywhere near that amount of time.

In September 1969, I went to a memorial service for a MACV Military Assistance Team lieutenant who had been shot in the head while getting off a helicopter during an air-assault operation. The service was held in the mess hall where the chaplain replaced the red and white plastic checked table cloth with white linen. He then sat a steel helmet, a pair of jungle boots, and an M16 rifle on the table in front of a metal cross.

The chaplain began the service by explaining that he had met the lieutenant we were memorializing two weeks earlier at the memorial service for the lieutenant he was replacing. It was the new, now dead, lieutenant's first day with the team. His tour certainly did not last twelve months.

**—MACV, IV Corps, 1969**

Ⅰt was the dry season—December—but the jungle floor was soft and even moist in places. We moved without a sound to recon jungle trails. We had been doing this for three weeks. Twenty guys. Tired, hot, thirsty, smelly, stubble-faced, dirty, whipped, and fed up. We looked like unwashed hell.

I was thirsty. The day before a bamboo spine had punctured my five-quart bladder canteen, causing the water to leak out. So I was out of water, and water obsessed me. I also had several bamboo puncture wounds on my hands and insect bites too numerous to count. Last night, I was awakened in the jungle blackness by something crawling on me. I tried to brush it off, but it got me first, right on the hand. "It bit me!" I said aloud. "Quiet over there," whispered my squad leader. So I waited for the scorpion sting to take effect. Maybe I'd get out of the field. But no, it wasn't a scorpion. Not even much swelling, just a welt and very sore spot.

We in the battalion recon platoon walked in a file through the thick jungle from eight in the morning till one and again from two until eight in the evening. The whole thing was tiresome, irritating, boring, and aggravating nearly beyond endurance. It was the hardest thing in the world to be tired, hot, and hungry, loaded down with sixty pounds of gear, moving for hours at the rate of fifty feet every ten minutes and waiting for the dogs of war to be set loose at any second. I was sick of it.

We have been moving this way all morning and now into the afternoon. I looked at my watch. Three o'clock. Five hours to go. Better not to think of it. Think, instead, of being short— a little over three months to go.

My squad leader was behind me, and we were near the end of the file. A new guy, I'll call him McCarron, a machine gunner, was up front near the platoon leader, because the lieutenant liked to have one of the platoon's two machine guns close by.

We had moved from the rice paddies in the Delta into the jungles northeast of Saigon near Xuan Loc several months earlier. Unlike the Delta, mines and booby traps were not a problem here. We had told ourselves it would be better in the jungle, but, of course, war is war. Shortly after the move north, McCarron joined the platoon with several other replacements.

He was tall and thin with a handsome, friendly face and a manner that seemed somehow disconnected from the nasty business of war. One would not apply the soldierly terms "tough" or "gritty" to McCarron, more aptly "fun-loving" and "puppyish."

But McCarron was a good soldier. He moved when told, even when the incoming fire was intense. A couple weeks earlier, his assistant gunner was hit, but McCarron kept firing the gun.

During our mission of trail reconnaissance, we had frequent contact with the sizable unit of NVA who were in the area. But the firefights were brief. We had not had a prolonged battle, not lost a man—killed or wounded—since our platoon leader, a West Point graduate, was KIA a month earlier. The firefight we had a couple of days ago was typical. At the first sudden explosion of fire, we hugged the ground. Soon, the rattle of the machine guns started up, and we crawled to the front, got on line, and moved through the area of contact as we continued to fire. It was over in minutes. No body count that time. The NVA usually ran away. I don't blame them. Why engage us in a prolonged battle and bring our artillery and gunships down on their defenseless rear ends? I was glad they ran. The only one who cared about body count was the battalion commander. Sorry, sir, I thought, staying alive was more important than your career.

We stopped and I bent over to get the weight of my rucksack off my shoulders. I thought to myself, "If I ever get outta here, I'll never carry a heavy pack again."

McCarron waited patiently. Sometimes he smiled at some wayward thought. His fiancée, perhaps. That was the thing about McCarron—his inclination to smile, which was strong and spontaneous. Despite all the hardships and danger around us, he was a happy man.

Back at the base camp, three weeks ago, he had told me with obvious pride about firing his M60 machine gun in a previous contact as if he were describing his skill behind the wheel of a sports car. He seemed to get a real charge out of it. He described the merits of keeping the machine gun rounds low to the ground as calmly as if he were talking about how to play softball. I think that the reality of killing people was utterly beyond him. To McCarron, it was just a job.

Before we started this trail recon mission, we had to cross a swamp. It was an awful place. We were up to our thighs in smelly muck for hours. No chance to rest; the stench was nauseating. I was near McCarron at the time and saw him struggling to get over a log with his machine gun. He stumbled and nearly fell into the mire. Catching his balance, he saw that I was looking at him and broke into a big smile. I thought, "McCarron, you'd smile at the devil in hell."

That smile—it was almost unnerving, a little maddening. When he had been in the field only a couple days, something happened that sobered him for a while. In the evening, he was in front of the position putting out the Claymores for the night when he disturbed a hive of bees. Repeated stings set him on a brief but spirited romp through the jungle. I can still see him examining the stings. But in a few minutes, McCarron was smiling again. He absorbed it, like all the other pains and burdens of being a soldier.

We kept moving through the jungle. I thought to myself, "Will this ever end?"

At the start of this mission, we had sat all day long in the hot sun waiting for choppers to carry us to the landing zone. Waiting can be the hardest. The boredom becomes almost unbearable. At lunch I opened a can of fruit cocktail and poured off the juice into the dirt. McCarron was eating next to me.

McCarron said, as if I was a source of great aggravation, "Don't spill that. Now you're going to attract ants."

I looked at him and said, "They'll be over here, and I don't care."

"Yeah," he said, "but what if they start crawling over here?"

I shoved some dirt over the juice, glancing with some aggravation at McCarron, who was looking down with a wry expression.

He was like that—unshakeable in his good humor, something of a pain, but a delight at the same time; something of a joker but deadly serious about his job as a soldier.

He talked a lot about his life in New York City—his job and the commute. He bragged, as if it were a note of honor, to have commuted two hours each way—by train, then subway— to work downtown. The earnest look on his face made me think he considered this a matter of great importance to me, too. He had worked for a financial firm, and, as I recall, had been drafted later than most of us. I remember that he said they had reserved his desk at work for him when he returned. He was proud of that.

McCarron was generous with the frequent packages he got from home. His mother must have been a superb cook, or at least a great baker of cookies and other things. There was a fiancée, and he proudly showed us a photo of them together. He had his arm around her shoulders. She was half his size and very pretty.

I was thinking about how thirsty I was, how much my pack weighed, and how I wanted to go home when a cacophony of sound, harsh and insulting, split the jungle stillness wide open. I fell to the ground and crawled for cover as I rolled out of my rucksack and checked my weapon and ammo. Everything slowed down. Every nerve in my body was at its height as a crashing wave of fear washed over my entire body—numbing me. Up front a machine gun was going and rifle fire filled the jungle. I looked about frantically, but could only see one other soldier. He was wide-eyed, shaking his head, as if to say, "Damn, not again!"

My squad leader shouted and waved frantically, "Get to the front! Get to the front!"

Several other guys and I scrambled forward, running at a crouch, dodging from tree to tree. We passed a soldier who was folded up behind a log, his head in his hands. We kept going, pressing forward toward the focus of the roar. We passed another soldier half-lying behind a tree, watching us hurry past, waving his hand and saying, "Go on. Go on." As we got closer to the firing, we crouched and dodged from tree to tree.

Our squad leader yelled, "Over there, to the right, form a line."

I could see the lieutenant, McCarron, and several others strung out through the area of contact. My squad got on line, kneeling and laying down fire to our front. I could not see a target, but fired single rounds. McCarron was to my left.

"Move forward with fire. Move! Move! Let's go. Keep the line in order," yelled my squad leader.

We fired, rolled over, got up, and scrambled forward a few meters strides. Then we repeated the process as we moved through the contact area. The sounds of outgoing and incoming fire were horrendous.

Off to my left, I glimpsed a man cry out sharply and throw his hands to his face as he dropped like a rag doll and lay hidden in the under growth. At the same time, the soldier next to me yelled and with a crazed look, held up his bloody thumb. "Get back," I yelled at him.

"Medic!" someone screamed to my left.

A few seconds later, the lieutenant shouted, "Grenade!" and scrambled forward, grabbed the grenade, and threw it forward.

I then saw the lieutenant fire a long burst into a NVA soldier hiding in the brush.

We keep firing and moving. Someone was still screaming for a medic. Finally, the firing died down, like a passing thunderstorm of incredible ferocity. I stopped behind a bamboo thicket, looked about desperately, even more scared than before. I had never been more thirsty; sweat streamed out of me; my fatigue shirt was soaked. My ears were ringing. An acrid odor filled the air.

"How is he, Doc?" the lieutenant shouted.

"He's hopeless, sir," the medic replied, his voice downcast.

I heard the others talking in shouts, but calmly, getting a perimeter set up, calling for a dust-off. What seemed like a long time passed, though probably it was only minutes, when I heard the thudding of chopper blades in the distance, then louder and louder, until it is was right overhead, its downwash roiling the treetops. Soon a cable came down through the canopy and I saw through the foliage several people working at something in the grass. They stood back. In a little while, I saw a body hanging from the cable rise up through the jungle. The face was shrouded in blood and unrecognizable. The body was long and thin with arms outstretched. His shirt, which was open and flapped limply in the downwash, and his torso was crimson. The body rose above the foliage. The chopper leaned forward, gained altitude, and flew away. I was very thirsty and thinking of death and killing.

I saw the medic hunched over and obviously depressed. I asked, "Who got hit, Doc?"

"McCarron," he mumbled and turned away.

I didn't hear him or did not want to. "Who?" I repeated.

"McCarron," he said. I've never seen a man look more hurt.

I learned later that we had contacted a unit of NVA, probably a platoon or even a company. The enemy had scrambled out of the area, leaving behind three men to hold us off—a team. Two were killed straight away; the other was wounded and lay dying, hidden in the under growth, as we moved forward. He carried an M16. When we came within sight, he fired a long burst, which hit McCarron, the other rounds flying in front of me and hitting the man beside me on the thumb. The NVA soldier then tossed a grenade, which the lieutenant threw back. Fortunately, the ChiCom grenade was a dud. McCarron, hit by several rounds from gut to face, died almost at once. The lieutenant finished off the NVA.

Sitting in the jungle that evening, I recorded the events of the day as carefully as I could in my journal. Some details—the grenade being a dud, the same burst that killed McCarron had flown in front of me and wounded the man to my right—came only later. I really didn't know McCarron well enough—or maybe I was too young or immature or hardened by the war—to feel any real grief at the time.

When we got back to the main base camp, the chaplain conducted a memorial service. The lieutenant read a glowing synopsis of McCarron's brief military career.

Later, I wrote a letter to McCarron's fiancée. She wrote back. It was heartbreaking: "My Billy . . . Why was my Billy killed?" She told of the priest and two officers coming to the door to notify her of his death.

We just went on, mission after mission. A few other guys in the platoon were wounded—no one else was killed, that I recall—in the remaining months of my tour. As the years passed I largely forgot McCarron, except for a passing thought brought on, perhaps, by Memorial Day or some mention of the Vietnam War in a book or on TV.

Many years ago I visited the Vietnam Memorial in Washington, DC. I lingered before McCarron's name etched into the wall, and those of other soldiers I also had known. But that was that. Until lately, I did not dwell on the war or McCarron's death. Strange, but now I find it has never left me, and never will. I can see him so clearly.

**—199th Light Infantry Brigade, III Corps, 1969**

Fort Benning, Georgia, in 1968 was full of second lieutenants being trained for Vietnam. My Infantry Officer Basic Course was composed mostly of others like myself who had no plans of remaining in the military any longer than we had to. Several military intelligence officers were also in our class—a requirement by their branch before they received specialty training. We all got along in class and socialized together during the brief times we had off—with the single guys who lived on post gathering at the houses of the few married lieutenants who lived with their wives in nearby Columbus.

One of my friends was an Oklahoma City attorney who was commissioned in the military intelligence. I have no idea why he was not in the Judge Advocate General Corps or why he had not been able to avoid service altogether. Everyone, regardless of branch, had to pass the Land Navigation Course that consisted of reading a map, using a compass, and keeping an accurate pace count. The lawyer lieutenant failed the course twice. Once he got so lost that an NCO had to search the Georgia woods for him. The word was that failing the course three times meant loss of your commission and an immediate transfer to Vietnam as an enlisted rifleman. I thought that was unlikely for him with the need for lieutenants, but it was still a threat.

Our training was so concentrated that we worked even on the morning of the 4th of July, but we were given the afternoon off—that is, everyone except the lawyer who had to take the Land Navigation Course for the third time. My wife and I invited several lieutenants to our rented house for a backyard 4th of July barbeque. Our directionally challenged friend was to join us after he finished the navigation course.

We waited for him to join us until nearly sundown before we put ribs and chicken to the grill. Finally, sometime after 8:00 p.m., the doorbell rang. I answered the door to find my wayward friend. He looked awful with torn fatigues caked with mud, and with scratches on his face and hands.

I handed him a beer as he said, "I failed again."

Before I could say that I was sorry, he continued, "I got lost, and they sent the sergeant into the woods to find me again."

After three despondent beers, he added, "I may as well tell you the worst part. You'll hear it anyway."

I said, "Nothing could be worse than getting lost, for the third time. You'll lose your commission and go to Nam as a grunt. You'll probably get killed."

He concluded, "Yeah, something could be worse. I lost my compass."

At least one man at the barbeque was killed in Vietnam is less than a year. I have no idea whatever happened to the lawyer from Oklahoma.

—**Fort Benning, Georgia,**
**Infantry Officers Basic Course, 1968**

★ ★ ★

I did a tour with MACV in the Delta before being discharged from the army in 1970. In 1972, I returned to Vietnam as an agricultural advisor with the United States Agency for International Development (USAID). Teamed with a former Special Forces captain, we assisted a veterinary team and even delivered a pure bred Duroc boar sent from Iowa to a hog breeding farm. Except for once driving into and through a firefight between ARVNs and NVA on a highway north of Xuan Loc, this tour in Vietnam was fairly quiet.

During my time with USAID, I also spent some time in Nha Trang. The town was lovely, but the scores of prostitutes on its streets were not. Most were amateurs in the oldest of professions—refugees trying to made a living for their families driven from the villages further north by the newest NVA offensive.

One afternoon, a cyclo driver stopped me along a Nha Trang street and asked, "You want girl? I take you special place. Vietnamese girl, Chinese, mountain girl; all, I have just for you. You want virgin?"

When I replied that I really was not in the mood for a virgin, he said, "But, sir! I have reference." He then proudly handed me a note, printed crudely in ballpoint pen:

TO WHOM IT MAY CONCERN:

This is to certify that Mr. Huong is a damn good pimp. He always gets you good pussy and his girls don't hardly ever have the clap.

Signed by a staff sergeant, C Company, 3rd Battalion 1st Infantry

—**USAID, II Corps, 1972**

⭐ ⭐ ⭐

By 1967, the antiwar movement back in the States was gaining momentum. The antics of the protestors were discouraging for us fighting the war, but occasionally we did get some good news about support back home. One of the soldiers in my company was the son of a union leader in New York City. A letter from his father included a single-page announcement directed "To All Members of Local 824 and Affiliated Locals I.L.A." The soldier read it, seemed unimpressed, and handed in to me saying, "Keep it if you like."

The announcement from the president of the International Longshoremen chapter invited its members to "Rally to March," and stated:

Let's all march to show flag burners, draft card destroyers, and objectors that we back our boys in Vietnam 200% and to show these unAmericans what real men are.

I.L.A. all the way for our boys in Vietnam. It's about time we back our boys behind the lines that are fighting for all of us.

Labor unions all over the country are behind this parade. Come one and all.

We will meet on 95th Street between Lexington Avenue and 3rd Avenue at 11:00 am. We want everybody to be there to show our faith to our country.

The announcement may not have been all that well written, but its impact was nonetheless powerful—at least to me.
**—25th Infantry Division, II Corps, 1967**

Random acts of kindness did occasionally happen, even in Vietnam. In 1967, we crossed Highway 1 on a long march back to LZ Liz. On the edge of a small village on the highway roadside, merchants clustered around the company to peddle their wares. For security, we tried to keep them at some distance. It was also against company policy for anyone to eat or drink anything sold by the locals.

Most of the venders kept their distance except for one boy about ten years of age. He had a sack of ice and bottled soft drinks. The boy persisted until a soldier took the bottle out of his hand and broke it on the highway. The boy looked down at the broken glass and spreading soda with tears in his eyes. A quarter of his business inventory had just been destroyed.

The company continued the march. I happened to look back to see a GI approach the boy and hand him a fistful of South Vietnamese currency. He said nothing as he moved on.
**—4th Infantry Division, II Corps, 1967**

Every battle of the Vietnam War was not fought in Southeast Asia. Just as many—and maybe more—took place on the "home front" that did not exist as a *place* but rather as *state of*

*mind.* For me, that state of mind took the form of a waiting wife—waiting for my husband's one-year tour to be over, waiting for the birth of our first child, waiting for R&R, waiting for every letter, waiting . . .

But a lot happened while I waited. Between April 1969 and April 1970, Senator Ted Kennedy drove off the Chappaquiddick Bridge, Neil Armstrong walked on the moon, the Charles Manson family went on a murdering rampage in Los Angeles, Woodstock shocked the country, and the Moratorium on War protests filled the streets of San Francisco.

It may seem a contradiction that anything as individual as waiting for a letter would have any relationship to world events, but everything touching the Vietnam War was related, and all things were contradictions. And so it was for me. I was a waiting wife, but instead of being part of group "left behind" while our men were at war, I was alone and on my own as far as the army was concerned. Soldiers went to Vietnam as individual replacements rather than as members of units, so waiting wives were scattered far and wide without a cohesive bond. We had nowhere to belong. We had no unit or unity.

After putting my husband on a plane for Vietnam, I temporarily moved back home with my parents. Within a couple of weeks, I discovered I was pregnant. I was thrilled. Then I was shocked when neither my parents nor my in-laws shared my excitement. My parents feared I would end up raising the child alone; his folks feared that it was asking too much to pray for his safety and the arrival of a healthy baby. And they worried that knowing he was going to be a father might cause their son to make a wrong decision that would be fatal. None of those reactions mattered, though, once I learned that my husband was pleased about the baby.

When my friend's husband also left for the war two months after mine, I moved to San Francisco to share a flat with her, just as we had planned before we all left Ft. Bragg. It was a relief for everyone.

Living in San Francisco in 1969 as a waiting wife, however, was not a respite. At first, my roommate and I thought we would associate with old school friends of hers who were still living in the Bay Area. We quickly found that most people our age were adamantly antiwar. In fact, their first words upon hearing about our circumstances became predictable: "We're opposed to the war." Where could a conversation go from there?

Our next efforts focused on the Presidio, just blocks from our flat. We could find solace "at home" in the military environs, we thought. I had immediately scheduled an appointment with a gynecologist there after arriving in the city, and I frequented the PX and commissary on a regular basis. Because the post felt like familiar territory, we decided that joining the officers' club there would provide us a safe place to enjoy a nice dinner occasionally—something we could look forward to when we could afford it. When we tried to apply for membership, the manger informed us that waiting wives were not allowed because some such facilities had become hunting grounds for would-be widows lining up the next $10,000 life insurance policy embodied by second lieutenants on orders for Vietnam.

In the meantime, my roommate found a clerical job that demanded only that she show up and open envelopes all day. I decided that I should likewise seek employment, and I set up interviews only to meet a wall of resistance. Employers in 1969 did not employ pregnant women, no matter the education or experience. Once recovered from the dejections, I tried to volunteer with the Red Cross at Letterman General Hospital on the Presidio. Apparently this organization, too, viewed waiting wives as predators. Even after showing my training credentials from Bragg, I was refused.

Following the barrage of antiwar and anti–waiting wife shots we had taken, my roommate and I hunkered down in our flat, venturing out only for work, errands, and special occasions. Even at home, though, Vietnam contradictions found us. My roommate was angry with her husband for volunteering for Vietnam; I was supportive of mine because it was what he had wanted for years. She was politically more aligned with her old friends in her philosophical opposition to the war; I backed the military. At home she attacked the war; in public she defended the warriors. Mostly she chose to ignore the daily newscasts; I followed every telecast that covered the war, looking to see if I could spot my husband.

Our outlooks and attitudes were so different and our rejection by civilian society so complete that we had nowhere else to turn our attention but to neutral, but intriguing events. The first was the Chappaquiddick scandal involving Ted Kennedy. My roommate called the incident correctly the first time she heard about it. I, on the other hand as naïve and unsuspecting, was sure a valid explanation for how the senator had survived and his "assistant" Mary Jo Kopechne drowned would surface. I needed to believe that lawmakers who sent my husband to war were moral men of principle. At the same pace that the whole Kennedy story revealed itself, my faith in government deteriorated, leaving me questioning the wisdom of war waged by the Kennedy ilk.

Before the Chappaquiddick incident left the headlines, another story grabbed our attention. I remember sitting in front of the TV watching Neil Armstrong walk on the moon and marveling, as I knitted a baby sweater, at a country that could put men into orbit but that could not (or would not) employ every weapon available to win the war against much more poorly equipped and trained enemy in Vietnam. My position was that if the United States was doing everything in its power to defeat the enemy and protect my husband, and if my husband were killed, well, I would somehow have to bear it. But if my husband were killed while the United States pulled its punches, well, I could not bear to think about my reaction. And all the while I was watching the first moon walk that evening, I knew my husband—if he was still alive—was sleeping on the ground in a faraway jungle. The world made no sense.

It made even less sense when actress Sharon Tate and her friends were slaughtered in Los Angeles. The story was gruesome, gory, and repugnant. Still my roommate and I pored over all the details we could glean from the daily newspapers, preferring the horrors of this Charles Manson family murderous and random spree to the horrors of the Vietnam quagmire.

While we spent the summer in retreat, thousands of our contemporaries gathered at Woodstock. As little as I comprehended war, I understood it better than the throngs partying and rolling in the mud in upstate New York.

By October, though, I was focused only on my immediate current event: R&R in Hawaii. Thrilled to be seeing my husband but apprehensive about his seeing me—now seven months pregnant—I waited at Fort DeRussy on Waikiki for buses bringing servicemen from Honolulu International in a state of high anticipation. True to form, my man was the last man off the last bus—his reasoning being that he, as an officer, was not going to push ahead of any troops.

We had a wonderful week in Hawaii. But our time together was gone in a blink. When we parted at the airport this time, I viewed the war quite differently. I was no longer gungho; I wanted my husband back. Period. I did not want him dying for what was painfully becoming a losing cause, regardless of the abilities and dedication of its warriors. It had been easier for me when I viewed the war more patriotically.

Back in San Francisco, I was surrounded the following month by streets of protestors waging the Moratorium on War. From our flat, we could hear the chants of the marchers. We felt under siege.

In December, I gave birth to a beautiful baby girl. My roommate endured the inglorious duty of being by my side in the labor room, and then she faithfully went to the Red Cross office in the hospital to request my husband be informed of the birth. Our daughter was five days old before I knew that my husband knew he was a father.

Of all the agonies of waiting, for me the worst and most persistent was waiting for every letter. My husband was stellar in his consideration: he wrote every time he had the chance. The missives from him ranged from three to five words to ten pages. I spent hours poring over each one, long or short. The real message, regardless of what he wrote, was that he had been alive at that time. In general, I received a letter five days after he wrote it, but sometimes when he was in the field (where he was for nine of the twelve months) for extended times, the letters took two weeks. Every time I received the muddied and crumpled envelopes, I looked first for the date inside. And then I calculated, thankful that he had been alive five days ago, seven days ago, two weeks ago.

I knew, of course, that had anything happened to my husband, the military would inform me. But I also knew that the military was not always as timely as it might be, so I continued to rely only on the letters I received as proof of his well-being.

Slowly and excruciatingly, the winter and early spring days moved through the calendar. Having a baby to care for kept me much busier, but still each hour took its full toll.

Then finally my husband was out of the field and in the rear in a safe job where he would complete his last few weeks in-country. Letters came quicker; our focus turned to the future. Then just as I began to relax somewhat, the post office went on strike and all letters stopped. I took it as a personal affront.

Fortunately, we had estimated his date on return, within a week's variation. During that week, I never left the reach of the phone. When the magic call finally came, I heard a crackle and then my husband's voice, saying, "It's over, honey. It's over." He was calling from Alaska where they had stopped to refuel.

It was nearing midnight when a lone, paint-battered chartered passenger jet lumbered up to the gates at Travis Air Force Base. The steps for deboarding rolled up to the door and war-weary soldiers trooped down and then walked in a single file line through customs and then onto waiting buses. As I watched the deplaning uniforms, I felt a wave of panic. I was meeting the plane my husband said he would be on, but no one else was waiting with me. Was I in the wrong place? Where was the crowd? Then I saw my husband's head pop up as he

exited the plane. The answer to my questions was that I was
the only person meeting this planeload of returning soldiers.
It was just one more—and the final—contradiction of expecta-
tions for us in a long, complicated war.

**—San Francisco, California, 1969–70**

On January 19, 1967, my company was patrolling Highway
19, the infamous Street Without Joy, in the Central Highlands. Alongside the road we came upon the burnt-out hulk of
a rusting M5 tank. The tank had been stripped of its gun and
everything else that could be pried loose. We could make out,
however, a small painted French tricolor flag and the insignia
that appeared to be that of a Polish cavalry unit.

I knew enough history to realized that the tank hull was
what little remained of the ambush of Mobile Group 100 that
had been ambushed and mostly destroyed by the Viet Minh in
1954 in the last major battle of the First Indochina War. And
here we were, going down the same road nearly a quarter of
century later.

**—25th Infantry Division, II Corps, 1967**

I was a C-141 copilot in Military Airlift Command (MAC)
assigned to the 53rd Military Airlift Squadron, 63rd Military
Airlift Wing, Norton AFB, California. MAC was not the most
glamorous assignment for a pilot in the United States Air
Force as we couldn't turn our plane upside down like the
fighter pukes could and we didn't get to blow anything up like
the BUFFs (B-52s). All we did was go round and round the
Pacific, hauling junk to out-of-the-way places and playing a

continuous game of cat and mouse with the ferocious thunderstorms that always seemed to be to our front.

Anyone could always spot a MAC crew member in any officers' club in the Pacific. He was a tired guy wearing a big watch in a sweated out flight suit trying to cash a check at the bar. We started calling it the "midnight airlift command" because we seemed to always be scheduled to fly at night and then had to try to sleep during the day.

In the spring of 1973, our crew had been flying around Southeast Asia for a couple of weeks hauling beer, boots, and household goods to all sorts of exotic places. At that time, the missions operated a little like the pony express, only backwards. Unlike the real pony express our horse never got tired, but we did, and we had to change riders every so often. The airplanes continued on around the system, but every twelve hours or so a new crew took the airplane, refueled, and continued on while the old crew got some rest and waited for the next plane to come in.

After a long circuit through SAE, we were finally homeward-bound when we stopped for crew rest at Hickam AFB, Hawaii. Just before we went back to the ready room after a few hours sleep, I got a call from the aircraft commander informing me that we were alerted for a homecoming mission. Everyone knew what that meant. Operation Homecoming was a mission everyone wanted to fly, to be part of bringing the prisoners of war home from North Vietnam. The news was absolutely electrifying.

POWs were first flown to Clark AFB in the Philippines where they received any necessary medical treatment and then they boarded flights to bases near their stateside homes. We met "Balls 7" (C-141 67-0007) on the ramp at Hickam and replaced the crew that had flown from Clark. Shortly after take-off, the former POWs, many of whom were pilots, began to come up to the cockpit to chat. At first they came one by one, but as the hours wore on they came in greater numbers. Eventually we had standing room only in the cockpit and everyone seemed to be really enjoying themselves. (Try that in an F-4.)

Our call sign was "Homecoming Air evac 7 triple zero 7" and the air traffic controllers gave us priority handling from the point we entered U.S. airspace until we reached our destination of San Antonio. As we went feet dry (crossed the coastline) over California, I announced on the intercom, "Gentlemen, welcome to the continental United States of America." A cheer went up throughout the aircraft and the former POWs who were in the cockpit hugged each other and hugged us.

The remainder of the mission was textbook—priority handling, a military band to welcome the flight to Kelly Air Force Base, Texas, and all the excitement and celebration associated with the homecoming. Our crew stood back out of the way and silently wished them well. What a great experience to be able to play even a small part in bringing those men, who had suffered so much for the country they loved, home to their families and friends.

**—63rd Military Airlift Command,**
**Hickam Field, Hawaii, 1973**

I thought 1969 was a shitty year in Vietnam. But come to think of it, 1968 was not so hot either. And neither was 1970. But 1969 was the year I decided we were not going to win the war. More important, I was beginning to realize there was really never any intention of winning and I was mad because no one had let me in on the secret. America had just landed a man on the moon, yet we could not seem to beat a bunch of undersupplied, undernourished, black-pajama wearing miscreants who had no air support, no artillery support, and no armor support (that I ever saw). To top it off, Uncle Walter Cronkite had just declared the war in Vietnam "unwinnable."

I had been raised on John Wayne, Roy Rogers, Hopalong Cassidy, and Superman. I really believed in "Truth, Justice, and the American Way" and that the good guy always won. Some-one had told me that we were in Vietnam to stop the spread of Communism. And I believed them. In fact, when the army was passing out the Kool-Aid in Ranger School, I had two glasses. But then things changed: I had found out that there was no Santa Claus, no Easter Bunny, no Tooth Fairy, no good guys, no bad guys, and no God. All in the same week. For a twenty-two-year-old kid from Texas, that was hard to take. Life sucked.

To cap it all off, a week before I was a hero. Within the last couple of months I had been awarded an Army Commenda-tion Medal for Valor, a Bronze Star Medal for Valor, and a Sil-ver Star—America's third highest award. During the time I had been in Vietnam, I had killed a lot of people. I didn't know how many then and I chose not to remember how many now. But it was a lot. Senior officers would come from all over the area of operations, fly out to my position wherever I was, and shake my hand. They wanted to touch the magic. Pretty heady stuff for a twenty-two-year-old. Pretty heady stuff for anyone. Then it all went to shit.

Seems some pothead claimed that one of the people I killed didn't stay dead. So I had shot him again. Maybe yes, maybe no. Maybe there was more to the story. Maybe not. But one thing was certain, the system that I had put so much faith in, the system I was willing to die for, was not taking any chances. They fed me to the wolves. The My Lai Massacre had only recently come to light, and my commanders were not about to risk their careers and reputations on one soldier. The new army edict seemed to be "better ten innocent be hung than one guilty go free." My unit at least was going to show the world that they did not condone incidents such as occurred at My Lai, no matter what the cost or who was hurt. As long as it wasn't them.

So I was placed under what in the civilian world would be considered "house arrest." I was not in jail; in fact, I still car-ried a rifle and ammunition. But I was pulled from the rice paddies and restricted to the battalion firebase. Life sucked. But it could have been worse. I could have been in jail. I could have been handcuffed to my bed with an armed guard. I don't include being dead as "being worse" because at the time, being dead looked like a pretty good option.

The army was willing to ruin my life, but my battalion was shorthanded and could ill afford to have someone like me just sit on his hands awaiting a trial that could take months to occur. So they put me to work. Someone thought I would be ideally suited for being a bodyguard—and it would keep me mostly out of the way.

In Vietnam, big-shot colonels and generals flew everywhere they went. The roads were too dangerous. And there was no such thing as an armored vehicle unless you drove a tank. Highway 1 ran just outside our firebase, all the way up and down the coast and through, or near, all of the major cities located along the South China Sea. I guess the French used the road to transport their rice to the major Vietnam sea ports. Again, I don't know. All I know is that the road was there and it was used all day by the Americans and all night by the Viet Cong. A hell of a deal.

Jeeps in those days had all the armor protection of five pounds of butter. There were no sides to speak of on the vehicles and, if they had a top at all, it was made of canvas. There was no such thing as a convoy (unless for a special occasion). Americans could drive to a larger firebase or, if lucky, an air field to swap or steal supplies, go to the beach to swim, or go to town to get laid. Some people actually had official business to conduct. Regardless of the reason for travel, everyone used Highway 1.

One of the few people who actually had an official reason to travel Highway 1 was the battalion chaplain (we will call him Chaplain Paul). If a squad or platoon was deep in the mountains or well off the road in some God-awful village, hamlet, or rice paddy, Chaplain Paul and his assistant would fly to visit them. But if the unit could be reached by road, then road it was.

Someone thought it would be a great idea for me to travel with Chaplain Paul and his assistant to provide security. If they came under fire, the idea was that I was to shoot back. I don't think Chaplain Paul was allowed to shoot at the enemy (but I always wondered what he carried in his Communion bag that made it so heavy) and his assistant had no idea which end of the rifle the bullet came out of. So I was it. Wonderful. I would have rather been in charge of burning the contents of the forty-plus cut-in-half fifty-five-gallon drums used to accommodate the outhouses on the firebase. Unfortunately, that job went to some lucky Local National who was paid $5.00 per day and who split his time between burning feces and marking off the firebase for late night VC mortar attacks. Me, I was stuck with babysitting the chaplain while awaiting trial.

Assuming I ever had a faith in God, it had pretty much dissolved by this point in my life. I think if a person was honest with himself, it was pretty hard to find God in Vietnam. I know some people said He was there and even others said they discovered Him for the first time in the war zone. But I wasn't one of them. Even when I was on the very top, I could never see the hand of God in anything I or anyone else was doing. Maybe in Saigon, somebody could see God. Maybe anywhere a soldier was not getting his ass shot off every night, or stepping on booby traps, or seeing his buddy blown all to hell, he could see God. But I could not see him. In fact, I wondered that, if there was a God, would he forgive us for the things we did "in service to our country" in Vietnam? Being stuck with Chaplain Paul every day that he decided to take a ride down Highway 1 and give a sermon was not my idea of a good time. Far from it. But stuck I was.

The first few days on the job were no real problem. We never ran into an ambush or roadside bomb (these days the roadside bombs have sexy names—improvised explosive devices or IEDs—but in those days they were just called roadside bombs; I think they killed just the same); in fact, we never even drew enemy fire, which I found surprising. More important to me, Chaplain Paul did not really expect me to listen to his sermons, I was free to stand away from the group and smoke or read if I wanted. That said, the squad or platoon command posts were rather restrictive, and there was really nowhere to go outside range of hearing the sermons. Chaplain Paul took his job seriously and we would try to reach four or five locations in a day on the road before we called it quits.

It was a Saturday in the summer, and it was really, really hot. It was late in the day, almost dark and we were finally headed home. Chaplain Paul had had an exceptionally rough day. In addition to five religious services (all with Communion) Chaplain Paul had conducted two memorial services. The memorial services were tough on us all. No one liked them, but I don't think many men understood that Chaplain Paul and his assistant had to see them all and had to participate in them all. Every man killed in the battalion had a memorial service conducted by Chaplain Paul. Every man. And not to make this out to be more than it was, or to lessen the impact of even one dead American, but my battalion lost more men in a month than are lost in a year by the entire command in Iraq or Afghanistan.

Chaplain Paul never complained and never talked about it (at least not to me), but regardless of the amount of faith he had, doing four, five, six memorial services a week—usually for multiple soldiers at each service—had to be mentally draining. I have often wondered if Chaplain Paul still sees the demons the rest of us see, even though he never did any of the actually killing.

Anyway, this had been a tough day for all of us. By the end of that fifth sermon, I think I could have given number six by myself and never missed a beat even without the Bible as backup. I was tired of hearing about God. To steal a line from a movie I saw thirty years later, "God hated me, so I hated him right back." It seemed to work.

One of the worst jobs in the battalion was "Bridge Guard." Highway 1 had a bunch of bridges. And on each one of these bridges, there was an American guard post, which was little more than a sandbagged bunker. Companies from the battalion rotated this duty with a company putting a squad or a platoon minus on each bridge in their sector. You sat there.

Forever. Just sitting. Waiting for someone to shoot at you. If
you had enough people on your bridge, you could send out
patrols to break the monotony. Sometimes the soda-girls would
drive by on their bicycles or motor scooters selling soft drinks,
candy, marijuana, and various social diseases, but even with
that, it was tough duty.

As we drove back to the firebase that evening we passed
the last bridge guard position. We were used to getting waves
from the soldiers as we passed their bridge so it had become
perfunctory to wave back, which is exactly what the Chaplain
did. But something on the bridge caught my eye. This kid waving looked strange. I could not put my finger on it; he wanted
us to stop, or he wanted us to do something. I didn't know.
Regardless, I poked Chaplain Paul and asked if he had seen
the look the soldier on the bridge gave us when we drove by.
As soon as I said it, I knew I had screwed up. The Chaplain had
us turn around. We would visit the bridge guards before going
home. Shit.

As we were getting out of the jeep and being met by the
men on the bridge, I reminded Chaplain Paul that it was getting dark and getting dark quick. It would not be cool to be
caught on Highway 1 after the sun went down. Chaplain Paul
just smiled and said, "Did you ever hear the story of Joshua?
Joshua stopped the sun to fight a battle. Maybe I can stop it to
pray a few minutes with these men." I am not certain, but I
think I answered with an expletive.

There were only four men on the bridge, the remainder
being out on a patrol and setting up for a night ambush. No
one would be back until first light the next day. This did not
deter Chaplain Paul. Although he didn't give them an actual
sermon, he recited some scripture verses and talked to the
four as a group. He then spent some private time with each of
the four men. As we were packing up to leave, one of the men
asked if the Chaplain could give them Communion. I again
reminded Chaplain Paul that it was getting late and we did not
have time for a Communion service, but I already knew my
plea was falling on deaf ears. I broke out the Communion

stuff. All four men received Communion. To this day I have no idea if they were all Protestant, all Catholic, or a mix. But they all received a Protestant Communion. The Communion over, we packed up, and headed home. We made the wire at dusk.

One hour after we left the bridge, it was hit with mortar fire. Three of the four men on the bridge were killed. The fourth lost a leg. I never went on another security mission with the Chaplain.

One week later, Chaplain Paul baptized me. One month later, my trial was held in Nha Trang. Chaplain Paul was there. Two weeks after the court-martial rendered a nonguilty verdict, I was back in the field with my old platoon. Five months later, I was home. Forty-five years later, I still do not know what I saw in that kid's eye that made us turn around—or how it was that I would find God on a bridge on Highway 1. Maybe Chaplain Paul did stop the sun.

**—173rd Airborne Brigade, II Corps, 1969**

When all the blood seeps beneath the soil
and common memory
When all the bones are crushed to marrow
or ashes float away to sea
When all the broken aircraft
and rifles rust beneath green trees
When the letters
and pictures crumble into yellow dust
When the last land mine explodes in a flash and fury
and when my nightmares turn into mere dreams
Then will I write the last Vietnam War story.

—**MACV, I Corps, 1967**

# Acknowledgments

Every effort has been made to ensure the veracity of the stories included in this collection. Some are from my own experiences, most are from fellow veterans with whom I was acquainted before the war or met during or after the conflict. The few that are from veterans with whom I do not have a direct relationship came with the recommendations of men I completely trust.

Some readers may observe that the stories are heavy from the 199th Light Infantry Brigade. I make no apologies. The 199th was my unit in Vietnam and where I made many lasting friends who were the first to step forward offering their war stories.

Most of the included war stories were gathered by e-mail correspondence with the contributors. A few came via U.S. mail, telephone interviews, and face-to-face interviews. A number of veterans made no response at all to my request for war stories. A few wrote back saying "no" or "no thanks." Others wrote saying they just did not feel comfortable discussing their participation in the war. One wrote, "Sure I talk at times about my 'war stories,' but as much as I hate to admit it, I really don't like to be reminded of some of them. I'd just like to keep some of the things I witnessed and some I participated in to myself." Another sent me a war story only to write a couple of weeks later asking that I not include it. He said he just did not want to share it with just anyone.

Some admitted that they had never told anyone about some of their experiences. One vet wrote, "My wife read my stories and cried."

Those who did respond often began with the same apologetic explanation, "My memories of Vietnam are mostly mundane—the day-to-day life of a grunt that is only of interest to those who were there. As you know, much of a grunt's life was boring and tedious."

Many veterans wrote saying that their tours were not likely of interest—and then proceeded to tell riveting tales of combat or hilarious stories of passing time in Vietnam. One veteran began, "For forty years, I tried to forget Vietnam and for the last two I have been trying to remember it."

Another veteran summed up his feelings writing, "To me the Vietnam Vet was the twentieth-century equivalent of slavery. Forced to serve and hated when freed."

Still another wrote, "We're not the Greatest Generation—we are a part of the 'big mistake' that everyone would like to forget."

As for telling the truth, one veteran wrote, "The stories are as accurate as I can remember them. They have to be. I realize that there are other people out there who were also there and would recognize if I exaggerated."

I am sure that it was difficult mentally for some to remember and write about their wartime experiences. Some had physical impediments as well. One explained that his stories were in all lowercase letters "because it is much faster when you can type with only one hand."

And finally, "There is only one story about the Vietnam War—we all just tell it differently."

Several veterans sent their journals or draft manuscripts of their combat experience offering the contents to be used anyway I saw fit. In one veteran's papers was a description of burning villages, throwing hand grenades in bunkers, filling in the village well, and killing all the livestock. He added that only one living thing was spared, "My policy was to never hurt a dog." Other vets called on the phone to tell me directly about their experiences. Some stories are ones that I recalled hearing around club bars, field bivouacs, or on long airplane rides to one military exercise or another.

It is also worthwhile to note that each person in a fight sees and experiences that event within their limited space of the battlefield. Two soldiers separated by only ten meters may see a battle entirely differently. Both of their stories are true.

Grateful acknowledgement is extended to the following men, who like their fellow veterans came forward to stand up for their country when lesser men hid behind draft exemptions or fled to Canada. The following individuals made this book possible and significantly contributed to what our armed forces and country are today: John Abernathy, John Allan, Al Allen, Ben Andrus, Frank Bonvillain, Jim Budde, Ray Burnard, Jim Butler, Mike Carothers, Ernie Chamberlain, Sam Chambers, Dan Cragg, Thomas Daly, Bruce Davies, Tom Dineen, Steve Edwards, Jim Fitter, Ron Fowler, Tony Geishauser, Jeff Grass, Tom Hargrove, R. Ren Hart, George Isleib, Mike Jackson, Jim Jardina, Jim Lanning, Bill Laurie, Roy Massey, Dale McJunkin, Jim McLeroy, Lamont Meaux, Kent Mills, Linda Moore-Lanning, Bill Morrow, Terrell Mullins, Vin Musgrave, Patrick O'Regan, Larry Prater, Jim Price, Steve Price, Rick Renaud, Bill Richardson, Bob Rosenburgh, Lee Sanders, Leroy Shafer, David Sherman, Larry Sommers, Ben Swett, Randy Thorne, Ben Tindall, Ben Trail, Don Ulrich, Duncan Williams, Wayne Williams, Leigh Wilson, and James Wyatt.